ARRP

WINTER WARRIORS

WINTER WARRIORS

Across Bosnia with the PBI

*UN and Nato Operations with the
2nd Battalion the Light Infantry 1995/1996*

Les Howard

Book Guild Publishing
Sussex, England

First published in Great Britain in 2006 by
The Book Guild Ltd,
Pavilion View,
19 New Road,
Brighton, BN1 1UF

Typesetting in Times by
IML Typographers, Birkenhead, Merseyside

Printed in Great Britain by
CPI Antony Rowe

A catalogue record for this book is available from
The British Library.

ISBN 1 84624 077 8

This book is dedicated to the 167 who gave their lives in the Former Yugoslavia under the UN flag, from 1992 to 1995: 159 military personnel, 3 military observers, 1 civilian police, 2 international civilian staff and 2 local staff.

Their sacrifice was not in vain.

And for Daniel and Conor, so you may get to know me.

If you are only ready to go when you are fetched,
where is the merit in that?

Field Marshal Earl Kitchener, 1915

Contents

Author's Note

Special thanks go to my wife Ela, without whose support
and encouragement this book would never have been
written. Also to RHQ LI, HQ Land Command, Glen Shaw,
and my publishing team at the Book Guild.

I would also like to give a special mention to the following
individuals, whose help, encouragement and example have
influenced and guided me more than they ever knew:
*Nick Bos, Tony Brain, Steve Carolan, Mickey Evans,
Barry Exley, Tony Finnegan, Mark Little,
Charles MacDowell, Ronnie McCourt, Sean McEvoy,
Chas Nwachakwu, Paddy Proctor, Steve Reeves,
Paul Trendle, Wilf Williams*

The photos are the copyright of the author. The maps are
copyright of IFOR, the poster is reprinted with kind
permission from the Royal Green Jackets

Tens of thousands of British soldiers served in the Former Yugoslavia during the war from 1992 to 1995 under the control of the UN, and to the present day under NATO and EURFOR. Everyone has a story to tell.

This is mine.

Over the Hills and Far Away

It had been dark for five hours already. There were no streetlights or welcome glow from any of the houses we passed. Intermittent moonlight broke through the clouds to cast an eerie glow over the snow covered landscape; one which we knew harboured real evil. In every house and every street, in every field and every wood, I could sense hateful minds planning our demise. We were not welcome here. *So many acts of barbarism had been carried out and they still had much more to do.*

We had left the safety of an armoured infantry battalion and were heading north into the unknown. Our only protection was from our three vehicle convoy of a Land Rover, two lightly armed and armoured CVRTs and for what it was worth a letter from the Croat Government guaranteeing safe passage.

We travelled on radio silence – we didn't want to advertise to the warring factions that we were coming. Apart from a few high-pitched squawks when data was sent, the net was quiet. For what seemed like the hundredth time, I felt for my rifle by my side. The smooth gunmetal of the barrel felt reassuring. Beside it were my driver's rifle and our webbing, close at hand, in case we needed to de-bus in a hurry.

I looked ahead and saw the Land Rover's rear lights glow faintly in the distance. Between us the large bulk of the Sultan command vehicle was illuminated by our headlights. The icy roads meant we were making slow progress. Every now and then we would slip or shudder as the tracks tried to grip the rock-hard black ice. I reminded my driver to keep a decent gap between us and the Sultan – good convoy discipline but on these treacherous roads at 40kph a sudden stop could mean us becoming a permanent feature of the vehicle in front.

I sat down in the cupola to take a break from the biting cold. I pulled up my driving goggles, took off my arctic mittens and settled onto the seat.

1

Everything took twice as long as the cold had seeped through the protection of my tank suit and had numbed my body. I switched on the night-sight and traversed the L37 in a 360. The monochrome picture was sharp and clear. I focused on the Land Rover; the painted white UN logo seemed to glow on its rear as it meandered along like a mother duck.

I scanned the road further ahead. The horizon was beginning to glow brighter. With another eight hours until daybreak it looked like the int reports were true. Our destination was burning.

I stood up again and stared ahead, confirming what I saw with the mark-1 eyeball. The light on the horizon flickered with little green fireflies darting across the skyline. It looked almost welcoming, like coming home to a flickering log fire. We slowed down and turned a bend and darkness shrouded us again. I did a 180 to check the rear and felt the Spartan speed up again as we hit another long stretch.

We hadn't seen any other vehicles since the explosion, but the memory sharpened my senses and kept me switched on to what could happen. I kept looking around. There were no friendlies out there, just evil men with murder on their minds, and they had four years of conflict to hone up the skills of their barbaric trade. They didn't want us here spoiling their daily diet of merciless self-gratification.

I completed the 360, leaving the hatch to the rear and the jimpy pointing to the left. I rested my back against the steel hatch, welcoming the extra protection it would give in addition to my flak jacket. I was beginning to get paranoid about getting shot in the back. The bad guys were not fussy about who we were and had a proven record of attacking the UN. I was determined not to become another notch on the butt of a sniper's rifle.

Up ahead the brake lights of the Rover flashed on and we started to slow down. I dropped down again and had a quick look in the night-sight. We were coming up to another checkpoint. As we slowed to a halt, the lights of the Rover picked out the ominous sign of anti-tank mines. There was no barrier and the Croats made no attempt to stop us. They didn't have to; we either stopped or blew up!

Two Croat militia soldiers stood smoking by a makeshift sentry hut on our left. They wore Soviet-style uniforms with locally produced HVO badges with the familiar red and white chequered design. They looked up and took their hands out of their pockets. They unslung their AK47s and held them by the pistol grip and stock, pointing the barrels at the Rover.

I stood up and looked towards the hut. Smoke from a wood-burning stove trickled out of a tin pipe and floated slowly away. Inside I could make out more men. One of them came out to see what the noise was. He looked pissed off because we had forced him to leave the warmth of the hut. He was obviously in charge and as if to prove the point he wore American Woodland-pattern combats instead of the old Soviet style. On his head was a side hat with a lifetime's hair grease staining the rim. A folding stock AK47 was slung across his back and around his waist he had a brown leather holster on a shiny black leather belt. He coughed up phlegm and spat it at his feet. He put his hands on his hips and jabbered something at the sentries. I got the impression we weren't welcome here.

The three Croats stood there and stared at us. They didn't move and didn't appear that they were going to. They just stared at us as though we had just appeared from another planet. The passenger door of the Rover creaked open and the Serjeant Major stepped out. The flak jacket accentuated his stocky build. He adjusted his beret and had a look around. He was a hard man and had an air of authority about him. Normally a comms recce would have been carried out by a corporal, maybe a sergeant, but his presence indicated how crucial the mission was.

I took in the scene as it unfolded. The Croats stood in a rough semicircle facing the road. They appeared to ignore our armour and stared menacingly at the softer targets of the Serjeant Major and the Rover. The convoy had closed up, but we had left enough room between each vehicle to manoeuvre. We kept the engines idling, welcoming the break from the chill factor of the ice-cold wind. A smell of burning was in the air, sweet and sickly. The smoke from the hut was drifting away from us, so it had to be from somewhere else. I had a quick look around but there was nothing to be seen. We were all alone, just us and the Croats.

The Serjeant Major lifted up his hands and slowly unfolded the letter. The Croat leader took a good look at him and grinned. Why did he look so smug? I looked back at the Serjeant Major and noticed that there was something missing from the picture – his weapon!

Fuck, what was he up to? I knew he wanted to be non-confrontational but these guys respected force, lived by it. Guns were status symbols and badges of rank. Having no gun meant you were weak, a nobody, an easy target!

The Croat leader moved forward and stood in front of the Serjeant Major. He wiped his nose with his left sleeve and grinned. He unslung his weapon and held it by the pistol grip and stock, pointing it at the Serjeant Major's groin.

My driver spoke over the intercom: 'Where's my rifle?'

3

'Just behind your right shoulder, next to your webbing.'

I looked down into the vehicle and saw his glove-covered hand feeling behind him.

'OK, found it.'

My driver had the same feeling as me – trouble.

The Croat leader moved closer, his AK still pointing at the Serjeant Major's groin. The Serjeant Major ignored the threat against his manhood and looked directly at the Croat. He held up the paper guarantee.

'I have free passage authorised by your government.' He glanced at the other two. They looked uninterested.

'Do you speak English? Do you understand?' continued the Serjeant Major in his thick Geordie accent.

The Croat leader walked over to the other two and they conferred for a minute. Their breath condensed as they spoke, giving the impression that they were having a smoking competition. The sentries looked back at the Serjeant Major and started gesturing and pointing with their AKs. They smiled as their leader turned and strode towards the Serjeant Major. He pointed at the paper held in his hand, barked some kind of threat and walked back to the hut.

The Croats were playing their usual game of threats and intimidation in the hope that we would turn around and go back. They were the local warlords and masters of all they surveyed and as such thought this entitled them to do as they pleased. We, on the other hand, had no choice but to stick it out. There were over two thousand troops preparing to deploy and they were depending on us for comms. We had to get through.

The Serjeant Major kept looking at the Croat leader as the driver's door of the Rover opened. The Sigs Serjeant appeared, stretched his legs and strolled to the front of the Rover. He, too, was wearing his flak jacket, but wasn't foolish enough to forget to wear his sidearm.

The two Croat sentries now began to take more interest and moved closer. They raised their AKs and held them with both hands threateningly. They called out to their leader and moved closer to the road.

The Croat leader came back out of the hut and gave us a look that said it was unbelievable that we were still there. He spoke something to the Serjeant Major in Serbo-Croat and looked over at his sidekicks. They didn't look amused anymore and moved up to the Rover. One stood in front close to the Sigs Serjeant, covering him with his AK, the other walked to the back door and had a look inside the window.

The leader now started to look agitated. He shouted at the Serjeant Major and pointed at the Rover. He gestured to the guard to open the back

4

door so that they could inspect for 'contraband'. There was no way we would let them look inside.

The Serjeant Major ignored him and using a strained but diplomatic voice again mentioned the free passage and not-to-bother-us spiel. Instead of getting frustrated, he seemed to be content to wait this one out. He smiled politely and stood his ground.

The Croat at the back of the Rover tried the latch on the door but it was locked. He called out to the Sigs Serjeant but he just stayed by the front with his arms folded, feigning ignorance. The Croat aimed his AK at the window and called out again. Again he was ignored. This really pissed him off and he charged around to the front of the Rover, almost slipping over on the ice. I could feel the tension mounting. He scowled at the Serjeant and pointed to the mines. He shook his head, shook his AK and returned back to his place by the other sentry.

A voice from inside the hut called out. The leader turned around and walked back inside. I looked at the hut. It was made of logs and planks nailed together, with clear plastic sheeting on the roof. Fir branches were draped across in an attempt at camouflage, and heaped on top was a covering of snow. A tin-pipe chimney came out of the back and was still puffing smoke. Hanging from the side was a line of small icicles, running back into the treeline. The icicles must have been hanging on a wire. Probably an antenna for a radio or line for a telephone. I realised why the leader was called back in. It was odds on he was informing someone about us. Probably his boss, possibly reinforcements, maybe a reception a little bit further on? Whatever it was, it didn't bode well.

The Serjeant Major still had not budged. We had been there for about ten minutes but it seemed like only seconds had passed. He looked calm and collected, quite the opposite of his Croat counterpart.

I could see the Serjeant shivering; not surprising, as the temperature had dropped well below zero. Condensation from his breath obscured his face and he was shifting his weight from left to right in an effort to stay warm. The commander of the Sultan was leaning back against the hatch, his arms by his side, trying to do the same thing.

The Croat leader reappeared and walked over to the Serjeant Major and stopped just in front of him. He pointed at the letter and indicated that the Serjeant Major give it to him. He quickly read the letter and looked up. He laughed as he gave it back and then mouthed something at the Serjeant Major. I didn't need to be a linguist to translate it; his body language said it all. *Fuck off and go home before we kill you!*

The Serjeant Major tried to say something but was cut short. The Croat

5

leader nodded at the sentries and started to walk back and forth in front of the Serjeant Major. He kept yelling in Serbo-Croat, shaking his head and gesturing with his hands that we could not pass. I looked at the sentries. They had raised their AKs again and were nervously stroking the triggers. Shit! Not a good sign. You could cut the tension with a knife.

I gradually slid down into the cupola and rubbed my hands together to warm them up. I only had my thin cotton inner gloves on and the cold was starting to seep through. I looked through the night-sight and very slowly traversed the L37 so that it pointed down at the Croat leader. I double-clicked the pressel switch. The familiar squelch sounded in the Sultan commander's headset. He glanced back at me and got the message. Slowly his right hand moved up to the trigger grip of his jimpy. I saw the barrel lower and turn as he did the same as me and pointed it at the group of Croats.

The Croats were so engrossed in their own actions that they didn't notice my disappearing act or the subtle movement of the Sultan's jimpy. In my sights were the Croat leader and the hut. To my right I could see that the other jimpy was covering the sentries. If the Croats got all menstrual about this and the shit started to fly, I had my reply ready. At 750 rounds per minute I could shred everything in sight within seconds. Multiplied by the Sultan's jimpy, we would definitely spoil the Croats' plans for Christmas with the in-laws!

The Croat leader was still not giving in and the Serjeant Major had still not budged. The situation was getting critical as the sentries moved closer. One sudden move and it would make the gunfight at the OK Corral look like a Sunday afternoon picnic. The leader now began to nervously stroke the trigger guard on his AK and stopped in front of the Serjeant Major.

The Serjeant Major looked down at the flash eliminator and prominent foresight of the AK. He stared probably a little too long, and when he looked up he saw the Croat leader grinning. The Croat knew he had won. The Serjeant Major looked over at the Sigs Serjeant. It wasn't the look of defeat he was expecting. The Serjeant stared at him and then without turning his head rolled his eyes in our direction.

The Serjeant Major looked back and saw the reason for the Serjeant's unexpected expression. We had the Croats covered with our jimpies and the situation had changed in our favour. Still keeping a straight face, he turned and looked at the Croat leader. He waited a few seconds, and for the first time since we landed in theatre, the Serjeant Major smiled.

The Croat leader looked confused. Why was this man smiling? He was beaten. The UN had a reputation of backing down, even running away, but we were still there. The Croat was starting to lose patience. I could see him nervously play with the trigger guard again.

I raised my thumb and stroked the firing button. One false move and he would have to be identified by dental records, if he had any. I played it out in my mind. First take out the threat and then traverse left, pepper the hut to stop the signaller calling for reinforcements. The other jimpy could take care of anything left standing. I felt warm and calm, the first time since we left the school in Vitez.

The Serjeant Major cleared his throat to attract the Croat's attention and nodded in our direction. For the first time since we had stopped at the checkpoint, the Croat leader took a really long look at us. The commander of the Sultan was leaning into the butt of his jimpy, pointing it directly at him, and the squat cupola had another machine gun pointing at him. I could see his expression change from confusion to shock. It was not what he had expected.

I could sense the Croat weighing up the odds. He seemed to be looking directly at me through the night-sight, his eyes burning with pure hatred. He turned and faced the Serjeant Major again and stood there for about twenty seconds. You could almost see the cogs turning in his mind. He played with the trigger guard again, looked behind him and saw the two sentries. They had already lowered their weapons and had stepped back. He now knew the bluff was over, and he had lost. The Croat had gambled but the unarmed British soldier in front of him was now holding all the aces. He had lost. Reluctantly, he pointed at the mines and gave the order to clear them.

The two sentries moved to the front of the Rover and began kicking the black TMA-3 and TMM-1 anti-tank mines to the side of the road. I kept my sights on the leader, who turned and went back into the warmth of the hut. No doubt he would contact his superiors and tell them that he had failed to stop us and we were on our way. The two sentries stood back as the Serjeant Major and Sigs Serjeant got back into the Rover.

'Ready to move?' I called over the intercom.

'OK,' replied my driver, 'I don't suppose I've got time for a piss?' He laughed nervously and gunned the engine.

As we moved off, I traversed the cupola, keeping the Croats covered. One of them raised his AK into his shoulder and pointed it at us. I didn't want to give him the chance to zero in, so in reply I gave him a burst from the cupola searchlight. That should fuck up his night vision for a few hours!

When we turned the next bend, I stood up again, traversed the cupola

7

and settled back against the hatch cover. The icy cold started biting again as we moved closer to our destination. I looked around the countryside and prayed that the Croats had not radioed ahead to warn their snipers. I put on my arctic mitts and started to shiver again.

Chapter 1

Germany, July 1995

We boarded the Hercules C130 at RAF Lyneham, dragging our kit with us up the rear ramp. Also on board were two military policemen and their prisoner, two Crab loadies and a half dozen pallets of soft drinks cartons. We sat down and listened as a loadie give us a quick talk on safety.

The chubby Crab looked bored and told us the basics: 'There's the bog, sit down and don't touch anything!' He scratched the arse on his tight-fitting olive-green flight suit as he walked to the flight-deck. He came back with a box of earplugs for each of us. He probably thought he looked really sexy with badges everywhere, Foster Grants and slicked-back hair, but to me he looked like Elvis in his Las Vegas days. We strapped into the plastic-cloth bench seats and listened as the engines started up.

The whine of the engines started to get high-pitched, and stayed like that. The airframe started shaking and above us, inside the fuselage, exposed cables vibrated like oversized guitar strings. Elvis had put on a headset and went to the windows to have a look-see at the engines and once he confirmed that they were still attached to the wings we started to taxi along the runway.

The engines started to get louder as we began trundling along, trying to get some speed up, but we quickly defied gravity and after a few minutes levelled out, heading eastwards to our new home. I looked around at my surroundings. The Monkeys were taking the cuffs off their prisoner; he wasn't going anywhere now, unless he had delusions about hailing from the planet Krypton. That left the five of us, all spread out and trying to get as comfortable as possible. I looked down through the porthole at the fields below. The gentle tapestry of green, yellow and brown seemed to cover the land as far as the eye could see. The beautiful landscape of southern England disappeared as we slipped into the clouds. It started to get chilly. Time to put my fleece on.

The noise inside the fuselage was deafening and the little yellow earplugs didn't really stop the noise, so I looked inside my day sack. I had a spare pair of ear defenders with me for occasions like this and put them on over the earplugs. That was much better, now I could relax. I looked over at the others. They all seemed lost in their own thoughts; just as well because conversation was pointless. I started to get bored quite quickly. I knew I should have brought a book.

I tried to nod off but gave up on that when the loadie handing out lunch threw a white cardboard horror box onto my lap. Inside was a small satsuma, a carton of blackcurrant drink, a chocolate biscuit in tinfoil, a packet of ready-salted crisps and a meat-tasting paste sandwich so tightly wrapped in cling film it was half its original size. I wondered what they were having in first class.

We tried to swap with each other but had to settle for what we had because the Crab cooks were being extra nice today and had given us all identical boxes. The meals took about five minutes to finish off, leaving us feeling hungrier than when we started. I looked over at the loadie. His lunch box was twice the size of ours. He dipped inside and pulled out a hot Cornish pasty. In between bites he sipped on a can of Coca-Cola. He then had a fat sandwich filled with chicken and salad, followed by a banana and a Mars bar. So that's what they were having in first class! It was them and us, no inter-service camaraderie here. No wonder the Army disliked the RAF.

After Elvis did his rounds with a bin bag, I shuffled to the back of the plane near the ramp. I pulled the curtain back and stood by the stainless-steel toilet. We hit some turbulence as I started to piss and I had a hard time keeping my aim. Staying upright took priority, so it looked like Elvis had some mopping up to do after we landed.

We left Wiltshire on a cool and blustery day and landed in Paderborn in glorious sunshine. We collected our kit, watched the MPs drag their prisoner off to a waiting minibus and waited for someone to identify himself to us. Then we waited some more. Finally one of our group, Corporal Nufer, who was not one for inefficiency, stormed off to see if he could find someone. Nufe looked like Richard Gere in *An Officer and a Gentleman*, had the build of Mike Tyson and the temper of a Mafia henchman! He was the perfect squaddie who strived for perfection in everything he did. Unfortunately he had a problem with the slackers who stole the oxygen meant for real soldiers. He came back a few minutes later with a rather shaken-looking individual who we found out was the driver sent to meet us. He was taking a nap in the car park when he had met the

'Nufe'. A quick bollocking and a helping hand soon woke him up. This was our first introduction to our new regiment – I hoped it would improve!

It was a short drive to Allenbrooke Barracks. We stopped at a gate and waited to be let in. The sign on the entrance proudly stated that it was home to the 2nd Battalion the Light Infantry, a battalion of our sister regiment. The armed sentry checked the driver's ID and opened the gate. I looked up at the tall gothic white buildings as we drove through and took in the grandeur of the place. It was much older than I thought it would be, not like the modern barracks I had expected. We stopped outside the Battalion HQ and unloaded our kit. A clerk told us we were to be billeted in the Transit Block until we were posted to our platoons. We humped our kit up the six flights of stairs and were given a large room to ourselves.

After handing over our documents we had a brief on what to expect. Over the next few days we would join the Training Wing where we would wait until the battalion found out what to do with us. That would start in the morning, so with that we all spruced ourselves up and went to the NAAFI for a few beers. The NAAFI, or Warrior Club as the name above the door said, was officially the private soldiers' bar, but it was used by most ORs. It was huge, and there was a show on tonight. Over 200 squaddies were crammed in watching a hypnotist as he made complete fools of anyone stupid enough to get up on stage. It was a really good show, and the huge crowd of young men and women were in good humour. Every voice I heard had a Geordie accent. Every other shirt was a Newcastle United FC top. I knew it was a predominantly northern battalion, but this surprised me.

I looked up at the hypnotist. He had persuaded a young fair-haired Geordie that another contestant was a beautiful girl in a bar. The crowd was in stitches as Blondie tried to chat up the other contestant. Blondie was giving his best chat-up lines, but the other guy was calling him a homo and pushing him away.

The hypnotist suggested to Blondie that he should take his clothes off, which he did willingly. I watched as the crowd jeered and shouted encouragements as one by one Blondie's clothes came off. The subject of the love-struck Geordie's advances had enough of this affront to his masculinity and went to take a swing at him. The hypnotist snapped his fingers and stopped the lovers' tiff just before any blood was spilled, and the two Romeos sat down, heads drooping, sleeping.

At ten thirty the Battalion Orderly Officer and some provost corporals came in to make sure that the bar closed on time. We drank up, went back to the Transit Block and settled down for our first night in our new home.

The next day we paraded at the Training Wing. There were a few different cap badges there, waiting for the DS to let us know what was going to happen while we waited to be posted to the various platoons. Some had arrived a few days before us, some only a few hours ago. There were a dozen lads from the LI, two from the RGBW and seven of us from the Royal Green Jackets. We had all answered the call on Part Two Orders on our company noticeboards for volunteers and were now formed up waiting apprehensively for what might lie ahead.

I had met four of the RGJ lads from my battalion a week earlier when we officially got our orders. Chris Emmins was a section commander in my company and one of our PTIs. The other three were from Support Company. Corporal Colin Nufer was from the Anti Tank Platoon. Corporal Bob House was from the Machine Gun Platoon, while Lance Corporal Perry Tuson was a sniper from the Reconnaissance Platoon. I was the oldest by far, as I had re-joined at the upper age limit for joining, but the fact that I had previous military experience went in my favour. It never bothered me that some of my seniors were younger than me. They had earned the right and that was fine by me.

This was the first time we had all met each other as a group. We all served in the same battalion but as we were in different companies our paths rarely passed. I knew Bob House from my JNCO Cadre and was pleased to see a familiar face. Chris Emmins had recently transferred in from the Royal Anglian Regiment and had just settled in when he packed up and left again. He probably had a bit of Gypsy blood in him. The other two I didn't recognise, but I had made a few enquiries and found that they were highly regarded.

We all had our own reasons for joining 2LI. For some it was to get away from their own units, maybe to improve their promotion prospects or get away from a dead-end job. For some it was a chance to see active service. I fell into that category, but there was an even stronger motive. For me it was a chance to be able to do something positive, however small, to help stop the horrendous things that we saw on the news. Night after night I had witnessed the terrible events in Bosnia unfold. I was angry that the combined military might of the West wasn't being used to forcibly stop the genocide, and I felt ashamed at being part of it. I felt useless and wondered what was going on out there. Maybe there were excuses why other professional armies were standing idly by while innocents were massacred, and for me it seemed incredible that the Brits were doing it as well. So when I found out that 2LI were going to Bosnia not as peacekeepers but as a fighting unit to confront the Serbs and needed men to make the numbers up, I did the one thing my dad always told me never to do in the Army – I volunteered.

The first thing the non-LI guys had to do was find out how 2LI did things. This was to ensure we fitted in and didn't stand out too much. Regimental pride is a strong factor in how a unit bonds. Every regiment has its own traditions, history and uniforms, and the LI are justifiably proud of theirs. Regiments do things in different ways and inter-regimental rivalries can be intense. It's these differing identities that bring the soldiers together and mould them into what is undoubtedly the finest infantry system in the world. And, of course, as 'new boys' we didn't want to fuck up!

At the Training Wing, the Directing Staff told us that we were to stay there while our paperwork was assessed and to fill the available post within the battalion. During that time we went on runs, carried out tests on weapon handling, NBC, first aid, signals, and AFV recognition. We all had done these tests hundreds of times before and it was second nature to us. It could have been very boring but I suppose that being bunched together with blokes from different units made us try just that little bit harder to impress so we didn't let our own battalions down.

After we had settled in for a few days, we were introduced to the CO, Lieutenant Colonel Ben Barry, who told us he was glad to have us along, and to the god-like figure of the RSM, WO1 'Diddy' Mathews, who echoed his boss but also warned us not to fuck up! We also had German lessons, an introduction to the local garrison, and an interesting guided tour of Allenbrooke Barracks while at the double!

During lunch breaks and in the evenings, we caught up on the news. BFBS, the squaddie channel, was available on the TVs in the NAAFI and we were kept up to date on the situation in the Former Yugoslavia. The other armoured infantry battalion from 20 Armoured Brigade was already there. The 1st Bn the Devon & Dorset Regiment were operating from Vitez, as Taskforce Alpha, and had been on live-fire exercises around Tomislavgrad in preparation for ops on Mount Igman. They were there as Force Protection for the UN, quite different from BRITBAT, the British UN contingent for UNPROFOR. There was talk about being on standby to relieve Sarajevo, along with Taskforce Bravo, the French element. It looked like war was getting closer day by day.

Safe havens were being attacked but there was none of the retaliation that was being promised by the politicians in the West. We started learning of new names like Mostar, Srebrenica, and Bihać. Ethnic cleansing was still the new buzz word, and pictures of Belsen-like prisoners were shown

13

(after teatime, of course – they didn't want to upset the pads while they had their pizza and chips!). NATO was trying to enforce a no-fly zone and dropped the odd bomb or two long after the Serbs had gone home for the day. As usual, the news ended with a light-hearted story about someone's cheeky pet or school sports day, but due to our imminent deployment the reality of the war in Bosnia stayed fresh on our minds.

The most unnerving news item for us though was the capture of 33 Royal Welsh Fusiliers in Gorazde. They were shown locked up and guarded by victorious and dangerously hyped-up Bosnian Serb Army soldiers. We chatted about how we would react if confronted with capture. The general consensus was that we would fight our way out of it, but I suppose the Fusiliers had the same idea. We didn't know the circumstances of their capture, but the discussions went on for days. It was a sobering turn of events.

After the first week, despite being from so many different regiments and backgrounds, we had all gelled together. The two non-Light Division lads had even learned to march properly at 140 paces to the minute instead of the tortoise-like 120, and had mastered the relaxed commands that were given on parade. In the Light Division (LI & RGJ), everything is done from the at-ease position, with few words of command, a legacy of the Napoleonic Wars when light infantrymen and riflemen needed a less rigid system of command and control while they protected the cumbersome lines of 'Heavy Infantry'. The bugle was used to give signals when drums were too unwieldy and became the symbol of all light infanteers.

By the start of week two, we had covered everything a dozen times over, and the DS looked at ways of keeping us busy while the AGC in Battalion HQ took their time processing our docs. We had our first introduction to the Warrior IFV, the main fighting system of the battalion. We filled in forms and more forms, and refilled the forms that were lost while going from one desk to another in the same office. We stated our preferences for postings, and I hoped that I wouldn't get stuck in a shitty job that no one else wanted. We opened up German bank accounts and drew some cash from the Battalion HQ to tide us over until payday at the end of the month. We had more German lessons and joined the Battalion on their weekly eight-mile cross-country 'fun run'.

By the end of week two, we were given more time off, like longer tea breaks, lunch breaks and early finishes. That was welcome because it was so hot we were constantly washing our sweaty kit, and getting it dry and ironed took time. We were even asked what training we would like to do while we waited for Battalion HQ.

On the second Friday, we sat down in the classroom waiting to find out where we were going to be posted. The day previously I had an interview with the Regimental Signals Warrant Officer, WO2 John Thirlwell, who seemed impressed by my experience and my course report from the Signal Wing at the School of Infantry. He said he would see what he could do, but his hands were tied by the decision of Battalion HQ. I had no interest in joining any other platoon and had set my hopes on sigs. I had been a rifleman in a platoon, then section 2I/C, but had caught the signalling bug on a Signals Standard 2 cadre. I changed jobs and became a platoon signaller, under Lt Fox, then Driver/Operator of the company FFR. It was a stroke of luck on my part when my Detachment Commander, 'Skippy', became ill and I took over. I quickly gained a reputation within my battalion as the 'man who can' when it came to maintaining comms on exercise.

Peacetime soldiering has its merits. I found it challenging and rewarding and was in a battalion with an excellent reputation and superb *ésprit de corps*. I was respected by my seniors for my abilities and I had good prospects for promotion. It sounds like I had it cosy in my battalion and had no reason to leave, but as I have mentioned earlier I wanted to do something positive about the war to stop me feeling so bloody useless, but my wanting to see active service meant the chance to actually do the job for real in combat, something that might have passed me by if I stayed. On exercise in the British Army conditions are as close as possible to the real thing without actually chucking ordnance at our own troops. Sections can charge up and down all day perfecting their tactics, but the life-threatening reality of incoming live rounds can only be found in a combat zone. Signalling is one of the few roles where your job in training or in front of the enemy doesn't change. Communicating remains the same regardless, and we were constantly reminded of that fact by our seniors in the Signal Platoon. But war isn't like carefully planned exercises where the correct frequencies for the terrain are picked beforehand or the times for the different phases are known by everyone in company HQs. Troops tend to move more often and the changing tactical situation is dictated by the enemy, not your own officers in a planning cell. Being shot at or bombed wasn't just reserved for the attacking infantry sections, and we would all need to be on top of our drills and skills. I was a highly trained and a capable soldier, and I wanted to put my skills to the ultimate test. We were told that 2LI had serious manpower shortages and certain platoons had priority. We were soldiers first and the needs of the battalion came first. So like the others, who hoped to carry on where they had left off in their own units, I sat there and awaited my fate.

One by one, our names were called out by the DS and we learned where our new homes would be for the next year. It was near the end of the list when I heard 'Lance Corporal Howard – Signal Platoon'. I felt relieved. There were a few disappointed faces around me. From the RGJ lads, the others had all ended up in the Milan Platoon (not a fashion-conscious platoon, but named after the anti-tank missile system it used!). Corporal Nufer was delighted, but the others were disappointed, especially Lance Corporal Tuson who was hoping for the Recce Platoon. The Anti Tank Platoon was one of those with acute manpower shortages.

Next was a list of personnel who were to report for further training. That meant Warrior driver and commander or Warrior gunner and commander. Everyone sitting there had come from a light-role battalion, probably never operating out of anything more exotic than a four-tonner. I liked the sound of being a Warrior gunner. I waited expecting the best. I was told to report to the Driver Training Wing on the following Monday morning at 8 a.m. Oh well, maybe next time.

We were dismissed and went outside. I had made friends over the last week with a corporal from the RGBW and went over to see him. He didn't look happy at all. Corporal Jamie Ross had passed SCBC and had more infantry qualifications than any of us, but had made one simple error – he declared he had an HGV licence. Now this warry son of Wiltshire, who should have been leading his section in desperate battles against the odds, was going to war as a truck driver!

I went into to the Sigs Platoon offices and reported to the RSWO. He welcomed me to the platoon and told me that he had arranged the Warrior driver course, and it would be essential to his plans that I passed. He needed multi-skilled signallers who could operate any equipment, in any role and in any vehicle. I was told to report to the Support Company stores and get accommodation in the Sigs Platoon floor in the Support Company Block. With that he looked back down and carried on with his paperwork. I guessed it meant that the interview was over, so I backed quietly out of his office.

As I walked past the Sigs Platoon garages, I stopped and looked in at the variety of vehicles. There were Sultan, Spartan, Warrior, Land Rover and the mainstay of the British Army Armoured Infantry for over thirty years, the FV 432. I could see what the RSWO meant by multi-skilled.

The company storeman was a cheerful Lance Jack who showed me around the Support Company Block. Sigs were on the top floor and we checked the rooms for vacancies. As a lance corporal I should have been assigned a single room, but those were all taken, so I picked a space in the tidiest room. Besides, my rank was only one step above a private and I never really let it go to my head. There is a saying in the Army that the rank of lance corporal is the hardest rank to get and the easiest to lose. There was no point getting airs and graces just yet. The room had spaces for four beds, but had only two taken in it. Hanging above each bed was a football scarf – one Newcastle United and the other Hereford United. So there was a non-Geordie in the platoon. There was also a certificate above his bed, a GOC's commendation from Northern Ireland. There was also a sofa, coffee table, stereo, TV and video. Very nice indeed! I sat down on the sofa, put my feet up on the coffee table, and looked over at the happy blanket stacker. Looking like a customer who had just had the perfect test drive, I grinned at him and said, 'I'll take it.' He looked confused, so I asked him to get me a bed and he gladly wandered off while I brought up my kit.

I was still unpacking when the first of my new room-mates came in. He sat down under the Hereford scarf and introduced himself as Pete Wass. He had the nickname 'Sass' as he was a fitness fanatic and wanted to join his local regiment. He was awarded the GOC's commendation for saving the life of a civvy on the streets of Ulster. He seemed an all-round decent lad. I was still shaking his hand when I heard the second room-mate enter. I turned around to see Blondie standing there, the participant from the hypnotist show. I smiled at him and introduced myself. Private John 'Mac' McGee clicked on a kettle and made himself a Pot Noodle, to tide him over until teatime, which was only about half an hour away!

These two were to be my insight into the platoon, and despite the age difference we became good friends. The room decorations were bought by themselves, and I guessed it was Pete Wass that kept it tidy. Mac was busy undressing and throwing his kit all around his bed space. With a huge grin hc slurped down huge mouthfuls of Pot Noodle, while trying to look for his pride and joy – his Newcastle football top.

Soon after we had another visitor from the room next door, Lance Corporal Trevor 'Roger' Moore. He was an easy-going Shropshire lad and was married to one of the AGC clerks. He was living in while he waited for a pad. The news came on the TV and the room went quiet. My new room-mates and I sat down and watched BFBS for the latest goings on in the Balkans. As Taskforce Alpha we saw that the D&Ds had their normal black and green camouflaged vehicles as opposed to the standard UN white. We were to take over from them but at this time 2LI's Warriors were being lined up outside the vehicle sheds and were being painted white, so it looked like someone in Battalion HQ had fucked up. It was

17

also the first time since the Crimean War that a British unit was being put under French control, something that the jingoistic British tabloid press somehow failed to moan about. In Srebrenica the Dutch UN contingent had apparently let the Serbs walk into the town, and now there were unconfirmed reports of massacres as the UN helplessly looked on. The last of the Welsh Fusiliers had been released and there was footage showing strained smiles as they were reunited with their battalion. This time there was no puppy-dog story to finish with; even BFBS were getting serious.

Many of the live-ins were back by now and getting ready for scoff. It was very informal in the Sigs accommodation and there was a constant stream of people popping in to borrow things or just chat. I was introduced to those who stopped to say hello and it didn't take long for them to mention the LI nickname for the Royal Green Jackets. I was a 'bin lid', a reference to the shape of the RGJ cap badge. That was a new one for me. The RGJ call the LI ''alf-ers', meaning that they were only half a cap badge. The RGJ cap badge has a bugle in the centre of a Maltese cross, surrounded by a wreath, and topped with a crown. The LI only had the bugle, hence 'alf-er. I thought 'alf-er was a stupid nickname and didn't have the right amount of bite, so when someone called me bin lid I just called them a wanker, which worked every time!

We all went over to the cookhouse for some scoff and to get to know each other. The cookhouse was huge, and there was plenty of seating. The JNCOs were supposed to sit apart from the privates, but no one really enforced it. Army food has had a reputation of being barely edible, but the food served up here was very good. The choice was varied and plentiful, with loads of imagination. It was a shame that the vista was spoiled by the miserable-looking slop jockeys who stood by and waited for the usual verbal abuse that came with the job.

'What's in the sausage rolls, chef?' a squaddie would ask, always loud enough so that his audience could hear how funny he was, and always seeming to think that he was the first person to ever tell the joke. I looked at the cooks. I wondered if my father would have identified with them. He was an amateur boxer and wanted to join the Paras for his National Service in 1954, but like so many young men of his era ended up in a totally inappropriate job – the Army Catering Corps. Two years in Austria trying to please a hungry army of occupation on meagre rations was a difficult job but he loved the challenge. Maybe the cooks today needed a challenge other than running the Army's version of school dinners.

We carried our trays away, found a table close to the orange squash

18

dispensers and sat down. It was in the mid-30s outside and the weak transparent orange-coloured liquid was in high demand. We chatted about the Sigs Platoon. The RSO, RSWO, Sigs Colour Serjeant, two serjeants and about thirty-three men made up the numbers. Included were the drivers and gunners for the COs and 2ICs Warriors, which were the responsibility of the Sigs Platoon. The platoon, like the battalion, hailed from the length and breadth of the British Isles. The Cornishmen were the quietest, with noise levels increasing as you got closer to Hadrian's Wall. No wonder I thought 2LI was a Geordie battalion. There was a corporal in charge of the Signals floor in the block, Corporal Pratt. His nickname was 'Imer', but I was yet to find out if it suited him. The platoon was made up of mainly older members of the battalion and about two-thirds were living out. The married 'pads' were housed in one of the garrison's many housing estates, where they had as close to a normal family life as the Army allowed. A few single lads had rented rooms to get away from the barracks, which left about a dozen live-ins.

I asked about the RSWO. He was a Geordie and was reputed to be an outstanding signaller. Rumour had it that he had a 320 HF radio set in his mobile home. HF is the most difficult method of combat signalling and takes a lot of skill and knowledge. Antenna lengths have to be calculated for each frequency and atmospheric conditions have to be taken into account. Real signallers understood HF and took pride in being able to use it. A big surprise was the fact that he was originally from the TA. He did an S-Type many years ago and decided to stay on. Not only had he survived the Regulars' dislike of the TA, but he had managed to achieve high rank in a technically difficult job. I was impressed.

I looked around at the packed cookhouse. There were no black or brown faces to be seen. I came from a multiracial battalion, where we had a good mix of all colours and creeds. It was surprising that 2LI had none, considering the size of its recruiting area.

We talked about the best places to go in Paderborn, which meant Movie Stars, the Toll House and Paddy Murphy's Irish Pub. The City Club and Black & Whites were the best discos, and a few even ventured into Sennelager to the Hollywood Nightclub. I was warned to keep clear of the Turkish bars, as the Turks were rumoured to be very handy with a blade if you looked at them or their women the wrong way. I was also warned about the Monkeys. At night they roamed the streets looking out for drunken squaddies. If they were unsuccessful, they just might pick you up out of boredom.

Named after Field Marshal Alanbrooke, the barracks was an interesting topic for me as I had always been interested in history. It had recently been refurbished and had once been a German Army infantry barracks dating back to the 1800s. There were even some horse troughs and stables in one corner where the officers had kept their mounts. It had been taken over by the British Army when the allies took Paderborn in the closing stages of World War Two and they had been there ever since.

That night myself and a few of the new arrivals lads went out to Paddy Murphy's and sunk a few beers while we watched the local boxheads try and sing along to an Irishman with a guitar. The most comical moment was the ad lib chorus of Smokey's 'Living next door to Alice'. With beer in hand, they roared 'Alice, Alice, who ze fok iss Alice!' It was hard to keep a straight face, so we didn't!

On the way back to the barracks we spotted the Monkeys, driving an immaculately clean purple civvy minibus at about 5mph, looking every bit like gay kerb crawlers cruising the streets for talent as they eyed up every male that they passed. I'm glad that I never ended up spending a night in the cells, wondering how they carried out cavity searches!

That weekend we heard that more reinforcements had arrived. Apart from some more from the LI, there were eight from the Paras. One of them, 'Sammy' Sampson, was an old sweat and had fought with 9 (Para) SQN RE in the Falklands War, back in 1981. Another of them, a lance corporal, was about to become the most recognisable soldier in the battalion. Elgar StMart was stocky, wore his Para smock like it was an Armani original, and was very, very black. If the Paras stood out from the crowd, then Elgar stood out like Ronald McDonald in a mosque!

The Paras, after the usual slagging and distrust, settled in, but there was nearly a mutiny when they were told to take off their beloved parachute wings! A meeting with the RSM and phone calls from, to and from the 5th Airborne Brigade followed. Eventually 2LI relented and the wings stayed up. I liked the men from the Paras; they had an infectious attitude and a casual professionalism, much like the Royal Green Jackets. I got on very well with them, especially Lance Corporal Stevie Locke. He was about my age and was always laughing and smiling. Unusually, he had passed P Company late in life, and was a fellow West Ham fan.

Chapter 2

The Warrior and the Old Statesman

On the way to start my Warrior driver training, I crossed paths with Lt Phil Fox, one of my old platoon commanders from the RGJ. He came out to Germany a month before me and was posted as a platoon commander in A Company. He was the best PC I had ever worked with and was glad to see a familiar face. We said hello and had a quick chat about what we were up to, then went our separate ways. He was cheerful and confident, a young man in his element. I knew he would do well.

Warrior Driver Training was carried out in the Driver Training Wing. Of the thirty students, most were new arrivals from the LI and RGJ. We were introduced to the DS and listened as they talked about the programme for the next three weeks. As with all Army courses, we were not allowed to touch the goods until we had learned how they worked. We started with a video introducing the vehicle that had enabled the British Army to outperform their allies in the Gulf War of '91.

We sat back and listened to Ringo Starr narrate over what seemed a boring selection of Warrior footage from Salisbury Plain. Left to right, and back again, the Warrior glided across the screen. After a minute, the view changed to a lane with steep embankments to the sides. I expected the Warrior to appear at the top of the screen, like in a Western, a cowboy riding along the trail. There seemed to be a wait of ten seconds and the Warrior had not appeared. A few of the class had already lost interest and were chatting away. Suddenly a Warrior flashed across the screen, followed by another, then another. Instead of the predicted ride down the lane, the Warriors had simply jumped across the embankments.

'No way!' shouted one student.

'Not a fooking chance!' shouted another.

The video finished and the DS came back to the front of the class.

'What you have seen is just one of the things that the Warrior can do.

With its turbo-charged 17.5-litre engine you can beat cars away from traffic lights, it can climb steep gradients at speed and it can turn and stop on a sixpence! If you are good enough, I just might let you drive one.' The DS looked around. He had our complete attention.

The morning was spent learning the basic characteristics of the Warrior. Capable of carrying its 25 tonnes at 75kph, it was a beast. It carries a crew of 3 plus 7 troops, and is armed with a 30mm Rarden cannon and co-axial 7.62mm chain gun. Our first and most important lesson about the Warrior was health and safety. The Warrior is full of dangers, from heavy steel hatches, the tracks, the hydraulically operated rear doors, and the 'turret monster', the protective cage surrounding the turret working parts. Many a careless squaddie had a scar or lost a part of a finger due to a lapse in concentration. I heard of at least one who had lost his life.

The next day we learned how to maintain the Warrior. The first job is called a first parade and is carried out before you start up any vehicle in the Army. Fuel, oil, washer bottles and lubricant levels are checked, then mirrors, tracks (or wheels) and body condition and, after starting it up, lights, horn and comms. During any long stop a halt parade is carried out, and after parking up a last parade is carried out, intended to leave the vehicle in a better condition than when it was found.

On the third day, after carrying out our first parades, we had our first drive in the Warrior. It was within the confines of the barracks, in the car park outside the Warrior sheds. As we drove up and down, we could see the platoons carrying out routine maintenance on their own vehicles and painting them UN white. To the platoons, the Warrior was as familiar as the family car, so no one looked up at our clumsy attempts to get to grips with this amazing half-million-quid heavily armed sports car!

The Warrior unusually has a normal steering wheel, unlike the levers found on all other tracked vehicles. It was small and sporty, and folded away to allow for access. The gear lever was on a shelf on the left, and the seat was height adjustable. In the normal driving position when driving, the seat and hatch are raised, and the seat is lowered in the closed or combat position.

My first drive lasted for only a few minutes, but it gave me an indication of how easy it was to drive and the tremendous power available. Stopping, I found, was an art. The Warrior *could* stop 'on a sixpence', but it would also throw the soldiers in the back into the turret monster and those in the turret into the raven sights. Apart from the obvious injuries you could cause, like cuts and bruises, you could end up getting a good kicking for it as well from the pissed-off crew. A good incentive to remember the passengers!

We learned about the signals installation of the vehicles and how to operate them, from the intercom to radioing other vehicles. We also learned about the volumes and different types of fuel and lubricants it used, so that we could maintain it and order the right amounts when in the field. We learned how to command the Warrior, and the necessary link between driver and commander. As the driver position is on the front left, your field of view is restricted to the front and left. The commander has the best view, and communicating what he can see is vital to the vehicle's safety, especially when we ventured out onto the perfectly kept roads of the North German Plain.

It was there that we learned to drive with confidence. At first, the DS commanded the vehicle, and then it was left to the students. We drove through picturesque villages and through beautiful farmland, all the while enjoying the brilliant sunshine. After many hours of 'driver advance', 'prepare to stop' and kerb crunching we all became proficient, and so moved onto the Sennelager Training Area to go cross-country. (And yes, it did beat cars away from traffic lights!)

We spent the next few days on the AFV (Armoured Fighting Vehicle) course, a rollercoaster of mud tracks and water obstacles. The Warrior covered every type of ground with ease. The scariest part was when we were ordered to drive down a near vertical ten-metre slope. We watched from the bottom as the DS showed us it could be done, but I can honestly say that it was one of the most frightening things I had ever been asked to do.

Sitting tensely in the driver seat, I drove up to the edge of the slope and stopped. Because the front of the Warrior obstructed my view, all I could see was a clear blue sky. The DS ordered me to advance, but every sense and feeling in my mind and body told me it was suicide.

'What are you waiting for?' said the calm voice in my headset.

I couldn't refuse in front of the whole class; I would never hear the last of it, so slowly I inched forward. It takes a lot of confidence in your commander to drive into what appears to be an abyss, but the DS had probably done this a thousand times, so I took the plunge and gently pushed the accelerator. The feeling of twenty-five tonnes tipping over the edge was like nothing I had ever experienced. The Warrior crashed down onto its front suspension with an almighty thud and rocked back. The dry earth suddenly came into view, but instead of hurtling down at high speed or tipping over in a labouring somersault, the tracks bit and we ambled down at about 5kph. A few seconds later I was at the bottom and thinking what all the fuss was about. I exchanged with the next student and walked over to the group that had already done the drop. No one mentioned the fear factor, but later on at lunch we all recounted how daunting it was, and how we couldn't wait to do it again.

The more mundane lessons were for vehicle maintenance, including the dreaded 'track bashing' (changing the tracks – so called because of the use of many large sledgehammers). Track bashing was a necessity, but no one relished it. It was messy and labour intensive and was the cause of many small injuries if you didn't give it 100 per cent. Then again you could stand back like the slackers that are keen to give advice but not that keen to do any work!

At the end of the third week, we were given the usual final written test, as well as taking the tracked vehicle test (H licence). In the written test I shared the top score with a lad from REME, with only a couple of re-tests in the remainder of the class. Everyone passed the driving test. Unusually it had been a 100 per cent pass rate, but the importance of the task ahead had probably given everyone a big incentive to succeed. I loved every minute of the Warrior driver course, and from the faces of all my classmates I knew I wasn't alone in my thoughts.

I went back to the Sigs Platoon office to give the RSWO the news that I had passed and I was told that next I was to report for more driver training on the 432, after I had taken two weeks' leave.

Leave? I'd only just got here! I couldn't believe my ears. The whole battalion was going on summer leave, and the RSWO said that meant the entire platoon, no exceptions. I was surprised but I wasn't going to say no, so I went down to the Company Office to get the flight details.

So after only six weeks with my new battalion, I headed back to England, but this time to London Stanstead, much closer to home. A travel warrant got me a train ticket to London, then the Tube to Barking to stay with my sister Mandy and her family. It was nice to see my mates again, and I got to see the Hammers lose 1–2 against Leeds in the opening game of the season. I hoped things would improve. I kind of guessed I would need a few morale-boosting wins to keep up my spirits while I was away. It should have been an enjoyable break, but I had two young boys, Daniel and Conor, from a short-lived marriage, and I was told by my ex that I couldn't see them as two weeks was too short notice. The social calendar at playschool must have been hectic that term. It was a difficult time for me. In a few months I was due to go to the most dangerous place on earth and it could have been the last time I saw them. So I did the rounds, seeing as many of my friends and family as possible, and headed back to Germany.

The FV 432 was introduced in 1962, the year I was born. It should have been phased out at the end of the eighties, but it was still in service, thirty-three years on. It was the old statesman of Britain's armour and the battalion had four variants: command post, mortar, ambulance, and recovery and repair. The 432 was obsolete and should have been replaced by a Warrior variant in the mid-eighties. In the Gulf War in 1991 it was a serious liability, as it could not keep up with the rest of the armoured battle groups. Trials, but most likely costs, had delayed replacements. Milan Platoon had recently handed over their 432s and were waiting to receive brand-new Warriors from the UK. Just in case, they trained to carry everything – they were determined not to be left behind and declared that they would manpack in Bosnia if they had to!

As with the Warrior, we learned about the 432 from the classroom first. Corporal Chris Woods from the Sigs Platoon was our DS, and our class of sixteen were split up into two groups. We were introduced to the mortar variant, with fully opening hatches on the top where the business end of a mortar tube does its work. We spent many hours standing up in the back, trying to catch the breeze as temperatures reached their mid-thirties.

We practised driving around the bollard course in the vehicle park, carrying out three-point turns and reversing as squads of soldiers ran by, sometimes in PT kit, sometimes in CEFO carrying someone on a stretcher, and always with a PTI shouting words of encouragement that would make a sailor blush. Outside the sheds, Warriors were being repainted black and green, and fitted with an extra five tonnes of Chobam armour. One day, while I was driving a Sigs Platoon Land Rover back from the cookhouse after collecting the day's horror boxes, I passed a group of men outside the Anti Tank Platoon offices. They were carrying out AFV recognition on the Milan, looking through the sights at tiny model tanks laid out on a poncho. The instructor was Corporal Nufer, and from the irate look on his face I bet he had their full attention!

The intensity of the Warrior course was replaced by a more relaxed attitude, mainly set by the DS Corporal Chris Woods from the Signal Platoon. All of the class had already passed their H licence, so really this was just a conversion course. It could have taken just a few days, but the Army had it down for a three-week course, so a three-week course it was. This meant lots more hours driving on and off road, and lots of long lunch breaks eating our horror boxes in the gloriously sun-drenched German countryside. On the AFV course at Sennelager we sat back and watched the Royal Engineers as AVREs filled anti-tank ditches with bundles of pipes and AVLBs bridged streams, followed by speeding Spartans. We were not the only ones getting ready for war.

I enjoyed my driver training, but the real work lay ahead. After gaining the 432 driver/commander qualification, ten weeks after my posting, I finally joined the Sigs Platoon. In six weeks the battalion would be deploying to Bosnia.

Chapter 3

Pre-Bosnia Training

Even though we officially began pre-Bosnia training two months prior to deployment, it could easily be said that the battalion had been preparing for years. The battalion had missed out on the Gulf War of '91, having handed their Warriors over to a light-role battalion (to rub it in, 2LI trained them as well). 2LI were also on stand-by for deployment to Bosnia for the last few years. The standard of the soldiers was very high; the battalion were the BAOR's top guns, having won the AFV Gunnery Concentration for the previous few years, and the battalion had recently returned from Ex Medicine Man, a large armoured formation exercise in BATUS, Canada, where they had fine-tuned their tactics.

The real reason why 2LI had lost out in the past was the problem of retention. When the old 1LI was disbanded in 1991, the two remaining battalions saw a major change in personnel as hundreds of men were moved from their 'homes' into the new 1 and 2LI. Even within a large regiment, battalions have their own identity, and many of the new faces resented having to change the way things were done. Petty jealousies and favouritism between personnel from the old battalions meant men were overlooked for promotion, or were given unwanted roles. The feeling that the battalion was going nowhere, the years of garrison life, and poor job satisfaction resulted in hundreds of men taking Premature Voluntary Redundancy. That meant more men were leaving the battalion than were joining from the Depot. The battalion was severely under strength and needed reinforcements before it could be considered as operationally viable. It was a catch-22 situation that needed to be turned around and quick. The new attachments that joined around the same time as me accounted for about 10 per cent of the battalion's fighting strength. After summer leave another thirty men from the RGJ, and some blow-ins from other regiments arrived, ensuring that the battalion was up to strength for the first time since Options for Change in 1991. Now it could get ready for war.

I did not realise it at the time, but my Bosnia training had started a few years earlier in the summer of 1993, when we were on exercise with 24 Airmobile Brigade. During a two-week exercise with the MND(C) on Salisbury Plain, my Company was ordered to the Copehill Down FIBUA village. We were to provide enemy for 1LI and a German Fallschirmjäger battalion.

But before that could take place we were thrown a wild card. A Dutch battalion of the MND had been put on notice to deploy to Bosnia as part of the United Nations Protection Force, and as they had absolutely no training in this role, they urgently asked for assistance. 24 Airmobile had no hesitation in tasking us to assist them by carrying out a realistic exercise to help prepare the Dutch for the unknown.

Together with the FIBUA Training Team at Copehill Down, a plan was devised to create a realistic scenario for the Dutch to prepare themselves for what possibly lay ahead. The Dutch would bring aid to a fictional besieged Bosnian village, while my company played the parts of besieger and besieged. As we had riflemen from many different ethnic backgrounds, we split up into militia and villager. Dressed in civvies, those of darker-skinned Indian, Cypriot, West Indian and African extraction, together with some very skinny Cockneys took on the role of starved and bomb-happy Bosnians. The rest, dressed up like Mexican bandits with belts of 7.62 crossed over their shoulders, became the Serbs surrounding the village.

The brief was simple – harass the Dutch and make things very difficult. Improvise, be awkward, aggressive, and copy anything we had seen the Serbs do on TV. Using empty anti-tank mines supplied by the FIBUA Training Team we blocked both roads into the village. The first attempt at gaining entrance into the village was from the northern access road, but the Dutch, accompanied by some Spartans from 51 Field Squadron RE, found it was mined and tried the southern access road. Again, the 'Peacekeepers' met the same reception, so the Dutch decided to wait it out. We ignored them, harassed them, bullied them, and then ignored them again. They were threatened at gunpoint, and some of the younger Dutch conscripts were pushed around. Many 'Serbs' played it very real, probably due to their urban upbringing, but true to their national demeanour, the Dutch stayed calm and polite, if not a little confused. It started to rain heavily but that didn't put us off. We simply held out and asked for bribes. The Dutch conscripts, bored and confused, began to congregate near the front of the convoy. That was the cue for some of the more light-fingered riflemen help themselves to the kit in the back of the unguarded trucks. Rations, clothing, the odd FN rifle and even some C4 plastic explosives found their way back to the Company HQ. The Dutch Commander tried to bribe his way past the road block, but gave up on that idea when he was informed that the rations he wanted to barter with had gone missing!

The Copehill Down Training Team was aware of the tremendous benefits that could be made of this impromptu exercise. They observed from the clock tower, orchestrating the events as the day went on, and issued us a video camera so that the events could be captured on film. So, as a complete surprise to the Dutch Commander, a British news team turned up, followed them around, adding to the authenticity. Our company 2I/C, Captain Charles MacDowell, who doubled up as our Battalion PRO, made a perfect reporter.

The scene was made more real as shots and thunder flashes could be heard in the village. After about four hours we got the nod from the Copehill Down Training Team and let the convoy through. The villagers cheered as they drove in and some of the Dutch conscripts became a bit emotional when they saw the filthy wet villagers in tracksuits surround the vehicles begging for food. The Dutch took over an empty house in the middle of the village and set up a barbed-wire perimeter. Unfortunately they left the vehicles outside the perimeter so again a few of the more light-fingered amongst us took what left, including all of the ignition keys!

The odd rifle-shot still echoed around the village, together with larger explosions as pyro was let off. By now most of the 'militia' were in civvies as well acting as refugees. The refugee problem was made worse as we brought in casualties and tried to break the barbed-wire perimeter for food. Our Company Medic made up one of the girls in the Company to look like a victim of a sniper. She was dragged by a dozen villagers to the Dutch sentries who panicked at the realism. Fake blood mingled with the rain as the Dutch medics gently put her on a stretcher and took her inside the building. Shots still rang out and thunder flashes wore at the Dutch sentries' nerves, making them flinch and duck. The rain never stopped and the Dutch quickly became tired and confused. We kept this up for about thirty-six hours, when endex was called. We went off to a well-deserved cooked breakfast. The Dutch just stood around, shocked by the sudden turn of events.

After we had fed, cleaned up and changed back into uniform, we settled down to a few hours' kip before the next phase of the exercise. The Dutch Commander met with our Company Commander, Major 'Rocket' Ronnie McCourt, and commended him on the realism of the exercise and hoped it would help his men in the months to come. He was almost apologetic when he asked for the return of their weapons, explosives and ignition keys, but he said we could keep the rations (too late, we had already scoffed them down to supplement our own!).

The videotape made during the exercise was so valuable as a training aid that it was kept by the Copehill Down Training Team and used to help with the training of UK-based British units getting ready to deploy. From the TV and newspapers we knew that the Dutch had a hard time of it in Bosnia, and I hope that we played a part in ensuring them a safer tour.

In the Sigs Platoon we prepared for the battalion FTX which would be the last training the battalion would carry out prior to deployment. We had to prep the vehicles as we wouldn't have enough time after 'Pre-Boz', the Bosnia Theatre-specific training period that all units deploying to Bosnia had to carry out.

Under the direction of the Sigs colourboy, Colour Serjeant Martin Carney, diffy and U/S kit was replaced and spares ordered. Steel ISO containers were packed with kit, as well as a few luxuries. A few TVs and video players were found a space, as well as some made-to-measure kit that wasn't listed in any Complete Equipment Schedule. Sigs training upped a pace, with refresher training and long-distance comms exercises being carried out.

When the unfilled positions within the platoon were allocated, I was given my war role, as Signals Detachment Commander for the RAP. I would be responsible to maintain comms with the companies and ambulances so that casualties could be treated as quickly as possible – after all, the MO and medics would have better things to do rather than to play with radios. I would have a 432, and on the side would be a huge red and white 'Don't shoot' sign. My hopes for the safety and the sanctity of the Red Cross would soon disappear as we learned that to the warring factions we were just another target – just more clearly defined!

We were hoping to get issued with the new all-seasons Soldier 95 combat uniforms before deployment, but were disappointed to find out that we would have to make do with our old kit. A fire in the RLC storage depot at Donnington had apparently destroyed thousands of tonnes of stores. That had now become the standard excuse for delays in issuing badly needed replacement kit. As we were due to go on active service, we expected to be given priority for kit, but it seemed that other units in the UK were higher on the list than us, so we had to make do. I couldn't understand why a soldier on ceremonial duty in London needed a new combat kit, but with wisdom reminiscent of the Crimean War, the powers that be at the MOD decided otherwise. We were issued some arctic kit to help with the Bosnian winter. It consisted of four pairs of thick woollen socks, a white face mask, Gore-Tex mittens and cotton inner gloves and a fluffy 'woodsman'-style hat. The hats were all medium but must have been measured on children, so only fitted the smaller lads. As usual, the Sigs Platoon was last to be kitted out; even the AGC cooks and clerks had hats that fitted. I wasn't that bothered, and like most squaddies had my own woolly hat that would do just as well. It was khaki and could roll down into a balaclava, and it had already come in useful on many occasions while on radio stag in the back of a freezing-cold FFR.

We were also issued with our light-blue UN berets and helmet covers. We all soaked the berets to get a good fit, and had a parade so that the Company serjeant majors could inspect them. After all, we didn't want to look untidy in front of the warring factions now, did we?

As we got closer to deployment, the RSM decided that we needed a bit of a morale-booster, and decided to wake up the battalion in the traditional way – to the sound of the bugle! At 06:30 hours on the dot, a bugler sounded reveille. It was a noble and romantic gesture, reminiscent of the days of Empire, but it wasn't appreciated by the Support Company platoons who were accommodated next to the Bugle Platoon. After about a week of ear-splitting wake-up calls, a few of the donkeys from Mortars decided to do something about it. They waited in the stairwell by an open window, opposite where the bugler would compete with the birds with their early-morning symphony. As he wet his lips and took a deep breath, the donkeys let loose a high-pressure jet from a fire hose, which knocked him sideways. Soaked, and with the wind knocked out of him, he stood up and looked over at the offending window.

'Now will you fooking shut up?!" barked a voice from the window. The bugler looked up, spat out water, and disappeared into his block. He never appeared again. Later we found out that the local boxheads had also complained to the CO, so the RSM had to reluctantly give up on that idea.

Even after savouring the delights of the local Bierkellers, I had managed to save a little and decided to take advantage of the tax-free goods available in the NAAFI. I bought myself a good-quality Canon compact 35mm camera, some films, a small battery-powered shaver and a

31

Walkman. Like most of us, I wanted to take some souvenir photos, but the Walkman was for morale, especially when boredom reigned.

'Pre-Boz' was a concentrated three-week exercise carried out under the supervision of the Specialist Training Teams in Sennelager. The battalion was arranged into platoon- and company-sized groups and did a series of stands designed to introduce us to the varying conditions and incidents we could encounter.

First, we were given an intelligence brief by analysts from the Intelligence Corps. We had all seen the news and had our own ideas on the situation. The int briefs were designed to introduce us to the current situation and the history behind the conflict. It was hoped that an understanding of the history of the region would make our role easier to undertake. We all piled into an old auditorium and watched on a big screen a clip from *Blackadder Goes Forth*, while we waited for the inevitable death by viewfoil to start. The laughs were loud, but over the next few days they were harder to come by as we faced the reality of what lay ahead.

A WO11 from the Intelligence Corps began the introduction from a podium in the centre of the stage. He explained, with the aid of maps, that Yugoslavia was a federation consisting of Serbia, Montenegro, Croatia, Slovenia and Macedonia, along with Bosnia and Herzegovina. It was ruled from 1945 by the Communist dictator Josip Broz Tito, a hero of the Second World War. The language was Serbo-Croat, and Communist rule had kept a firm grip on these varied ethnic groups. These were mainly the Orthodox Serbs, the Catholic Croats and the Muslim Bosnians. After Tito's death in 1980, for ten years, a rotating presidency came into place, with each of the major ethnic groups taking it in turns to head the government.

In 1990 the status quo began to disappear as nationalism began to gain ground within the ethnic groups. Backed by Belgrade and Zagreb, nationalists started to arm themselves as they declared autonomous regions within Bosnia. The countdown to civil war had begun.

The fuse was lit for the conflict in Yugoslavia in June 1991 when Croatia declared independence. The Serb minority, actively supported by the Serbian government and the predominantly Serb Yugoslav People's Army (JNA), defeated the inferior Croat National Guard and created their own Serb Autonomous Region of the Krajina, roughly one-quarter of the country. With assistance from Belgrade, the Serbs began to remove all non-Serbs from the region. This was the start of a new and chilling phrase that would become known in every household around the world – ethnic cleansing.

Slovenia declared independence soon after Croatia. The Serb minority with the aid of the JNA tried to overthrow the government, but were defeated after ten days of heavy fighting. In October 1991, Slovenia gained international recognition as an independent state. However, against the backdrop of the fighting, in November 1991, Macedonia was able to become independent without a shot being fired. In January 1992 Croatia was recognised as an independent state.

The real problems lay in Bosnia and Herzegovina. Caught in the middle between Croatia and Serbia proper, the bordering regions were overrun by both Serb and Croat nationalists creating their own autonomous regions where they quickly set about cleansing anyone who didn't fit their own nationalist picture – mostly the Muslims. In April 1992, Bosnia was officially recognised by the international community as an independent state. This forced the Bosnian Serbs to declare an independent Serbian Republic of Bosnia. Radovan Karadzic, the Serbian president, ordered his military commander, Ratko Mladic, to link all Serb-controlled areas of Bosnia and remove all non-Serbs. The Bosnian Defence Force was totally unprepared and was no match for the Bosnian Serb Army. By Christmas the Serbs were in control of around 60 per cent of Bosnia. Encouraged by this, the HVO, under Mate Boban, created the Croat Bosnian state of Herzeg-Bosnia. This led to the Muslim–Croat war in central Bosnia. From May 1993 to March 1994 ethnic cleansing was carried out by the Croats with the same brutality as the Serbs were doing in northern and eastern Bosnia.

The account might not have been 100 per cent historically correct or accurate, but it was only intended to give us an idea of why the conflict started. The Int Corps didn't get bogged down in the blame game. We were being sent to help stop a war, not to take sides, but it was apparent that the Serbs were the major offenders. The talk was short but it did give me the answers to several of the questions that many of us had pondered over during the last few months. I looked around the auditorium at the mass of DPM. Many of the privates were bored, not really able to take in so much info at one time. In contrast, the NCOs seemed to be more alert, many taking notes.

The weather in the Balkans had made Yugoslavia a favourite destination for holidaymakers across Europe for the past ten years. During the summer, temperatures reached the low 40s, and news coverage often showed troops working in T-shirts. All very nice, but we were about to learn what the weather gods had in store for us. It was no coincidence that the Winter Olympics of 1984 were held in Sarajevo. The

Dalmatian coast, warmed by the Adriatic Sea, remained quite mild, but in the mountainous interior temperatures dropped dangerously low. We were informed that at night we could expect temperatures of minus 10 around Vitez, dropping to minus 20 around Sarajevo. Then we were told the bad news. Wind-chill factors in exposed areas would drop temperatures even further, depending on the location. On the move, vehicle crews, in their exposed positions, would feel the worst of it. On Mount Igman we could expect minus 30, and I knew that we might have to put a Rebro on other mountains. I made a note to pack all of my cold-weather kit, even the dreaded army-issue long johns.

Next was a talk on the role of the UN. Contrary to popular belief, the UN was not sent in to stop the war. In September of 1991 the UN imposed an arms embargo on all of the Former Yugoslav Republics. This was followed by Resolution 770 calling for all members to facilitate the delivery of humanitarian aid to Bosnia-Herzegovina. Basically, the UN went in to protect the aid convoys and nothing else. The United Nations Protection Force, or UNPROFOR, deployed to Croatia in September of 1992 to support the UNHCR in the supply of humanitarian aid. Based in a former JNA barracks in Split, the British element, BRITFOR, deployed over central Bosnia, on Operation GRAPPLE. In the early years UNPROFOR struggled to protect the convoys and their own bases. Slowly, the mandate changed and became more forceful. Safe Areas were set up, and the UN reluctantly agreed to use force to protect them. NATO was asked to enforce a no-fly zone, and they also began to use air strikes against any weapons found too close to the Safe Areas (Safe Havens). This sounded promising, but the UN rules of engagement (RoE) were complex and restricting, resulting in lengthy delays; it was often days before any action could take place.

Another factor in preventing the use of force was Russia. As fellow Slavs, they looked upon the Serbs as allies. The Russians might have sided with the rest of the UN in their attempts at providing aid, but they made it plainly obvious that they objected to the use of force against Serbia proper. It was a delicate situation and the last thing NATO needed was Russia and its mammoth military machine openly supporting the Serbs.

The UN main participating nations of France, Holland, Canada, Italy and Spain, as well as the British, were well known to have a military presence in Bosnia, but there were many smaller nations who also contributed: Norway, Pakistan, Bangladesh and Malaysia, as well as an old friend of Britain, New Zealand. A surprise to many of us was the deployment of former Soviet troops. Ukraine had a motorised battalion in the northern sector. There was also talk of the German Army deploying for the first time since the end of the World War Two, but a move into Bosnia would be politically sensitive so they would be kept in Croatia, a one-time ally of the Axis powers.

To identify the contingents on the ground, they were given shortened names. MALBAT was the Malaysian battalion, CANBAT from Canada, and so on. Not surprisingly, due to their more aggressive attitude and for stretching the RoE, BRITBAT also became known as 'Shootbat' by the other UN contingents!

Lt General Smith, a former commander of the SAS, had taken over from Lt General Rose, also a former commander of the SAS, as Commander of Military Forces in Bosnia, so command in theatre remained committed to a more forceful stance, even though the UN was bogged down by its own over-intricate RoE and political niceties. We had hours of briefings and films explaining the complexities of the role of the UN and when force could be used. The UN was getting a hard time in the world's press for failing to take control of the worsening situation. The UN military contingents in theatre didn't have the numbers to match the aggressors, but made up for it in professionalism and firepower. The main problem was political willpower. The efforts and sacrifices of the man on the ground were being severely hampered by the politicians' lack of will.

We were informed that many UN commanders had given warnings of Serb intent, only for them to be ignored. Mortar attacks on the market place in Sarajevo grabbed international headlines because of the shock value, but the real atrocities were made possible by the belief that by giving besieged towns a designation of 'Safe Area' the Serbs would respect them and not attack. We heard of how some of them fell despite warnings from UN observers, battalion commanders and Joint Commission Observers (JCOs). The JCOs were General Rose's men on the ground who reported directly back to him. It was classified information that they were SAS, but as the UN had promised the Serbs that special forces would not be deployed they were given a *nom de guerre* to disguise the fact they were in theatre. A lot the intelligence that came back from many of their little excursions was now being passed on to the hundreds of soldiers sitting in the auditorium in Sennelager who were preparing to leave the comforts of barrack life for the most dangerous place on earth.

We started to get some feedback regarding the attack on Gorazde. The Royal Welsh Fusiliers were hopelessly outnumbered and, despite warnings from their CO, the UN failed to act. Surrounded, the Fusiliers could do very little, and reports of great heroism were starting to emerge. Constantly shelled and fired upon, the 300 or so Fusiliers had a hopeless job of protecting the thousands of Muslim inhabitants. Small groups of Fusiliers were captured as they tried to stay in their positions to the last possible moment to prevent the Serb advance. After three weeks the Muslim defenders and the men from the valleys had held the town.

The Serbs, looking to save face, turned their attentions to Srebrenica, where the Dutch contingent, despite pleading for help, watched helplessly as the Serbs overran the town. Reports of genocide were beginning to emerge, but as yet there was no confirmation. A sixty-day ceasefire between the warring factions had been negotiated but it was very fragile. All factions had broken it already, but again the Serbs were the major offenders.

It was a hard job for the Int Corps to try and sell being a part of the UN as a good cause, but the formation of the Task Forces Alpha and Bravo was welcomed by the battalion who were looking forward to getting to grips with the Serbs. Now we were told that any serious acts of aggression could be met with force up to company level without authorisation from higher command. We all had seen the film footage on BFBS of the D&D Warriors and Light Guns of 19 Regiment Royal Artillery firing at Serb mortar and artillery positions around Mount Igman, while in the skies above NATO air strikes pinpointed tank build-ups. Now we were getting ready to spearhead the punch that would break the siege of Sarajevo.

As the area around Sarajevo fell under French control, we would be supporting their efforts. The French would have liked to do it without our assistance, but they lacked the one thing that would provide the necessary firepower and protection – the Warrior. French armour was designed for rapid deployment, which meant reduced armour for higher mobility, a relic of the Cold War when the French would need to travel long distances quickly to join up with their American and British allies in Germany if WW3 broke out. The British, already in Germany, relied on heavily armoured and armed formations for protection. For peacekeeping, the Warrior had an enviable reputation. The French were also very aware of that, and had no hesitation in asking the old enemy for help when it looked like they were going to be ordered to break through the BSA lines.

The Warrior was tough. We were shown news footage of a Warrior driving over an anti-tank mine that exploded throwing up a large cloud of dust and smoke. The commander nonchalantly looked back at the camera, shrugged his shoulders and moved on! The Serbs were calling the Warrior the 'White Death' due to its capability for withstanding attacks and the accuracy and speed of its armament. All very comforting to those of us who were going to have to rely on them in the very near future.

It wasn't just the Warrior that had an effect on the other UNPROFOR nations. The average British squaddie was also influencing the way they worked. Sickened by snipers preying on civilians and the fact that they couldn't officially help them, BRITFOR troops deliberately drove their vehicles in the line of fire to offer the civilians some kind of protection. It meant that if fired upon the Brits could return fire and, hopefully, give the gutless snipers the good news. It sounds like a good tactic, but if you consider that the Brits were doing this in soft-skinned Land Rovers as well as their armour, it shows the incredible bravery of men who were not prepared to stand idly by and witness cold-blooded murder. Soon, this tactic was deployed by most UNPROFOR units and began to change the way the UN soldiers were perceived by the local Bosnians.

We were updated on the other British units that were already in theatre. There were Challenger 1 tanks from the Queen's Royal Lancers, Scimitar CVRTs from the Light Dragoons, and the 1st Battalion the Royal Regiment of Fusiliers were in Saxon wheeled APCs. Various engineering support was there in the form of bridge layers, assault vehicles and EOD. All these got nods of approval from the assembled squaddies. The mention of the Royal Signals, Royal Logistic Corps and Royal Electrical and Mechanical Engineers was met with the usual shrugs that said of course we expected them there, but the mention of the RMPs gave way to groans of disapproval.

A less savoury lecture from the RAMC involved the various medical problems we could experience if we weren't careful. Larger-than-life close-ups of some very repulsive photos were shown, each for the different types of ailment we could experience if we didn't take notice. Sexually transmitted diseases vied with the results of digestive problems for our visual delight. The most memorable photo was of some poor sod that had 'spaghetti arse'! Not nice at all, and if anything would keep us from drinking the local water, thoughts of that image was it. It was funny, but not many men were hungry that lunchtime.

Outside on the training area, stands were set up by the Royal Highland Fusiliers to give us an introduction to the Bosnian environment. At the ranges we zeroed our weapons and carried out our APWT. We fired the jimpy from the prone position, and from the turrets of the 432. Here we practised walking the rounds on to a target by following the 'splash' on the ground. At night we followed the glowing tracer rounds.

We were introduced to a fairly new development in force protection. The Hesco Bastion was born on motorway construction sites where ground stabilisation was required due to collapsing excavations. A grey sack of geotextile material was filled with small stones and sand and wrapped in a wire mesh. Sand and stone is a good absorber of energy and has been used in sandbag protection for centuries, but sandbags can become unstable after a few hits from explosions and there was the risk of collapse. Now the sandbag had grown up. Standing about 1.5m high, Hesco Bastions are filled by an excavator and used in rows to form a blast wall. For the shelters another row was built on top and from there a corrugated roof covered in interlocking layers of sandbags completed the structure. A staggered entrance provided complete 360 degrees of cover, and lighting could be rigged up if needed. It was a proven life-saver already and was used extensively throughout Bosnia by the UN. Another form of protection was the standard steel container that is more commonly seen on the back of a lorry. Very tough and readily available, they were used as accommodation, stores and bomb shelters in confined places or in an emergency.

From all of the news and int reports we knew that one of the biggest problems was from mines. We had lectures on the types that were most commonly used by all of the warring factions. Most were of Soviet design, but a few older European types could be found. We were reliably informed that there were no mines of British manufacture in theatre, but to a squaddie a mine is a mine, and you don't stop to look at the 'made in' logo after it has just exploded under your feet.

Another problem was that most of the minefields in Bosnia were not set out, identified or mapped. Many areas were mined twice, and sometimes more, as confrontation lines changed hands week by week. The JNA used ready-made signs, but the Bosman Serb Army (BSA), the Bosnian Muslim Forces (known as the BiH – *Bosnia i Herzegovina*) and the Croat Defence Council (HVO – *Hrvatsko Vijeœe Obrane*) used less noticeable warnings like dots of paint at the base of a tree, crossed branches or small piles of stones. It was a chilling reminder that mines, whoever laid them, were used in Bosnia not to deter or deny access, but to kill.

Mine clearing is hard work. It looks fine when Hollywood portrays it on the big screen. The mine is always sticking out above the ground and probably has an edge or a prong sticking up. Tripwires glow with dew, and the heroes are all sure-handed experts at bomb disposal. In reality it is very different. Mines are very well hidden, and trip devices are not always seen. The tactical situation means that you are constantly looking in all directions, not just at your feet. Infantry soldiers do not carry mine detectors; they have enough equipment to carry as it is. That is a role for the Royal Engineers, and they are not always close by. Also, in disregard of international law, many mines were now made from non-metallic materials such as plastics and even wood, so the anoraks' favourite weekend gizmo would be useless looking for them.

So, reminiscent of photos of the eve of the battle of El Alamein, the DS (Army course instructors) crawled on their bellies, using a steel prod or bayonet to feel for the unwelcome thud of something solid. Shaky hands would then slowly remove enough earth to make a positive ID. Small markers would be left locating anything for disposal by the RE or our own Assault Pioneers, while white or orange mine tape would mark out a safe route. To make the exercise more realistic, small detonators were placed around the training area, ready to scare the shit out of anyone who didn't give 100 per cent. I had sat through this lesson and carried out the drills dozens of times, instructed by the Assault Pioneers from my own battalion, but as the instructors kept on telling us, remember the rule of Ps – planning and preparation prevents a piss-poor performance, but with mines a piss-poor performance could be fatal. So when it came to my turn and with that gem of wisdom in mind I got down on my belly and got dirty.

From there we went through a series of live-fire exercises covering many of the situations we might come across in Bosnia. We had all carried out live firing exercises of one kind or another, but these were specially written by the RHF, who had just returned from a tour of Bosnia, and were designed to mimic the conditions we would encounter.

In section- and platoon-sized groups we practised rescuing wounded men from minefields while live rounds whistled over our heads. We probed forward on our bellies to retrieve them, coming under fire from snipers. We returned fire and extricated the casualty to safety.

We patrolled and came under machine-gun and mortar fire (pyro-technics). We fell back using fire and manoeuvre, when Warriors from the RHF arrived, using their chain guns to suppress the enemy (figure eleven targets), while we sought safety in the backs before they sped off.

From two-man trenches we manned defensive positions and waited to be attacked. In daylight we listened for fire control orders while figure elevens and twelves popped up at distances of 600m down to 50m. The attacking rows of targets represented a charging enemy, while dozens of thunderflashes and smoke grenades added to the realism. At night, tired and hungry after the day's training, we would wait while section commanders and 2ICs watched out for movement with their night-sights. A contact was initiated by a remotely fired trip flare, and the targets would begin to pop up. Because night-sights don't work in bright light, those with normal sights would take out the targets until the flare faded. Then those with night-sights would carry on, until Schermuly flares fired by the section commanders went up, when the roles changed again. Again, more thunder flashes and smoke grenades going off just in front of us added to the realism.

We also learned to identify the direction and distance of incoming rounds. We sat in an open field while rounds flew about over our heads, with instructors from the Small Arms School Corps pointing out the subtleties of listening to the crack as it flew overhead and counting the seconds before the bang reached us. This was a little bit unnerving, even for those that had done this exercise before, as you had to rely on the steady hands of those firing, but we understood the value of the exercise.

We heard loads of stories first hand from the Jocks of what to expect. Many had stories of incoming fire and stressed the importance of our training. The Jocks were good instructors and seemed to have a genuine interest in passing their hard-won lessons on to us.

Classroom lessons covered revision of the basics and some new topics, too. First aid was revisited with the battalion's RAMC medics covering a bit more than the required ABCD. Concentration was high, especially as it was likely that we could be using our skills very soon. NBC was always a boring subject, but no less important. The threat in theatre was low, but we had good int on JNA stockpiles of chemical weapons and so stepped up training in case Belgrade decided to up the ante.

AFV Recognition had recently taken on a new dimension. After the collapse of Communism, the new combined German Armed Forces took control of thousands of former Soviet tanks, AFVs, aircraft and other assorted equipment. Also, many of the UNPROFOR nations used Soviet-supplied or licensed equipment. Now the enemy was our friend. Identifying the slight differences between a mud-covered Serb or Bangladeshi BTR 60 was almost impossible, and the last thing we wanted to do was take out a friendly.

An added twist was that a whole host of WW2 vehicles and equipment had been commandeered from museums and storage. Mothballed T-34s, German and American half-tracks, American armoured cars and even Sherman tanks were seen in the fighting. Ancient artillery pieces, along with mortars and rocket launchers, were recommissioned and used alongside their more modern counterparts. Improvisation was the order of the day, especially for the impoverished Bosnians. Steel pipes became mortar tubes and munitions were locally made. Damaged equipment was never abandoned and quickly found its way back into service in one form or another. Cars, jeeps and trucks had sheet steel welded all over to make makeshift APCs, and some even had rudimentary working turrets.

We were given useful little booklets provided by the Int Corps. The *Rat Recognition Guide*, produced by 18 Intelligence & Security Section, was an accurate list of equipment in use by the warring factions and became an invaluable *aide-memoire*. We were getting a mounting pile of handouts for each subject and they made compulsive reading in the weeks before we deployed.

At the end of 'Pre-Boz', we carried out a three-day FTX, covering basic armoured formation drills and scenarios based on what we might find in Bosnia. Here I joined the RAP. I drove the Command Post 432, and another signaller drove the Ambulance 432. Both of us were responsible for maintaining the vehicles and communications, while RAMC or 2LI CMTs commanded them. We loaded up the med stores, personal kit, food and water. Joining the rear of the Battalion HQ column, we moved from Allenbrooke Barracks and headed onto the Sennelager Training Area.

The first phase of the exercise for us was to practise the Diamond Formation. This is the standard tactical formation used by an Armoured Battalion HQ, where the elements form the shape of a diamond. The RSM and Provost Staff are at the point facing the enemy but behind the companies, with the HQ in the middle, and the other elements at the other corners. The RAP is positioned close to the bottom of the diamond, and the distances would be set by the ground conditions, tactical situation and available cover. The idea is that the RAP is as close to the battle as is safe for casualties to be treated. From there, RAMC ambulances would take away the seriously wounded to a nearby field hospital.

On the Training Area, we were led by a regimental provost onto the track plan. This ensured that all vehicles followed the same route, and in theory only one set of tracks would be visible from the air. Despite this, we saw the RSO's Spartan flying around, apparently lost. The battalion was moving on radio silence so we didn't know what was going on. We moved into a large wooded area and began to set up the RAP tent and equipment. The medics were quick and set up in minutes. Operating tables and oxygen bottles stood next to boxes of surgical equipment and medicines. It looked like a miniature scene from *M*A*S*H*. All that was lacking was music blaring from a Tannoy and the beautiful female nurses! In the CP I set up the map table, logbook and stationery. I didn't need to put up a mast, as comms were good, but made one ready just in case. With the ambulance cleared of equipment and everyone ready, we shut down the engines, hung the loudspeaker on the back door and, like so many squaddies before us, put a brew on.

In the meantime the RSO was still lost. Someone must have given him a map and instead of waiting to be shown in, he tried to find Tac himself. Camouflage from the air is a priority, so once in location the cam nets are always put out immediately, making the vehicles and command-post tents almost invisible. To add to his confusion, the forests on the training area were very big and crisscrossed with tracks from years of armoured activity. The RSM's group were still putting out the Tac signs, so after following the wrong tracks and passing by his intended location, he was called by an impatient zero and asked where he was.

In an effort to explain that he was close by, the RSO got on the net: 'I have stopped close to your location. I can hear engine noises coming from my rear.' There was a pause and then we all burst out laughing. In an attempt at maintaining security on the net, the RSO had made it sound like the reason for his delay was that he had a serious bowel problem!

The exercise from then on went through the motions as planned. We had calls for the ambulance and treated many fictitious wounded, who after a few hours of hanging around the RAP were returned through the system to their companies as battlefield casualty replacements. The net was full of Batco and contacts from the companies. Everyone was busy. That evening, instead of using the net to send the RAP Sitrep and Logrep, I wrote them down and following the track plan, walked about 500m to Battalion HQ. I gave the message to the duty watchkeeper and had a chat with some of the Sigs guys. Here, the smell of hot chocolate, coffee and cigarettes prevailed. In the confined space of a command-post tent it wouldn't be long before that was replaced by the musk of dozens of hard-worked and unwashed bodies.

The FTX was going well, and I was warned off that a move was imminent, one of the advantages of personal contact. Noting the details, I walked back to the RAP. Once back I informed the MO of my news. He decided to pack away all the non-essential kit so that when the order 'prepare to move' came we would have more time to sort ourselves out and prevent anyone from throwing any teddy bears about.

After the first day we moved from a tactical stance to one of high visibility. This was the peacekeeping phase of the FTX and involved a lot of patrolling, convoy escorts and setting up temporary bases. The role of the Bosniacs went to the RMPs, who manned a series of checkpoints. We waited ages to get convoys through many of them, only to find that after a few vehicles had gone through, the Bosniacs would stop the remainder and split the convoy. This was designed to frustrate us but we had been warned of this time and time again and so sat it out. In Bosnia, some aid convoys had been separated from their escorts in this way which resulted in the aid being taken by gunpoint at the checkpoint while the escort happily drove off thinking all was well.

We all learn from our mistakes, especially costly ones where lives and property have been taken, so we trained with two escorts, one front and one rear, so that in the event of a similar ploy, the convoy would still be protected. The Monkeys took great delight in messing us about, so we just sat there and played out the scene. The Monkeys probably thought that they were doing a great job of pissing us off, but the average infantry soldier is quite happy to sit on his arse and do nothing, so the contented looks from the crews were definitely not what they expected.

Three days does not sound a long time for a military exercise prior to a major deployment, but it was the culmination of months of hard work and much was achieved in that short period. The command and control of the battalion, companies and platoons was rehearsed, as well as tactics and logistics. The Warriors had a good shake-out as well, with very few problems. Lessons from the past three weeks had been put into practice and, apart from a few expected hiccups at the start, the battalion performed extremely well. At Endex the Sigs Platoon paraded for the CO, who was all smiles and he thanked us for our efforts. We all smiled back but the main thought was embarkation leave, and the nice man would let us go after we cleaned up and put all of our toys away.

So after we washed down the vehicles and kit, parked up, restacked shelves and paraded for dismissal, those on the first embarkation leave said their goodbyes and headed home. Some, mainly pads, stayed, the majority flying back to the UK. Those of us waiting for the second leave period went back to work on the Monday morning and finished packing the remaining kit for deployment. Warriors were packed and waterproofed before being driven to the train station and loaded onto flatbed carriages, then transported to the North Sea to await loading onto a ferry. A few lucky sods would be taking in a Med cruise on their way to Bosnia.

During this period, we spent most of the evenings out of the barracks. Paddy Murphy's, The Savoy and the Toll House became our retreats, while we tried to clear our heads for a few hours. We needed a release from the pressure of training and you just couldn't do that in the NAAFI surrounded by reminders of who we were. There was a group of about a dozen of us from the new arrivals and Sigs Platoon, who used to meet up in town. We had a great time and if you saw us, you would be forgiven if you thought we were a local pub league football team on holiday. At weekends we would end up in the City Club, and afterwards grab a pizza or gyros for the walk back to barracks. We looked as if we hadn't a care in the world, but munching away, we were lost in our own thoughts, thinking of our impending departure.

Chapter 4

Pre-Embarkation and Deployment

When it came to my embarkation leave, I stayed in Germany. I would have liked to go back to the UK to say my goodbyes but I wasn't entitled to a free flight, and after sending back some money to my ex I was left short and couldn't afford to pay for one. Staying in Germany wasn't too bad. I helped my room-mates sort out their kit and had a few good nights out without the worry of getting up for work in the morning. A memorable one was when Hendo Henderson and me got up on stage to sing at a karaoke night in Paddy Murphy's. I wasn't too keen but Hendo was up for it, so I thought what the hell. My mother's side of my family are very good singers and I have many aunts and cousins who sing professionally in Ireland. Unfortunately I didn't pick up those particular genes, and from the sound of Hendo his singing gene had mutated into the shrieking gene many generations ago. We murdered Jackie Wilson's 'Higher and Higher' and even the normally enthusiastic German crowd booed us off the stage. The DJ running the night was in bits laughing at our attempt and gave Hendo a tape of our effort as a reminder of the night, which I promptly told him to destroy!

When everyone was back from leave, we heard of rumours of a compulsory drug test (CDT) being carried out, but before a list of personnel could be posted for testing we had a shock in the platoon. Two of our lance jacks turned up at the Med Centre and confessed to taking drugs. It meant that they were immediately put on restricted duties and had blood tests. We had no doubt that they had taken drugs as they had a bit of a reputation, and the threat of a CDT had forced the matter into the open. If you are caught taking drugs you are instantly kicked out of the Army with a dishonourable discharge and loss of pension. But if you voluntarily admit to taking drugs, the Army has a responsibility to rehabilitate you, meaning light duties and a full pay packet to pay for your habit while you sort yourself out. Both were living out and needed time to sort out jobs, so it suited them to hang around once we had departed. I don't think it was the thought of going to war that made them walk in and chat to the MO, but they needn't have bothered as the CDT team never materialised.

As one of the two was a company detachment commander it was a big blow to the platoon. It meant the RSWO had to transfer one of our lance jacks to that company and reorganise the Platoon Orbat. He was severely pissed off at the inconvenience and we kept out of his way for a few days. In return we got a lad from anti tanks who was close to being lynched by his oppos for being a nutcase. No one wants a troublemaker, and especially one who wasn't trained in your role, but we were desperate for manpower and after an interview in front of the RSWO without coffee the new lad quietly settled into the day-to-day running of the platoon.

For the rest of us life carried on as usual. The colourboy always found work for us and if there was an exceptionally long pause during proceedings the full screws would line us up and watch as we carried out area sweeps of the building perimeter.

One morning the Sigs Platoon was called into the platoon office for an important brief by the RSWO. While we waited and found a space to sit, Hendo pulled out the tape of the karaoke night and played it to the whole platoon. It was worse than I remembered and totally embarrassing. Hendo seemed quite pleased and even started to sing along, which started a barrage of flying Batco wallets and pamphlets, all headed in his general direction!

The RSWO came in and seemed happy that the platoon was in high spirits. He went through the Orbat, flights and platoon admin. The Platoon Orbat was pretty much sorted before the FTX, but the loss of two experienced signallers meant a few changes. We had to take over three Rebros that covered Task Force Alpha's AOR. Comms would be vital for the battalion's deployment, and as the RSWO didn't want the platoon to let him down he would only be putting his best signallers on them. They were important jobs, and I was surprised to be given one of them. It was probably due to the fact that one of the lance jacks he had down for that job was now putting his feet up waiting to talk to a drugs counsellor. Apart from the full screws that ran Main, Tac and Echelon, there were a few dirty looks from the other lance jacks. It was a prime role and huge vote of confidence from a very demanding RSWO. I knew that I wasn't the original choice, but I was still chosen ahead of my peers, and it gave me a great boost.

46

Next we went through the procedure for getting the flights. It would take five days to get the battalion to Split in Croatia and the RSM wanted it to run smoothly and without any cock-ups. The Advance Party would consist of the head sheds who would take over essential jobs from their D&D counterparts. On Main Body 1 would be those who would be needed to take over some of the other key posts. That included the three Rebros. We were told to read Part Two orders on the Support Company noticeboard for the lists of all flights.

Later on the Sigs colourboy issued our UN brassards, which we had to wear from the moment we left Paderborn. It had a green shoulder flash with 'Light Infantry' written in yellow. Under that was a small Union Flag, and under that, badges of rank were worn. At the bottom was the white and blue UN badge, big and bright. I couldn't see them staying smart for long. We were also given an Op Grapple 7 'tour' sweatshirt, to be worn when off duty. I wondered at the choice of the code-name of the operation. I thought that names were only used the once and care was taken not to repeat names to prevent confusion with other operations. I don't think the Army had done their homework on this one. Grapple had been used previously for the very high-profile operation by the RAF in the Christmas Islands in 1950, when they dropped the first H-bombs. I knew we were being prepared for conflict that could potentially bring in the Russians on the side of the Serbs. Maybe someone was trying to tell us something?

The Support Company CQSM issued all the living-in squaddies with two boxes to store kit to be left behind, one for military and the other for civvies. We were to store them in the attics of the Company Blocks when we deployed. Electrical items like TVs, videos and stereos could be left in the company stores. We were also issued MFO boxes, one between two men, which would hold our spare kit and a holdall with civvies in for leave. Our spare military kit would go in our green canvas holdalls. To identify our Bergans, we were given a small wooden tag. Ours was a yellow 'T' and we had to write on it our name, regimental number and platoon. Like many of the platoon, I tied it on to the top with para cord.

The last hurdle before deployment was Op Eval, an evaluation of the battalion's operational readiness. For a few days' tests were carried out on a random number of the battalion's personnel to see if they were up to the job. It was the last hurdle before deployment and I imagine that there were more than a few worried senior officers in Battalion HQ. A unit that fails has to stand down while another unit takes its place. It's rare, but units have failed, so we all let out a big sigh of relief when word came through that we had passed.

* * *

The pace of life in the battalion slowed down in the last days before deployment. Everything had been done so it was just a matter of waiting and going through kit lists we had been given showing the essential items we needed to pack, as well as items to take in the holdall. We set about packing our Bergans. Non-issue warm-weather kit was a priority. I packed two sets of Marks & Spencer's thermal underwear that my sister had sent me, a Berghaus fleece, and my SAS arctic smock. Of the issued kit, a set of coveralls, a Norwegian shirt, T-shirt, towel, spare boots, socks, foot powder, the arctic kit, bivvy bag, poncho, tent pegs and jumper HD spare all went in, topped off by my helmet. This was followed by essential items like my spare water bottle, housewife, toilet roll, candles, spare AA batteries, head torch, spare notebook, spare 35mm films and some spare tapes for my new Walkman. NBC kits were to be stored in theatre, as the threat was still low, so we were ordered only to take our respirators. I didn't trust this, so packed a spare vacuum-packed NBC suit in one of the side pouches. I wasn't going to be caught out stuck on a Rebro while some spotty blanket stacker wondered why he still had a set left over!

My webbing was already packed since I had cleaned and sorted it out after the FTX, but I still went through it in case I thought of anything else. I replaced the tape used to tidy up the loose straps, and rewrote my name and 'Last Four' of my army number on all of the parts. The ammo pouches were supposed to be for ammo only, but I also had a US-issue speed loader which fitted in nicely with the magazines. In my water bottle pouch I had a Teflon mug and water bottle, with a few dozen puri tabs stuffed into the little pocket in the pouch lid. My rear pouch had emergency boil-in-the-bag rations, brew kit, gas cooker (less canister – they weren't allowed on the flight so would travel with my MFO box), racing spoon, comms cord, hexi blocks (for emergencies), lighter and storm matches. I never used my mess-tins for cooking in the field so stored them in my Bergan. That gave me a bit more room in an otherwise small pouch. My respirator case was next, which, apart from the respirator itself, included a spare canister, vacuum-packed inner and outer gloves, detection paper, combo pens and decontamination powder. Between them and the left-hand ammo pouch was my bayonet frog. The bayonet was in its scabbard and sat nice and tight on the belt. In a rifle regiment a bayonet is called a sword, but as I was in a line regiment I bowed to their customs. My webbing could have carried more, but I needed space for ammo, rations and any other kit I might be issued. It would have been easy to add another pouch and fill that up with bits and bobs, but I came from a light-role battalion, where we carried everything, and weight is a premium. You learned to cope with the minimum of kit and I wasn't going to change the habit.

My room-mates both tried on my webbing and liked the fit, so asked me to help sort out theirs. Years of life in an armoured battalion where the vehicles carry your burdens had made their webbing look like a line of washing. We took them apart and started from scratch. We discarded the crap, put it back together, tried it for fit and taped off the straps. Word soon got around and I ended up doing another half-dozen sets of webbing. One of the nigs, Private Smith, was straight out of the Depot and his admin was in bits. I picked up his webbing and the water bottle pouch fell off. The straps were all different lengths and the belt would have fitted the not so inconsiderable girth of our colourboy, not the six-stone streak of piss that stood before me. I helped him the best I could, but I don't think he had the capacity to learn too much at any one time. How he made it through basic was a mystery to everyone, but to their shame, they never went out of their way to help him either.

SOPs stated that we had to carry our FFD in the top left pocket of our combat jackets, as well as our ID and morphine syringettes when we were issued them. Almost everyone had spares. We knew that with modern automatic weapons or shrapnel bursts we might get more than one wound. Some had FFD pouches on their webbing straps or just taped on. I carried two in my upper left pocket as that was the obvious place to look, and another two in my webbing with my own first aid kit, in case I needed to use them on someone else (you are never to use your own FFD on someone else in case you need it yourself so that was why I carried spares). I also had some tampons along with paracetamol and plasters – tampons are very useful in soaking up and stopping blood in wounds as well as their more regular function.

We were ordered to leave out our doss bags, as we would travel with them. The idea was if we were caught out by delays we wouldn't be stuck for somewhere to sleep – we would doss down wherever we found space. We would also travel with a daysack that held our wash kit, towel, any other personal kit we felt we needed. I carried my mess-tins, KFS, Walkman, spare batteries, a book, camera, book, socks and spare under-wear. Knowing the Army, it would be a long journey with lots of hanging around.

In my combat jacket I carried my personal kit. Top right had my Silva compass attached to the button hole by para cord. In my left-side zipped pocket I had a set of TAMs, a camouflaged zip holder for my stationery set of marker pens, waterproof notebook, small Nyrex folder orders book, a stainless-steel shaving mirror, ROE cards, HF emergency frequencies, a small Serbo-Croat to English phrase card, mini Maglite and a military protractor. In my two bottom pockets I had my NI gloves and woolly hat. I tried the jacket on and thought it was too heavy and bulky so the TAMs went into my holdall. I probably wouldn't need them but I decided to keep them close by just in case.

It's amazing the amount of kit a modern squaddie carries, issued or not. Many in 2LI had bought assault vests or chest rigs, as constantly getting in and out of armoured vehicles can be difficult with normal webbing, especially the hatches. I had tried a chest rig before but found it restricted access to the pockets on my jacket and, because you cannot unzip it on a tab, made me overheat. The assault vest was a much better idea as you could unzip the front but it was expensive, and like many squaddies I felt that I shouldn't have to pay for decent kit out of my own pocket. The kit you are issued can get you through basic training but you soon learn that you have to buy a lot of extra items just to operate efficiently and comfortably. Half of the stuff I carried in my webbing or on my person was non-issue but it was the only way to survive.

Once my kit was sorted and my personal stuff was packed away, I went into town to get my hair cut and stock up on toiletries. The haircut speaks for itself, but I needed to get a small and large bottle of shampoo, a whole load of disposable razors, soap and some roll-on deodorant. I wasn't sure what would be available in theatre, so I wanted to make sure I had enough to last the whole tour.

That night we sat in our room eagerly watching the news. The fragile ceasefire was still holding despite the frequent violations. Each of the warring factions was blaming each other, but the feeling we were left with was that the Serbs were openly carrying on with their agenda for a Serb-only Balkans. We waited for news about Task Force Alpha and were rewarded with shots of the gunners of 19 Regiment RA wading around in mud-filled gun pits. A few of us headed to the NAAFI for a beer. It was busier than normal but the usual banter and laughter had been replaced with quiet and serious conversations. This wasn't too surprising. Tomorrow the Advance Party would be leaving for Croatia.

The next day we watched as the Advance Party paraded on the drill square and loaded their kit and weapons bundles onto some four-tonners. Once the kit had left they boarded some coaches and headed out of the barracks to Paderborn Airport. I wished I was going with them but I only had to wait another day. Or so I thought. On the way back from the cookhouse that afternoon I stopped by the Support Company office to check the noticeboard, only to find that my name had been removed from the flight list. I spoke to the Company Clerk but he said it was orders and I would be going the day after. I told him that I was due to take over a Rebro in two days, but he said my name was removed so that someone with higher priority could go. I was OK with that but when I checked the list again I noticed that the new name was another clerk from HQ Company. It looked like the switch was a favour so that one of his cronies could say they were one of the first from the battalion in theatre. I doubted if he was being sent to panic the Serbs with his typing speed. It was pointless arguing with the clerk so I went back and unpacked some civvies and went to Paddy Murphy's for a beer or three.

The next day I went down to the Sigs Platoon office in my tracksuit and hung around doing odd jobs. The RSWO was on the Advance Party and he would find out soon enough that I wasn't going to turn up today. It was a long day just waiting and trying to think up things to do, so I went back to the accommodation and kept myself to myself. I lay on my bed and wondered what was happening over there. Pete's TV had been packed away and not knowing what was on the news was getting to me, so after twenty minutes I went over to the NAAFI and sat down next to the dozen other blokes who were watching BFBS, desperate for news.

The NAAFI that evening was depressing as everyone was in a sombre mood. I went into town to Paddy Murphy's and met up with some of the non-LI lads. Thoughts of our own mortality make us react in different ways. I wrote letters to be given to my sons and sister if the worst happened. For others it was spending as many seconds as possible with their wives or girlfriends before they departed. It seemed that this lot had more base desires and had just come back from the Beehive, one of Paderborn's brothels.

On 30th October 1995 Main Body 2 arrived at Paderborn Airport and after the usual hold-ups as lists were checked and double-checked we walked out onto the tarmac. Sitting there in the late-summer sunshine was a gleaming white jetliner with UN stencils on the side. Many of us were happy that we would be travelling in comfort instead of a Herc, but our smiles soon disappeared when we realised it was a Russian-built Tupolev 152 airliner. As we entered the cabin we read the logo on the side of the fuselage: '*Balkan Airlines. The Official Sponsor to the Bulgarian Football*

Team, World Cup 1982'. The inside was narrow and cramped. It looked like something straight out of the sixties, with Formica and pressed steel in abundance. The rows of PVC-covered seats were disrupted by a gap of about three metres where the wings met the fuselage. It was handy for dumping our doss bags into but it had an uncanny resemblance to a sheep pen. We found a seat and squeezed in. I was sitting next to Corporal Bobby Belshaw and he didn't look too happy. It turned out that he had a distinct fear of flying and being on an ancient-looking Russian plane wasn't doing his confidence any good. To be honest, I wasn't feeling too clever either.

Soon after we had boarded we began to taxi to the end of the runway. Everything seemed OK and I began to relax. We waited for a few minutes for clearance and then started to move forward. I closed my eyes and listened as the engine noise increased. It kept on getting louder but I couldn't feel that we had left the ground. I opened my eyes and looked out of the window. We were still racing along the runway. The engines began to scream but we didn't seem to be going fast enough to take off. The engine pitch increased further and the fuselage began to shudder. I wondered how long the runway was and hoped it could cope with an underpowered and decidedly shaky aircraft. It was a huge relief when we felt the Tupolev lift gently as it changed from being earthbound to a laboured flying mode.

We carried on climbing and levelled out when we cleared the thin layer of clouds. If we thought things were going to get better, we were mistaken. The fuselage might have shaken less but the engines still screamed worryingly. Bobby was whiter than the paint job on the outside of the plane and looking around he wasn't the only one. I started to count down the minutes until we landed.

Chapter 5

The Former Yugoslavia and Slipper City

The Tupolev hit the tarmac at Split Airport on the Croatian coast with a bone-crunching thud and carried on screaming down the runway. It was still screaming when we passed the terminal building and finally stopped screaming when we slowed down at the end of the runway, the bit normally reserved for emergencies! The relief on Bobby Belshaw's face was a picture, and most of the lads cheered when we finally stopped to turn around. It was a close call. As we turned to taxi back to the terminal, I could see the starboard wing sweeping over the grass where the tarmac ended.

As we disembarked we grabbed a doss bag each and sorted them out after we got into the arrivals area. The first thing we noticed was the heat. Split was basking in glorious sunshine and we were not really ready for it as we all wore full combats with norgies and jumpers HD. We were allowed through customs after showing our passports and met up with our baggage after a quick bus ride to a British Army logistics base just opposite the airport. From there we went to the old JNA barracks that was serving as the British Army HQ in Croatia, and settled down in some makeshift transit accommodation. Because it was so far from the fighting and was renowned for the easy life of its inhabitants, it was known by those going up country as Slipper City. The REMFs here had an easy life and lived in relative luxury.

We got together in blob formation and listened to a quick brief about the dos and don'ts while here, like stay out of trouble, no leave passes and don't walk on the flower beds. We were told we would be heading up country first thing in the morning. The rest of the day was ours, so after getting rid of our warm clothing we grabbed our eating irons and mugs and headed off to the cookhouse. There was a huge queue outside, but we were bathed in sunshine so we didn't mind at all. We took in our surroundings and observed the scale of the logistical build-up. There were thousands of tonnes of stores, vehicles and containers and amongst this were the Portakabins that housed the units looking after all of this. Opposite the cookhouse was a small group of Portakabins, and in front of them was a small play area, complete with tyres hanging by ropes from the branch of a tree. A cook taking a fag break outside the cookhouse saw what we were looking at.

'It's for the Monkeys to play with,' he said, nodding at the swings.

'Do they have monkeys in Croatia?' asked one of the naive young squaddies.

'He's talking about the Red Caps,' said a REME Corporal, 'Look at the sign outside the cabins.'

We all focused on the sign for the camp RMP Detachment and laughed at the joke.

'You haven't heard the best one,' chirped the cook. 'The tyres have been up for years and they ain't twigged it yet!'

There wasn't much to do after scoff, so we sat around outside the accommodation block and soaked up the last of the evening sun. It seemed idyllic in Split, like a holiday camp. Everything was so relaxed. You could tell apart the bronzed base personnel compared to the pastier-looking troops in transit. That evening we bunked in one of the temporary accommodation tents. It looked like a marquee you would find at a wedding but it wasn't as plush as it looked. The place was a tip and hadn't been cleaned in months. The doors were hanging off their hinges and couldn't close properly. The lucky ones had a bed, and the even luckier ones had a mattress on it. Most of us had to sleep on the floor on our foam kip mats. There was no need for this and the bloke in charge of the accommodation should have been busted back to Private for allowing it to happen. If it was run by the infantry it would have been immaculate, like a show house on a new housing estate, but our hosts had other ideas on how to treat their guests. It just went to show the contempt the REMFs had for the infantry. I bet their accommodation wasn't this bad!

Chapter 6

The Road to Vitez and the Relics of War

The next morning we had an early breakfast and collected a packed lunch. From the 2LI temporary armoury located in an ISO container we collected our body armour and rifles and bombed up with 180 rounds ready for the journey up country. After loading a mag onto our rifles we gathered the rest of our kit, and boarded the ancient coaches that would take us to Vitez, in the heart of Bosnia. We all stored our webbing and sleeping bags on the overhead shelf, many of us pocketing a couple of loaded magazines in case of emergency. As we passed the barrack gates the German Army guard were subjected to the usual Nazi salutes and raspberries they have endured since the end of World War Two. God they must have hated us.

We drove through Split in the early-morning traffic, taking in the sights, just like regular tourists. The city looked normal and apart from the military activity it looked as if the war had no effect on it. We joined Route Circle and headed north-east. All the main routes used by the UN in the Former Yugoslavia had a code-name and was based on a British Army system that we were well used to. I sat back and relaxed as much as the once-sumptuous seats allowed. The roads out of Split were fine but became very bumpy as the road surface became more and more potholed as we travelled inland.

The landscape was quite picturesque and looked just like mainland Greece. Vineyards and olive groves competed for space amongst the freshly tilled land, while scores of people gathered in the last of the year's harvest. It started to get hilly a few miles inland, and this slowed us down considerably. Our charabanc swayed like a drunken hippo with every twist and turn and the engine laboured with every rising gradient.

After we passed through a tunnel that went under a mountain at Vukić we looked at a convoy of buses and cars that were parked along the side of the road. The vehicles were full of HVO soldiers on their way back from the front. They were a ragged bunch, mostly bearded, and in an assortment of uniforms. The only thing identifying them as Croats was the red-and-white checked badges showing the Arms of Croatia. A few women were there, as well as children and even a goat. They looked weary and melancholy and those that could be bothered looked up at us with guarded expressions.

Not long after the tunnel we passed the border. We were now in Bosnia. To highlight this, we started to witness at first hand the ravages of the conflict. Lone houses were devastated, riddled with thousands of bullet holes, scorch marks rising from doors and windows. Most houses had no roof. The panorama was made surreal by just as many untouched houses, with children playing in perfectly kept gardens. Unlike the scenes we had seen on the news, this wasn't carried out by the Serbs, but by the Croat HVO, who were just as efficient at ethnic cleansing as their old enemy. The scene changed from Beirut to the Swiss Alps and back again. It was sickening to think that neighbours might have had a hand in the destruction next door.

We carried on along Route Circle witnessing scenes that Europe thought had been left behind at the end of World War Two. The bus driver must have had complete faith in the coach and his own driving because he drove like a nutter. With complete disregard for lane discipline or oncoming traffic, he tried to keep his speed up as if his life depended on it, ignoring the jarring effects of potholes and cutting as many corners as he could. It didn't take long for me to suffer because of his driving. I had leaned forward to get to my horror box when the coach hit a mother of a pothole and the whole coach bucked with the impact. I cracked a tooth on the flash eliminator of my rifle, which was held between my knees. The impact was so hard that I swear I saw stars. There was no blood, but I had to take a couple of paracetamol for the pain. It didn't feel too clever so I reminded myself to see a RADC dentist when we arrived.

Soon we were passing around a large blue lake, Buşko Jez. The road was cut from the side of the cliffs and it twisted and turned precariously about fifty metres above the lake. From my window seat I could see straight down into the clear blue water. Not very reassuring, as I was on the left, and we should have been driving on the right, but it did take my mind off my throbbing tooth. It was a great relief to all when we left the lake behind and disappeared into forested mountain passes and valleys, moving closer to our only stop, Lipa Camp, about 20km past Tomislavgrad. Here we could stretch our legs and empty our bladders as we waited for an escort.

At Lipa, the guard was provided by TURKBAT, who seemed happy with the concept that less is more. We only saw one guard on the gate – it must have been siesta time for the others. An immaculately clean and shiny white M113-variant stood on guard next to some Hesco bastions. It looked as if it had just been delivered from the showroom and was obviously the Turks' pride and joy. It gave me the impression that the Turks didn't like venturing further than the camp gate. I sincerely hoped that someone else would be our escort.

My prayers were answered an hour later when we were told to get back on the bus. We were continuing on to Vitez with two New Zealand T50-NZs as escort, another variant of the ubiquitous M113 family. In comparison to the Turkish M113, the Kiwis' vehicles were muddy and the white paint was chipped and well worn. They had add-on armour to the front and sides: the front of sheet steel, and the sides of corrugated blocks of steel. The black painted UN markings were still visible through the dust and mud, while a small light-blue UN flag fluttered on the top of a whip antenna. The Kiwis looked professional and had a couple of blokes poking out of the mortar hatches as top cover, as well as the commander in a machine-gun cupola.

The T50 belched a white cloudy smoke as it accelerated in front of us. We followed behind and moved out onto Route Triangle, taking us deeper into Bosnia. We watched the Kiwi soldiers with interest as they kept their heads low, scanning left and right over the tops of their Steyr AUG assault rifles. I'm not sure if the coach driver appreciated being cooped up between the even slower T50s, encumbered by the add-on armour, but it made the journey a lot more comfortable for us. We passed the Royal Engineer bases at the Redoubt and Invicta where the guards seemed to be more alert. The further inland we moved, the worse the devastation became. Most of the single houses bore the scars of war, and some of the small roadside hamlets were now just piles of rubble.

Now and then there would be an excited shout from within the coach as someone spotted a burnt-out wreck of a tank or AFV. Some of the wrecks were fresh, with machine guns not salvaged and no signs of rust. Small holes in the sides or on the turret showed the hit from an anti-tank round. If they could do that to a tank, what chance would we have in a flimsy tin can of a coach? I willed the Kiwis to get a move on. We passed a few checkpoints, some stopping us, the others not batting an eyelid as we churned up the dusty road.

Route Triangle ended at a town called Prozor. This was the first major town we saw after Split. All the houses were pockmarked with bullet and shell holes. Some had makeshift window coverings made from plastic sheeting with UNICEF or UNHCR stencilled on it. On street corners people were selling anything that had a value, and often things that we in the UK would consider rubbish. Raggedy children were selling petrol in lemonade bottles or from battered military jerrycans. Toothless old crones, dressed in bundles of clothes, held out skinny hands offering single cigarettes. These people were desperate and were selling anything that once had value. They didn't look up at us; they learned long ago that we wouldn't stop. On the street corners, armed militiamen stood around in small groups, smoking and trying to look macho. With all the desolation and despair around their posing didn't impress us much but I'm sure it appealed to the wretched locals.

From Prozor, we headed north to Gornji Vakuf, changing onto Route Diamond. Overhead, two Lynx helicopters flew by; their TOW missile launchers and door-mounted machine guns giving them a menacing look. Gornji Vakuf was badly damaged as well. Sections of the town had been razed to the ground; more piles of rubble for the kids to play on. Here and there a few women waddled by, looking obese under their coats. We knew it wasn't from overeating, and in this heat it couldn't have been comfortable. The reason was simple. They wore as much as they could because when the fighting started, they ran, and the only way to survive the cold nights and upcoming winter was if you carried with you as much you could. The easiest way was to wear it, and in Bosnia you learned quickly how to survive.

We drove by the HQ of 20 Armoured Brigade and its adjacent helicopter base. The tiny MALBAT soldiers on stag looked all teeth and camouflage as they smiled at anyone and anything that passed by. The blue body armour and helmets looked oversized and made them look like army cadets, but I knew that appearances were deceptive. It was these guys that came to the rescue of the US Rangers who got caught out in Mogadishu, Somalia, back in October 1991. The brigade location looked OK, a good place to stay. In fact most of the bases we had seen so far looked fine. I wondered what Vitez was like, but didn't think too much about it because I was due to deploy to a Rebro as soon as I got there.

Just past Gornji Vakuf the overworked Royal Engineers were busy at work repairing the seriously damaged roads, so we had to take a diversion via Bugojno on Route Emerald, and met up with Route Diamond after adding an hour to the journey. The devastation seemed to get worse as we drove north, but sitting on the coach and viewing it all seemed to detach us from reality, like watching a film from the comfort of a cinema seat.

The smell of washed bodies, deodorant and clean uniforms didn't match the horror that unfolded before us, so we just kept on watching, waiting for the intermission.

That happened at Vitez. From our int briefs we knew that Vitez was the centre of some of the heaviest fighting, but that didn't prepare us for the scale of the devastation. Collapsed and shell-damaged houses, shops and factories, piles of rubble and burnt-out cars all littered the outskirts. Our first stop was the garage, the location for Echelon. The escort carried on a few more ks to Camp Kiwi in Santici as we turned into what was once the town's bus depot.

We all got off the coach and shook off the cobwebs from a very long and uncomfortable journey. For me, it meant getting rid of the pins and needles in my feet that had been bugging me for the last hour. All those who were to be based here got their kit together and were met with their department heads. It was here that we started to get a feel for our new surroundings. The smells and sounds of a confined military base permeated the air. The throaty roars of diesel engines competed with the shrill sounds of power tools in the REME workshop. Smoke, oil, fuel, food and the smell of sweaty bodies mingled with dust being blown in from outside the base. It was a quick pit stop and as soon as the driver reappeared from the toilets we were ordered back on the coach for the last few hundred metres of our journey from Split. Closer inside the town, a few houses had survived, and surprisingly on the main street a couple of shops had managed to open for business, even though it looked like they had sod all to sell.

At Vitez School blue-helmeted French squaddies waved us past their white sandbagged guard post. The coach driver pulled up in the car park where lines of Warriors, Land Rovers and Bedford trucks were to one side, and French VABs and VBLs on the other. Private cars were also dotted around, which we later found out were owned by the locals employed in the camp by the UN.

After unloading the coach we stood by our kit. We watched as British and French squaddies passed by, oblivious of the new arrivals. All were fully kitted up and carried their weapons. It was obvious that the alert state was high so we didn't wait to be told, we donned our kit. Body armour was done up, webbing and helmets worn, rifles slung. I took the magazines from my map pocket and replaced them in my webbing, then replaced my daysack onto my Bergan – sorted. I didn't need a bollocking this early in the tour.

News of our arrival soon spread and group by group we were met with a rep from our platoons and shown to the accommodation park. Here, dozens of white steel Portakabins were set out in rows like a cheap holiday camp. We poked around for a while until we found a few empty ones. I picked a bunk and threw my Bergan and holdall onto the green plastic covered mattress. The accommodation was basic, exactly the same as the offices you would find on a building site. They were all wired for power, but the bulbs were missing in ours so we went looking for another empty cabin to commandeer a few. When we got back, we opened a window to let out some of the stale smell that the last occupants had left behind and closed the door behind us.

When we had stowed away our kit we ambled back to the school along the wooden duckboards that formed the paths between the cabins. I read the names that were written in black marker on the doors. The cabins further away from the school seemed to be all infantry, and closer to the school were the clerks, cooks and Royal Sigs, who lived there for the duration. The school was the HQ for Task Force Alpha, and the home of BRITFOR. Tac was up on Mount Igman, overlooking Sarajevo, and both were controlled by the D&Ds until we had enough men to take over. Like all other buildings, it hadn't escaped the bitter fighting and had strike marks from all sizes of rounds on its grey exterior. The RSWO came out and welcomed us to Vitez. He explained that we would put relief in place as soon as it arrived so that the D&Ds could start to pack up and go home. The signallers from Main would start to share duties with the D&Ds in the school, until we had enough men to take formal control. With that, the RSWO looked at me and Bobby Belshaw.

'Why was you'se not here yesterday?!' he exploded. 'We were supposed to take over two of the D&Ds Rebros but we let them down because you two didn't turn up. You made me look like a complete twat!' So much for not getting an early bollocking! Bobby looked confused, but I took a copy of the movement order and showed it to the RSWO.

'The Company Clerk removed us from the list and swapped us with a couple of his mates at Battalion HQ. I tried to tell him that it was vital that we were on the flight but he said one day wouldn't matter.' There seemed to be a competition between the senior clerks to see who would be first in theatre, as if that made them heroic and indispensable.

The RSWO was livid: 'That little runt! Wait till I get my hands on him!' He took a deep breath. He had more important things to worry about than a jumped-up little pen-pusher.

'OK, sort out your kit. Bobby, you'll be moving up country tomorrow;

H, you'll go the day after. In the meantime check in with Fred; I'm sure he could do with a hand.' With that he walked off. Serjeant Hodgsen came over and smiled at us.

'Welcome to Boz, lads. Follow me and I'll show you around.' He covered the basics, like Main, cookhouse, toilets, Serjeants' mess, officers' mess, and most importantly – the bomb shelters! He also pointed over to a single house on the edge of the car park.

'Female accommodation. lads. Take a good look, it's out of bounds.' Fred turned and smiled. 'Get caught in there and don't think you'll get a ticket home, you'll be scrubbing dixies for the duration!'

In comparison to the RSWO, Fred was in good humour. The signallers from Main and Tac walked into the school and reported for duty. That left me and Bobby, so after we stored our rifles in the LI armoury ISO we headed back to the Portakabins, collected our eating irons and mug, and went for scoff.

That evening we went to the soldiers' bar located on the edge of the camp. It looked like it was once a restaurant and was quite well done out. The ceiling had timber beams that were supported by thick timber columns. Large arched windows were on one side. The glass had tape across them just like old World War Two films of the Blitz, but apart from that, it looked very normal. It even had a pool table, but it looked like it hadn't been used in months. On operations the British Army has a 'two can' rule. That means you cannot consume more than two cans of beer per day. Well, that's the way it's supposed to work. There was a small counter where a stunningly beautiful Bosnian girl of about nineteen served as barmaid. The rumour was that she had gone through the RHF at 50DM a go, but she looked too innocent for that. The romantic in me hoped that the rumours were not true, but in war survival is a strong instinct, and morals take a back seat.

The bar was full of tired-looking D&Ds waiting for transport back to Split, some Royal Signals and loggies who were based in Vitez, and us. We stood around one of the columns and chatted about any gossip or news that anyone had managed to find out, drinking cans of Tennent's and John Smith's. By ten the bar started to empty so I said goodnight and drifted off back to the accommodation.

The evening was very warm so I slept outside my doss bag. I still had my trousers and T-shirt on, but as the Muslim–Croat peace was holding out around Vitez I decided it was OK to take my boots off. I left them with my combat jacket, body armour, helmet and webbing at the foot of the bunk, just in case the alarm went up and we had to dash to the shelter.

The next day I awoke early, not without a little anticipation for the job ahead. I grabbed my wash kit and headed for the showers. The water was cold, but as the day was already warming up it didn't bother me too much. In any case, my mind was on more important things.

After breakfast, I got stuck into my own admin. Bobby was busy sorting out things for his own deployment, so I walked over to the stalls that some of the locals were permitted to run on the outskirts of the car park. It was a lovely day without a cloud in the sky and it reminded me of my last holiday in Spain. Some French soldiers were loading their VABs, getting ready to go out on convoy escort. The blue-helmeted soldiers were busy strapping up their body armour and putting magazines into their FAMAS rifles. I nodded my hellos as I passed them and got a few nods back. They stood back as huge grey clouds of smoke belched out of the exhausts as the engines started up. They waited until it had disappeared then opened the rear doors and boarded.

The locals had a thriving business from the Vitez garrison. It was obvious that because the local economy was in bits the only way to get some hard currency was by trading with the UN. There might have been very little in the local shops but the stalls seemed to be full of stuff. You could buy the locally produced fags that gave smokers an early-morning cough that sounded like a 432 starting up in winter, or copies of Marlboros and Rothmans that gave smokers an early-morning cough that sounded like a 432 starting up in winter. You could also buy cheap T-shirts that only lasted one wash before they would only fit a deformed orang-utan. The slogans printed on them catered for the more discerning REMFs who wanted to impress the local talent when they got home. '*I survived Sniper Alley – Sarajevo*' seemed to be the best seller.

There was also a large choice of 1980s new and used German porn mags, no doubt the focal point of many a squaddie's visit here. There was even a variety of condoms to choose from, but looking at the age of the jazz mags, I guessed that the use by date might have been a bit suspect. Also on sale were postcards, obviously dating from Communist days, as the photos were of idyllic scenes showing bountiful harvests, with fit and happy locals in national dress or the familiar old woman dressed in black leading a donkey. From what I had seen, there wasn't much harvesting going on, and I bet the donkey had been made into a stew long ago!

I wasted about ten minutes looking at the merchandise while the Bosnian stallholder and his wife tried to impress me with the choice and quality. I didn't know when I would next get to visit a shop and so stocked up on a few luxuries and morale-boosters. Coca-Cola seemed to be an omnipresent luxury that the world couldn't do without. From ultra-rich Caribbean retreats to war zones, Coke was a common sight. Aid might be difficult to bring in, but Coke seemed to have no problem. I bet if aid was smuggled into needy regions on the back of a Coke lorry there wouldn't be any starving refugees! I picked out a dozen cans, half a dozen Mars and Snickers, a disposable lighter, and a pack of wafer-thin playing cards that I hoped would last for at least a few games of patience.

It didn't take long after the UN arrived for the local businesses to be given concessions to provide services. Bakers, barbers, laundry, transport, cleaners, the stalls and the bar made basic living conditions for the squaddies less austere. The British Army had a long tradition stretching back to the Peninsular War of paying the locals for services in support of the Army, and these were usually controlled by the quartermasters and CQMSs. For the UN, it also meant that it could contribute positively to the local economy and build up some much needed support within the local communities.

On my way back I noticed that the French were still waiting in their VABs. The commanders were in small turrets at the front, while at the back pairs of soldiers were sticking out, ready to provide top cover. They were waiting for a convoy to form up in the car park. An officer was looking at a notepad by a dirty white lorry with UNHCR stencilled on the side. He was probably cursing the civvy volunteer drivers who were ruining his timings. It looked like the French suffered from the 'hurry up and wait' syndrome as well. Passing by on foot was the perimeter patrol from the D&Ds. Vitez was still a medium-risk area, so they still wore helmets instead of berets. Despite the monotony of walking endless circuits of the base, the guys looked happy, probably because they were due to fly out in the next few days.

After hiding my booty at the bottom of my holdall, I cadged a lift with one of the Sigs Platoon to Echelon at Vitez Garage. Here I met Colour Serjeant Carney and one of his gofers. I managed to get hold of a couple of packets of AA batteries (Walkman – for the use of), and some det cable. Det cable is a pure copper cable used in demolitions and is a great electrical conductor. Standard D10 comms wire has steel strands for strength, but that can give a poor connection when connecting radios for Rebro. I didn't know if the signaller at Rebro I was deploying on was using det cable or D10, so I took some just in case. The colourboy was going through his lists, so didn't have much time to talk, but did manage to shout over at me: 'Make sure it works and don't sign for anything that's not there!'

I like to think that I don't look stupid, but I suppose that he was just under a little pressure settling in, so I didn't take it the wrong way. I was well versed in the Army's way of checking and signing for things and had an excellent teacher with my own colourboy back in my battalion, Colour Sergeant Tony Finnegan. I had a close working relationship with him. Tony was an excellent soldier and always knew how to get the best out of anyone who worked with him. Sometimes he would despair when I tried to order kit that we were not scaled for, or when I painted the FFR in a retro D-Day pattern, but he understood that I was keen and motivated by a desire to be the best at the job.

As it was tea break we decided to take a trip to the Kiwi base at Santici. There was a PX there and I wanted to see what they had to offer. The Kiwis were well used to the Brits visiting them, and didn't bother to check us out, instead just raised the barrier and waved us in. The PX was in a Portakabin and kitted out just like a shop, complete with shelves, displays and a cash register. They had multi-fuel cookers on sale, but I didn't have the cash, so instead I bought a few canisters for my old epi-gas cooker, while the others stocked up on cheap but genuine Marlboros and Camels.

I knew that the RAMC dentist was visiting today, and so I took the opportunity to get my tooth checked out. The dentist was busy so I had to wait for an hour until I was seen. The news wasn't great – the tooth had cracked all the way down to the root and had to come out, but he didn't have the time to do an extraction as he was due to leave for another location so I would need to see him when he came back. I told him that I was due out on a Rebro at Kiseljak the next day and didn't know how long I would be there. It turned out that he was the only RAMC dentist in theatre and was constantly on the move covering the whole of the British AOR and some other units as well. Unfortunately Kiseljak wasn't one of the stops. However, he did stop at Mount Igman once a month and I should get up there to see him as soon as I could, as I risked getting an infection if I left it too late. I took down the dates of his Igman stop, thanked him and went back to the car park and jumped in the back of our Rover.

The streets of Vitez had started to come alive by now, with the usual street sellers and militiamen hanging around. There were even a few cars and trucks on the main street. I would have liked to drive around and see more of the town, but we were operating under strict rules not to leave the designated routes as mines, sniping and hijacking were a big threat, so we carried on back to the school.

For the rest of the day I did some odd jobs for Fred and got my kit ready for the next day. We heard on the grapevine that peace talks had started in Dayton, Ohio. We had no word on what that entailed and didn't think that the Serbs would sign anyway. That night I celebrated my birthday a day early in the bar with those of the Sigs Platoon that had made it so far. The new arrivals were eager for news, and as veterans of a few days' standing we gladly told them all we had found out. The 'two can' rule was stretched slightly, and we shot the shit until the bar closed. Walking back to the accommodation, we were told a few times to keep the noise down. Morale was high, and we were looking forward to getting stuck into the job. We were confident, and confidence is infectious. In a few days we would have full control of the radio net, and that would allow the rest of the battalion to deploy. Sigs Platoon would be the first fully operational sub unit of 2LI.

Chapter 7

The Rebro, the Hotel and the Brick Factory

We moved out from Vitez on Route Pacman, attached to a small convoy heading for Mount Igman. As 2LI's Warriors were still en route, we had to rely on the French for protection. We had taken over a motley collection of vehicles and were busy getting them checked out, so as the Rovers were being used elsewhere, we took a four-tonner. SOPs for BRITFOR were that all road movement had to have minimum two military vehicles with at least one armoured. The idea was that if a convoy or patrol got bumped those in soft-skinned vehicles could take refuge in the back of the armour and then bug out. I don't know if the French operated the same way, so I prayed we wouldn't have to find out. In front was a driver and Fred, the Sigs Serjeant, and in the back, sweating under our body armour and helmets, were myself and Private 'Hendo' Henderson.

For most of the journey we only saw a few civvy cars on the road and no other UN vehicles. The villages we passed were virtually empty, and no one was tending the fields. The sight of shell-damaged houses was becoming familiar, and I started to look beyond them. I began to notice features like the spire of an old church or the tower of an old mosque. As always both were shot to bits. Piles of cut timber were stacked up along the sides of houses, ready for the winter, and there was evidence of repairs to doors and windows. A few houses had trickles of wood smoke rising from chimneys. Whether it was survivors of the fighting, returned refugees or the new occupiers of a 'cleansed' house it was impossible to tell. Those people I did see outside them looked old and weary and barely gave us a glance. I had almost expected the locals to act like the liberated townsfolk that you see in a World War Two newsreel. There were no waving women and children, no flowers being thrown at us, no cheering.

It took about an hour to get to Kiseljak, and we only realised that we were there when we saw the gates of the Brick Factory close behind us.

We stopped in the vehicle park to the south of the factory and got out. The ground was muddy and, despite the sunshine, hadn't dried up. There were dozens of D&Ds lying about on their Warriors taking in the last of the summer sun, while a few Warriors returned from a patrol and churned up the ground with more than a few unnecessary 360s. It was no wonder the mud didn't get a chance to dry out.

We identified the Rebro quite easily, due to the coax connections that stretched across from the tented area and led to some broadband antennas fixed to the top of the factory's chimney. The D&D signallers were overjoyed to see us, and had all of the kit laid out on the vehicle tarp ready for us to inspect. Fred went off to empty his bladder, so myself and Hendo gave the Rebro a once over.

The Rebro was set up in a standard 432 and not the command variant. It wasn't a fault on the part of the D&Ds, as they had taken it over from another unit, but it wasn't ideal. A Rebro uses a lot of battery power, and the command variant has additional batteries for the radios. Using a bog-standard 432 meant that you had to keep running the engines more often to top up the charge. When Fred got back we first paraded the wagon and found a major problem – the engine oil was milky, a sign that there was a coolant leak in the heat transfer system. One of the D&Ds said that he had reported it over a week ago but had heard nothing since. More likely, thoughts were of home and it wouldn't be his problem anymore. The coolant leak wasn't good news and Fred told me to keep an eye on it until our own REME could get down here, as it was a workshop job and would need a pack replacement. The rest of the wagon wasn't in the best condition. The ancient rubber seals for the hatches had dried in the Bosnian sunshine and were starting to disintegrate, meaning that it would leak like a sieve when it rained – not good coming up to winter. The rear door wouldn't lock properly, which meant that it couldn't be padlocked if I had to go to the cookhouse or toilet. It was OK for the D&Ds, paired up on the Rebro – they could cover for each other – but I would be on my jack and couldn't afford to leave the radios or my kit unattended.

The wagon's bodywork was covered in a film of dust but visible were a dozen or so small dents and scratches where the bare metal had started to go rusty. The D&Ds said they were strike marks from night-time sniping, but the official version was spent rounds from 'celebratory fire'. As was common in the Balkans, the local men fired their AKs into the air to celebrate almost anything, from birth to death. Mostly though, a night on the piss and a good fart was the most common excuse to spunk off a few rounds on full auto! The trouble was that unless someone was hit, Higher

Command always dismissed it as celebratory. The only good news was that it only happened at night when the locals knew we were away from the Warriors and trying to get our heads down. The bad news was that the Rebro was smack in the middle of the base and totally exposed!

The D&Ds also mentioned that the perimeter had been regularly broken into, normally during a 'celebratory fire' episode. The local militia and criminals had used the disruption as cover and while the attention of the guard was diverted, they sneaked in and stole jerrycans of fuel and the tools strapped on the vehicles. Despite the obvious dangers, Higher Command had refused to acknowledge the shooting episodes as aggressive and did nothing about it. The D&Ds surprisingly still parked their Warriors right up against the wire, giving intruders excellent cover. I saw that the jimpy for the 432 was still packed in its wooden crate, so I made a mental note to get acquainted with it later on.

The CES checks took just over an hour and revealed a few missing items, which Fred made a note of. We packed away the rest and waited for the D&Ds to remove their personal kit. Fred had arranged to rejoin the Igman escort on its return to Vitez and had a few hours to wait. While Fred stayed at the Rebro and had a fag, me and Hendo did a quick tour of the camp.

From an old sandbagged OP on the side of a hill just outside the base perimeter we looked down on the Brick Factory. It was used as the base for the Task Force QRF, and we could see the D&D Warriors and 432s parked up and ready to move out at ten minutes' notice. Lined up in the Engineer Park were the REs, AVREs, AVLBs, CETs and Spartans, ready to support any push on Sarajevo and beyond.

Closer to the factory building was the tented accommodation area where the company personnel stayed while the Corimec accommodation was being built. The tents were supposed to be temporary and were protected from sniping from the direction of the town by a Hesco blast wall. To the side were five toilets, one for the officers, one for the SNCOs, and the other three for the ORs, and each had a shiny stainless-steel tank supplying the water. It didn't take a genius to work out that with about ten officers, thirty SNCOs, and two hundred squaddies, there would be problems. The water should have been topped up frequently but that wasn't the case and usually the tanks for the ORs would run dry after a few hours. We checked the water in the showers, and surprise, surprise – nothing. I opened the door to the boiler cupboard and had a look. The hot water boiler was for domestic use, and only had a capacity for half a dozen showers max before it ran cold. With a never-ending flow of dirty soldiers, the boiler was constantly trying to top up and couldn't cope with the demand. A quick peek into the less used and much cleaner SNCOs' toilet and I found an abundant supply of hot water. A brassard with sergeant's stripes on would come in handy at wash times. I wondered if Silvermans would deliver.

A small distance away from the tents was a small construction site, where the new Corimec accommodation was being built. These were white Italian-designed and manufactured kitlike Portakabins that were designed to link together and form larger blocks. Unfortunately there was no sign of work going on, so it looked like 2LI's immediate accommodation would be in tents.

The perimeter of the base along the main road into the town was well protected by Hesco bastions, floodlights and barbed wire, but the vehicle park just had a barbed-wire fence, and that was in a state of disrepair, loose and full of gaps. No wonder it was easy to sneak in at night.

In the main factory building, the RE had their own CP set up, so I introduced myself and was briefed on their role. Apart from the assault Engineers attached to Task Force Alpha, there was a large Recce element in the Brick Factory, responsible for surveying all the routes in the area. The cookhouse was set up in the factory's original staff kitchen and was staffed by cooks attached to the RE and D&Ds. The bombed-out walls had been replaced by wooden frames with green plastic sheeting, and there were trestle tables and benches that could cater for about a hundred per sitting. Because of the limited room, meals had to be taken on at different sittings, the RE was first and the infantry were second. As I was operating the Rebro on my own, I arranged with the head chef to be able to get fed early so that I wouldn't be away from my wagon for too long and it wouldn't upset anyone if I was seen jumping the queue. I also found out where the cartons of drinking water were stored and arranged it so I could take some whenever I needed it.

The RE were also busy refurbishing some other areas of the factory, and I stopped to look as I passed by. The Engineers were sweating away as the D&Ds sat on their Warriors and watched, safe in the knowledge that as QRF they wouldn't be ordered to help as they were on ten minutes' notice to move.

By the time we got back to the Rebro, the D&Ds had removed all their kit, so I signed for the 432, and I moved in. The first thing I did was confirm to Zero that I had taken control, and then made myself comfortable. Fred and Hendo poked their heads inside and said their farewells, got back into the four-tonner and joined their escort. The charge in the batteries was getting low, so I ran the engine, and called over the UBRE that was topping up the lines of Warriors. After the UBRE driver had finished I made myself at home, organising my own kit and taping up a copy of the CEI onto the wire-mesh doors of the crew compartment. The D&Ds left a map, so after I had folded it to show the area we were operating in I taped that up as well. The radio installation was OK, and as I guessed, they used D10 to link the sets, so I replaced it with det cable. Then I cut some green comms cord and made a clothes-line between the storage compartment and hung up my damp towel to dry. With my personal kit stowed away in the storage compartments, I sat back and listened to the engine idling away, happy that I was at least settled in.

Once the batteries were fully charged I made a brew from the just-boiled BV and continued listening to the net. The traffic was sporadic, mainly from passing convoys and RE route Sitreps. As I listened I began to familiarise myself with the various callsigns in the area. Normally, the British Army change callsign indicators daily. For example, I was H21H, or Hotel Two One Hotel, as it was pronounced. Tomorrow I might be Z21H, the next day F21H, and so on. In fact, frequencies and codes also changed daily, but the Serbs were suspicious of this and claimed that codes and frequency changes were aggressive in nature, especially as the UN was originally deployed in Bosnia in a peaceful capacity. So as not to upset the Serbs, the UN agreed to keep the same operating frequencies and not use codes. It meant that the Serbs, highly trained in radio interception, had an easy time monitoring the UN's radio traffic. It also meant that I wouldn't be using Batco and would stay as H21H for the remainder of my time on the Rebro.

The inside of the 432 is very spacious. It was designed to carry a section of ten riflemen in the back, so I had plenty of room to stretch out. One of the bench seats would be my bed, the other would be for my rifle, helmet, webbing and anything else I needed to be at hand. I decided not to go for evening scoff, partly because I wasn't hungry, and partly because I couldn't lock the rear door. So as the sun began to set on my first day on H21H, I sat on the rim of the commander's hatch, drinking yet another brew, and listened to the net on the commander's headset.

While taking in my surroundings, I wondered how I was supposed to man the net *and* get some sleep. The RSWO had said that I was to remain here for about a week, until the battalion had taken over from the D&Ds and the platoon had settled in. After that I expected I would rejoin the RAP. It was a cardinal sin to leave a net unmanned, but there was no way I could stay awake for a week. The net would be at its quietest at night, but that wouldn't guarantee that I wouldn't be called. Quite often if a callsign was not answering, the duty watchkeeper at Zero would panic. Instead of waiting to see if the other callsign was in a dead spot, or was unable to answer straight away because of tactical reasons, the Rebro would be called to confirm that comms were fine. Not good practice, but watchkeepers were not signallers and often failed to grasp the subtleties of security and good drills.

I finally decided to see if I could survive on a few hours' kip a night, during the quiet hours. Over the last three years as an infantry signaller I had developed a knack while on exercise for being able to sleep with a headset on, and slept so lightly that I could hear if I was called. With the added danger and tension of being on active service, I hoped I could keep this up for an extended period of time.

As the evening drew on and got colder I heard the distinctive crack of an AK as small bursts were let off in the vicinity of the town. There was a beautiful display of green tracer as its trajectory brought it almost horizontally across the vehicle park, creeping dangerously towards the Rebro. I didn't wait to see where it fell and scrambled inside the wagon, closing the hatch behind me. I was glad I did as I heard a few rounds pinged off the side of the wagon. I thought the locals were supposed to approve of our efforts against the Serbs? I was about to call it in when the RE CP came up on the net and reported it. A hundred k away, safely tucked up in the school in Vitez, Zero told everyone who was listening that there was nothing to worry about as it was just celebratory fire. Maybe the locals heard it was my birthday! I decided it might be a good idea to stay locked inside the wagon at nights.

I took off my helmet and body armour, lay back on my doss bag, and picked up a word-search magazine. My hands were shaking after my belated welcome to Bosnia and I couldn't concentrate, so I put it down. I started to shiver but it was probably the cold. I expected a drop in temperature at night but this was a bad sign. For the next few hours it remained quiet outside and I began to relax. I opened a can of Coke and settled down to my first night on the Rebro. It had been an eventful birthday!

For the next few hours I did a crossword puzzle while listening to the net. I was thinking that it was quiet enough to get my head down when a report of heavy machine-gun fire from a Royal Fusilier callsign died mid-sentence. I checked the sets. Both were working fine, and the battery charge was still high and in the black. Zero was trying to get back in touch but there was no answer. I checked the connections and again everything was OK. I was beginning to fear the worst for the Fusiliers when there was a knock on the rear door.

A red-faced D&D squaddie poked his head inside and said I should go out and take a look at the coax. After the 'celebratory fire' episode I was apprehensive but there wasn't a sound now, so I put my body armour and helmet on, slung my rifle and went outside. He showed me to a spot between two of the accommodation tents where an antenna coax was hanging like a washing line. There should have been two lines, and the D&D apologised and said it broke when he tried a short cut back from the toilets in the dark and it nearly garrotted him! The poor sod had been holding it in until the local celebrations had died down and in his rush he forgot about the coax. I took out my Maglite and checked the connections under its tiny red beam. They had come undone and were fine, but the strap taking the tension had snapped. The connection could easily come undone again, so I made a quick repair job with some electrical tape and returned to the Rebro.

Zero and the Fusiliers were talking again, and everything was back to normal. The fault had been found relatively quickly, but if the connection had failed during the night and not reported the net could have been down for hours. The next morning as soon as it got light I would need to take a good look at both coaxes and check their condition. Already I was beginning to realise that the siting of the Rebro might need to some improvement.

The next morning I was up just as dawn was breaking. I put on the BV and had a shave with my battery razor. I made myself a large tea and opened a pack of biscuits brown. To the tune of the Stranglers' hit, 'Golden Brown', I began to sing to myself, 'Never a frown, with biscuits brown', as I snacked on the Army's version of ship's biscuits. A few days in theatre and I was singing to myself already. I hoped it wasn't the first signs of me going bomb-happy!

The net was starting to get busy with traffic, and I was beginning to recognise some familiar voices from 2LI's Signal Platoon mixing with the West Country brogue of the D&Ds. The battalion build-up was almost complete and the Warriors had arrived from their Mediterranean cruise. The support elements were in place, and in a few days the companies would deploy.

Already I had a few jobs to do, so hanging the loudspeaker on the back of the rear door I went outside. There were a few new shiny strike marks just above the exhaust, but nothing was damaged. Next I checked the antenna coaxes. The route to the chimney was about fifty metres and was crossed by two paths: one leading to the toilets where the coaxes were suspended between the tents, and one where it was laid across the ground close to the chimney. I scrounged some pallets from the back of the D&Ds' stores tent and made a crossing point at the base of the chimney and wrapped some mine tape on the suspended sections between the tents. Next I fixed the latch on the 432. It only took half a dozen hits with a sledgehammer and it was working perfectly. I knew I should've joined REME! With a couple of dozen Warriors sitting twenty metres away I didn't feel the need to mount the jimpy, but gave it a pull through and oiled the working parts. Better safe than sorry. I left it out of the crate and strapped up against the engine compartment. It was a small comfort to know it was ready.

Now that I was able to padlock the rear door I could go and grab some breakfast. The batteries were getting low but would last for another hour or so. I quickly got ready, told Zero that I would be 'off these means for figures ten' and ran over to the cookhouse. The slop jockeys weren't ready to start serving, but after a quick explanation of who I was they let me grab a sausage and egg banjo and a brew in my thermal mug. I was back inside the Rebro in ten minutes and grabbed the spare handset to inform Zero that I was back, getting the usual reply of 'Roger, oot' from one of the now ever-present LI signallers.

After scoff and a cold wash, I checked the engine oil. It was still the same colour but a bit low. I looked through the oil cans in one of the rear storage bins and found a full one, so added that in the hope that it would help improve the situation and prevent the engine from seizing before the arrival of REME. For the rest of the morning I kept an eye on the battery charge, waiting for the last possible moment before running the engine again.

The base became alive with activity after breakfast. The D&D Warriors started up while a steady stream of Rovers, four-tonners and Spartans came and went. It wasn't as warm as yesterday, but it was still bright and sunny. It was still early and I had nothing else to do but sit on the commander's seat, listen to the net and watch the world go by.

At lunchtime, after checking in with Zero and making my excuses, I headed over to the RE CP. Here I managed to speak to Echelon on the HF Admin net. In thinly disguised code, I was told that the 2LI move was to be the following day and the D&Ds would move back to Vitez once relief was in place. That meant that 2LI would move into the D&D-held locations and formally take them over, leaving the D&Ds free to pack up and go home. I also got the Met report for the next few days. It said it should remain dry but a cold front was coming down from the Urals and was expected any day. The RE signallers were a friendly bunch, and we chatted about their daily tasks. Their Recce Spartans often left before first light, not to return until the sun was setting. They normally worked in pairs of vehicles, but sometimes relied on Warriors for protection in more risky areas. Sometimes the warring factions didn't want mines lifted in sensitive locations, or they didn't want the RE poking their noses around mysterious excavations. Many of the mass graves found in Bosnia were first located by the RE, despite warnings from Mr Kalashnikov and his friends to keep away.

At the cookhouse I spoke to a cook and asked if I could take some fresh milk. Back at battalion I would normally have been asked a million questions and then told to piss off, but instead I was told yes, anytime, and would I like anything else? Why yes, a fresh loaf and a tin of marge would be nice. And a tin of choccy bars. So after scooping some gorgeous-smelling beef stew and spuds into my mess-tin, I went into the back of the kitchen and availed of the cook's hospitality.

That afternoon one of the off-duty RE signallers came over for a chat. It was nice to have a bit of company and stopped boredom from setting in. It was also a way of finding out how other units operate and maybe pick up some tips. Infantry signallers are not too different from RE signallers, apart from the fact that the RE hardly ever manpacked their radios. He was on his second tour, as were a lot of his squadron. In fact the Squadron 2I/C was on his third tour. Despite the UK government's insistence that the Army was overmanned, the resulting cuts after Options for Change had severely overstretched many units. The RE was a prime example of how wrong the politicians were.

I asked him if he could man the net for a few minutes while I answered a call from nature. He was happy to sit there and check out the 432. He normally operated from Spartans and it was his first time in one. While I was out I decided to take a quick snap of the base from the sandbagged OP that myself and Hendo had looked at two days ago. I had a compact 35mm camera and hoped that the shot would come out OK.

Later on that evening while running the engine, I got in touch with Ech and asked them if there was any news on a visit from REME. The engine was running rough and was starting to overheat. I was assured that REME would be out to me as soon as possible, but from the tone of the reply I doubted if they understood the severity of the problem. I was worried that the engine might be getting damaged while running it, so even though the batteries were not fully charged I turned it off. I didn't get much sleep that night. I kept waking to check the battery power. At about five the next morning I had no choice but to run the engine. It definitely didn't sound too healthy, but what could I do? Comms were a priority and the last thing I wanted was to be in charge of the Rebro that let the battalion down during its first task under UN control!

Not wanting to leave the Rebro in case the engine seized I skipped breakfast. I opened the rear door and was shocked at the change in the weather. It was very cold and the dark clouds moving quickly across the sky were preventing the sun from showing its face. I fished my Norwegian out of my holdall and quickly changed, welcoming the warm feeling the soft fleecy material gave me as I put my combat jacket back on over it. I only wished that I had a chance for a shower before putting on something clean.

I walked around to the front of the 432 and listened to the engine. It was making a whining noise and there was a sweet smell of burning. I opened the front cover and had a look inside the engine compartment but everything looked OK. The battery charge was still low, so I crossed my fingers and waited inside the 432, shivering from the early-morning cold.

It wasn't too long before the net came alive with chatter from the leading elements of 2LI. A Company, together with their REME, medical, anti-tank and mortar attachments, had started the road move to Kiseljak. It wouldn't be too long before the first Warriors drove into the vehicle park. Already I could hear the D&D Warriors warming up and the excited noises from the occupants as they stowed away all of their remaining kit.

As I watched, the D&Ds' Warriors formed up into columns, the first snowflakes of winter slowly floated down and quickly melted into the muddy ground. The D&D Warriors that still had their mortar hatches open quickly closed them. It started to fall more heavily as the D&Ds finally moved out on the first leg of their journey back to Paderborn. The silence that they left behind was welcoming but eerie. The sudden reduction in manpower made me feel very exposed, left all alone in the middle of the vehicle park. The snowfall progressively got heavier, quickly covering the landscape with a fluffy white blanket. Visibility was down to the barbed-wire perimeter. A Company were moving on radio silence, so I didn't know how long they would be. The most dangerous time in a war zone is the first few hours, when the troops are still acclimatising to conditions and concentrating on getting into position. It would be easy to make mistakes that could lead to casualties. We were as trained and as ready as we could be, but the Fates can be unkind. It was a critical time for the battalion. I waited, looking at the base entrance and watched the snow falling.

I was contemplating mounting the jimpy when the first Warrior turned the corner of the Hesco blast wall and pulled up a few metres away from me. After a quick look around, the commander jumped down and began directing the platoons to their own parking areas. Already the beautiful white carpet of snow was being churned up into mushy brown goo. It snowed for about two hours, finally petering out as their Mortar detachment finally trundled in with their 432s.

After each platoon had parked up, they were shown to the tents. There were a few moans as they were promised Corimec accommodation back in Germany, but Mount Igman had taken priority, so the contractors had packed up and moved out, leaving the buildings incomplete. As A Company would only be there for one day, then move up to Mount Igman, they didn't bother unpacking too much kit. After the initial excitement of the road move from Vitez, A Company settled down and waited apprehensively for the move up to the front line.

Looking around me, I couldn't believe the drastic change in the weather. I ran up to the OP to take another photo of the base. Even though the snowfall lasted only a few hours, it was heavy enough to cover as far as the eye could see. The change was surreal and hinted at what the weather gods had in store for us.

Unfortunately for me, my engine was still a problem, so on the way back I stopped at A Company's REME Light Aid Section and asked one of them to have a look. I could have guessed the verdict. Don't run the engine again or it will seize. I got back onto the Admin Net and spoke to Ech. Again I was told the solution was in hand and sit tight. Easy for them to say, but I would be deep in it if the Rebro went tits up! The downside of the first part of the changeover of responsibilities was that the increased radio traffic between locations would eat power from my batteries. Batteries don't like the cold either, and that drained power just by sitting there, so I prayed that someone in Ech was taking me seriously.

So, instead of clock-watching, I was drawn into another way of dragging out the day – watching the battery charge dial on the radios. The cold was starting to get to me, so I closed the driver's and commander's hatches to stop draughts, and sat closer to the engine compartment. Lunch was a quick chip butty and some lemon screech, followed by more dial-watching. I hardly noticed A Company's presence all day while I stayed put, and even missed the daily UBRE top up. By nightfall the batteries were low again so I risked running the engine for an hour. SOPs called for no vehicle movement at night unless absolutely necessary, so the lack of radio traffic helped.

That evening I sat there, trying to read *Sharpe's Eagle* but couldn't concentrate. I even tried to complete a word search but gave up on that as well. I was even too scared to turn on the BV for a warming brew in case it depleted the charge; lucky I had the cans of Coke I bought in Vitez if I got thirsty. After midnight I set the alarm on my watch and laid back. I could hear the sound of machine-gun fire close by, but I was too tired to worry about it. Sleep seemed to come easily.

At daybreak I awoke feeling stiff, cold and wet. I had forgotten to get into my doss bag and the snow had started to melt through the seals in the mortar hatches, dripping all over me. So much for the wagon being NBC-proof! I rubbed the sleep from my eyes and checked the charge. Good, almost full. I thought about going for a quick shower before A Company woke up, but a few others had the same idea as me and there was already a queue, so I made do with a cold wash from a plastic basin. I had to wait another two hours for breakfast, but luckily A Company's duty signaller let me make a brew from his Warrior's BV to help kick-start the day.

As with the D&Ds the day before, A Company were ready to move out just after breakfast. They looked apprehensive and even the NCOs refrained from the usual bollockings that they normally gave out to anyone who caught their eye. The singing and band playing from the Great War as battalions marched to the front might have been replaced by the quiet professionalism of a modern army, but the fears inside each and every man were probably the same. There was none of the gung-ho antics you often see in Hollywood war films. No banging together of helmets, no hoo-has, no high fives, just a quiet resolve and an effort not to look scared. That morning the young men of the Second Battalion the Light Infantry prepared to put their lives on the line so that the people of a foreign land that most had never heard of before the war started might live in peace and without fear of dying. I wished I was going with them.

It seemed like they were waiting for hours when confirmation finally came down from Vitez to move. With a single command from the Ops Officer, A Company moved up to the front line on Mount Igman, B Company moved into the Brick Factory, while C Company remained in Vitez. At 09:30 hours on Guy Fawkes Day 1995, 2LI formally took command of Task Force Alpha and its supporting elements and were ready to take on the BSA around Sarajevo.

B Company's arrival coincided with more snow, which quickly turned into mud again in the vehicle park. As with A Company, they parked their HQ close to the Rebro with the platoons parking up along the perimeter. I informed the Company 2I/C on the problems with break-ins, so B

Company parked a few metres away from the perimeter to give the sentries a clear view of the wire. Once again, the lads in the platoons were not too happy with the tents, especially as they were now surrounded by half a metre of snow. The temperature during the day hovered just above zero and, from the look at the dark clouds, would stay that way.

Already the seats in the wagon were soaking, so I borrowed a broom from the B Company colourboy and swept off the snow from the top of the mortar hatches. There were dozens of dents and scratches around the top of the wagon and the tarp had a few holes where it had been hit by small arms fire. I unrolled it and tied it down over the top. It would probably leak as well but it was better than nothing and would have to do until REME turned up with a replacement wagon.

On the net I heard that on Mount Igman A Company was having a hard time of things. Heavy snow was falling, and the Warriors, still with summer tracks on, were struggling in the snow. Dug in close to the BiH bunkers and trenches on the front line, they had come under grenade and rifle-fire. At night, in temperatures that quickly dropped to minus 10, they slept in shell scrapes deep in the snow, close to their Warriors. A two-week turnaround was planned, with the companies taking turns in each location. It was fine for the D&Ds during the summer and autumn, but I wondered if A Company and the gunners from 19 Regiment RA would last long in such an inhospitable climate.

By now every time I ran the engine I had the worry that it might be the last time. It was making a terrible screeching noise and the sweet burning smell was getting more pungent. There was still no news from Ech so at the end of my fourth day I grabbed my webbing, rifle and helmet, locked up shop and trudged through the snow to the RE CP.

I was worried that a breakdown in comms might result in disastrous consequences for A Company. On every course a soldier attends he is told to say to himself 'what if?', to try and foresee any problems that might trip you up. I applied that method to my present situation. What if the Serbs tried one last desperate attack on Sarajevo before the winter closed in? What if A Company got into difficulties and needed the QRF? What if the QRF were tucked up in bed because the Rebro was fucked and they didn't get the message? I had a recurring vision of the Para signaller in *A Bridge Too Far* who pleaded desperately for XXX Corps to come to their aid and imagined A Company's Det Commander doing the same, waiting for me to answer!

I was full of despair and anger for not being able to remedy the situation. It wasn't any one person's fault, just an unfortunate turn of events resulting in a neglected APC, but it would be my name that would be attached to any failure. I called up Ech on the HF Admin Net and asked them if they had any news. The answer was stark and simple. No.

The sun was starting to break through the clouds as I walked back to the Rebro. I was so busy with my own thoughts that I didn't realise that the snow had stopped. It was still very cold, and the dark clouds hinted at even more snow. For once the Met guys had been bang on with this one. On Igman four extra Land Rovers were sent to cope with the snow, so that troop movement could be maintained until the winter track turned up. The suddenness of the snow and freezing weather had stunned the planners who were expecting a slower onset of winter.

After missing lunch I started to feel really hungry, so after the usual call to Zero and padlock on the back door, I walked over to the cookhouse. I could feel the temperature cool as it started to snow yet again so I decided to eat in. It was freezing cold and the queue had died down from the evening rush. In the kitchen the cooks worked miracles. Even though they used a field kitchen on a trailer, the food was superb. The cooks were all badged AGC but were attached to the various units in theatre. In the Brick Factory we had cooks from the RE and 2LI, and I think that the competition between the different units showed in the quality of the food. A field kitchen is not state of the art; in fact it had hardly changed since World War Two. It is basically gas rings on a trailer, with steel boxes on top as ovens, but with flair and a little inventiveness the same cooks that doled out 'school dinners' back in barracks produced a varied and excellent menu three times a day, seven days a week, with no days off, using mediocre Army tinned rations supplemented by whatever fresh food could be found locally or brought in by container. The cooks never really got the compliments they deserved from the queues of hungry squaddies, but it was noticeable that there was none of the usual complaining either. I sat down at an empty table and attacked a steaming hot lasagne. About halfway through, it was cold – a constant problem now with the weather, but it never stopped anyone from finishing their food. Before I headed back I filled my thermal mug with tea and grabbed a few apples. From the back of the kitchen I picked up a pack of water cartons for the BV, some tea bags and a carton of milk. That should keep me going until breakfast.

That night, as I was cleaning my rifle I heard some pinging noises on the front of the wagon, like someone throwing stones. It only lasted a few seconds and I quickly forgot about it. The next day I was doing my vehicle checks when I noticed the glass was smashed on the left-side headlight. Close to it were tiny patches of bare metal shining through the dusty paintwork. Inside the lens of the headlamp was a squashed copper-covered lead bullet. It looked like the locals wanted me to celebrate with them again. After breakfast I showed it to the duty watchkeeper in the RE CP. He rolled it around his fingers and examined it. He looked up at me from his canvas chair and, with as much concern as he could muster, said, 'I hope it didn't wake you up?' He laughed to himself and threw it in the bin.

On the way out I passed a swearing RE Corporal, moaning about the thieving bastards who had stolen some jerry cans of petrol. It looked as if the locals were up to their nocturnal tricks again.

I was only back from breakfast a few minutes when the engine finally slowed to a complete stop and seized. The batteries only took a small charge and would give me a few hours tops. I called Zero and told them the news, still getting the standard reply of 'Roger, oot!' There was nothing left but to carry out my contingency plan.

I had an idea and while checking to see if the coaxes would reach B Company's Warrior ØC a smiling Fred pulled up beside me in a Land Rover. I was pleased to see him but time was running out. I must have looked a bit excitable so he told me not to panic and that help was on its way. Sure enough a few minutes later a 432 and a 434 turned the corner of the blast wall, just like the cavalry in a Western film, and stopped in front of the Rebro. The 432 was a replacement for my wagon and we quickly set about swapping over the Rebro. Fred explained that they had found a spare 432 but it also needed a pack change and that's why there was a 'slight' delay in bringing it out. Again, it wasn't a command variant, but it was very welcome all the same. After a comms check, we did the CES and vehicle checks. This time everything was perfect. The engine was new and the rubber seals were in good condition. We closed down the old wagon and connected it to the REME recovery 434 via steel towing bars so the reccy mech's could take it back to Vitez.

I was hoping that the signaller who drove the replacement 432 would be my relief and that I'd be returning to Vitez for a well-earned rest and a desperately needed hot shower. Fred let me down gently: 'No fooking chance!' He looked at me and almost apologetically said, 'You'll just have to wait out and see what happens. Shouldn't be too long though.'

So after I had given Fred my laundry bag and a few blueys to post, they drove off and left me on my jack again.

The comms were running fine, and after the road move the batteries wouldn't need to be charged for many hours yet. Most of B Company was

81

at lunch, so I decided to grab a shower at last. My combats were filthy after working on the wagons and it would be nice to change into a fresh set. It was a blow not to be going back to Vitez, and to make up for it I used the SNCOs' showers. The water was beautifully hot, and it was a relief to scrub away the grime of the last week. While I was in there an Engineer staff sergeant came in to shower but didn't pass any comments. I walked back to the Rebro feeling 100 per cent better than I did before and ready to take on another week.

When you take over a location from another unit, there will always be problems of one kind or another that don't suit your way of operating. One that became apparent very early was the siting of the antennas on the chimney. They were great for distance, but there was a dead spot right under them, leaving vehicles with no comms as they passed by the Brick Factory. To change this and to put the Rebro in a more sheltered location, it was decided to co-locate the Rebro with the RE Command Post and put up our own masts.

It was a relief to move as I continued to have problems with the coaxes, and due to frequent snowfalls the mud was getting deeper around the Rebro by the day. Mud was getting everywhere, in the vehicles, in the tents and in the building. The vehicle park was getting to be a problem. Many a careless squaddie found that it was easier to walk the long way to get to the vehicles rather than cut straight across the mud. The constant heavy traffic had created deep furrows that were hidden under the permanently fluid mud, and sudden falls into the sludge were a daily sight. It was impossible to carry anything heavy, as it upset your balance, and it pushed you deeper into the clinging sludge. The mud would go over the top of our high-leg boots, and stick to your combat trousers. At night, in the darkness of the tents, a squaddie would have no option but to get into his doss bag with the bottom half of his legs caked in mud.

In the mornings most squaddies would try to pick off the dried-on mud from the inside of their doss bag, and then pack it away until the next time it was needed, without being able to air it. In no time, doss bags started to stink with the combined smells of dirt, body odour and vehicle lubricants. The only place able to clean the bags was Vitez, and it sometimes took longer than a day to return them. As it wasn't advisable to be without one overnight in winter, the pong had to be put up until you returned to Vitez. For the companies on rotation it would be between two and four weeks. For those of us on Rebros or in Tac, it could take a bit longer to be able to get into our doss bags without getting a whiff of '*eau de skip*' drifting up.

82

In addition, if your body and combats went unwashed for long periods, combat zits began to appear like a rash. They were same as normal zits, but much bigger and more explosive. Your skin started to get itchy and even bouts of celebratory fire couldn't distract you from having a good scratch. It was no coincidence that doss bags were sometimes referred to as scratchers!

The mud also brought rats, which became more than a nuisance. They were often found in the tents nibbling away at personal kit trying to get at the rations and plaguing the bins by the kitchen. Some were the size of a cat, and a few squaddies were seen feeling for the safety catch on their rifle if they came across one. To combat any nocturnal visits switched-on section commanders took the pick helves from the Warriors and put them in the tents in case an emergency whacking was needed!

Even though I was operating on my own, I often got to see some friendly faces as they passed through the base. Jamie Ross and some of the MT Platoon were on Op Water Babe, supplying clean water from the brewery in Sarajevo to the troops on Mount Igman. He was filling up his tanker with diesel from the UBRE and came over when he saw me. He looked clean and fresh, and after navigating his way through the mud greeted me with a hug like a long-lost brother. Despite his reservations about getting posted to MT, he declared that he was really enjoying himself. MT was getting to see more of Bosnia than any other unit in 2LI, and he even had a chance to do a little black-market shopping in Sarajevo!

The road up to Igman and into Sarajevo through BiH lines had been discovered by British civvy drivers working for the Convoy of Mercy. Using ex-British Army Bedford MK four-tonners they crossed the previously impenetrable horse tracks that were dotted over the mountain and were the first aid vehicles to enter Sarajevo without losing half of their loads in 'payments' at Serb checkpoints. This remarkable feat changed the way aid was delivered, and the UN was quick to exploit the route. In the summer the road was bad, in the winter it was treacherous, and for many drivers it was akin to a baptism of fire. Many civvy drivers fell victim to Igman as they risked everything to deliver aid across the mountain and into the besieged city.

The Igman Sector was controlled by the French, and Jamie moaned about the fact that it was easier to get through a BiH or BSA checkpoint than a French one – even though the water was intended for them as well! He said he was glad he wasn't staying on Igman overnight. The cold was unreal compared to ground level and made ten times worse by the wind-chill factor. I would have liked to chat for longer but it was just a pit stop for Jamie and the rest of his wagon train, and they had to get back to Vitez Garage and hand over their trucks for the next convoy.

After waiting for approval from Main we found a good spot for the Rebro next to the end of the factory building. It was in a sort of cul-de-sac offering excellent protection, surrounded by the base generators and an earth berm made by the RE, very close to the RE CP. Once the 432 was moved, we remoted the sets into the CP, and set up a Rebro for a much-needed VHF Admin net by clipping in another two 353s. Instead of using the chimney antennas, we decided to set up our own around the Rebro. A comms check forward to the Rebro at the base of Igman and back to Echelon at Vitez Garage proved workable, and a radio check from a departing RE Spartan proved that the dead spot around the Brick Factory was no longer a problem.

To make things easy, B Company, the RE and me shared the duties in the CP. This meant that I would stag on for two hours and then be off for six. This gave me plenty of time to maintain the wagon and keep the batteries fully charged, but most importantly I could get a decent night's kip at last!

The weather was slowly getting worse, so the CP 12×12 canvas tent was fitted to the back of the wagon to help keep out the wind, and I covered the wagon with the vehicle tarp as a precaution to keep out any leaks. I commandeered some more wooden pallets from the RE defence stores and made a raised walkway through the mud from the CP to the Rebro, and inside the tent to the back door of the wagon. To mark it so there wouldn't be any mishaps in the dark I put out some steel pickets and tied Day-Glo orange mine tape between them. I stood back and admired my handiwork, satisfied that I would be comfortable here. Only an idiot would fail to see the path.

Life should have been quite normal from now on, but as I was beginning to realise, life was never normal in Bosnia. I should have been more comfortable, but with the severe drop in temperatures the inside of the steel hull of the 432 was like a fridge. Gloves were the norm, and sometimes the only way of warming up during the day was to sit right up against the engine compartment when it was running. I heard on the grapevine that a new German-made diesel heater was being fitted into all 432s in the next few weeks. I couldn't wait that long and managed to acquire a kerosene heater for the tent. Fuel was plentiful, as the RE had a small POL point around the corner, and they didn't mind me taking a jerrycan every few days. On full blast the kero heater kept the chill out of the air, and at night I put it inside the interior of the wagon. I know it was risky but I didn't want it knocked over in the pitch black of the inside of the tent. As if to rub in the hardships to come, my morale-boosting hot showers had now stopped as the B Company guys had also used the SNCOs' and officers' toilets and ran them dry. Now they were kept locked, with the keys having to be signed out from the CP.

It was a complete bummer, but through adversity solutions are often found. A frequent visitor to the Rebro was the UBRE driver from MT Platoon, who, I found out, was homeless. The MT Platoon had sent him to Kiseljak to support the QRF, and he was living like a Gypsy from the cab of his lorry. Every evening he would drive to the Hotel Kiseljak and fill up his UBRE from the bulk fuel storage facility there. As he was working with fuel he was allowed at least one hot shower a day to help prevent dermatological problems, and the MTO arranged it so he could use the amenities in the hotel gym.

With all the 'celebratory' flying around he didn't feel safe trying to sleep in the thin metal cab of a petrol tanker, so we quickly came to an arrangement. He could set up his camp-bed in the tent and get a proper night's sleep, while he would take me to the Hotel Kiseljak where I could use the showers that were jealously guarded by the Royal Marines from the forward HQ of the ARRC. To make things more homely, we even adopted a pet kitten that was sniffing around the Rebro for food and warmth. Not surprisingly, it was christened Rebro.

Apart from when I was stagging on in the CP, each evening after the company's Warriors had been refuelled I would try to accompany him to the hotel. The journey was only a short five-minute ride from gate to gate, and covered the length of the town's main street. Kiseljak was a Croat enclave in a predominantly Muslim region and just like Vitez had suffered badly from the fighting. The pavements were empty apart from a few street sellers, bored locals and, from the look of them, possibly a few ladies of the night. As it was a short journey we travelled without an escort. This attracted a few stares from the many armed gangs that operated under the banner of the HVO, who hung around looking for mischief and the chance to make money. Fuel was a bigger commodity than gold, and the warring factions had a history of hijacking lone vehicles. A petrol tanker would be a considerable prize. The UBRE driver mentioned on more than one occasion that he was glad to have me along riding shotgun.

The Hotel Kiseljak was probably the pride of the town before the war and was fairly new. Despite the customary shell damage it had been repaired enough to be suitable for the UN to rent and because of the high rates charged it was making somebody a very rich man. The hotel was brimming with troops. Apart from the HQ element of the ARRC, which seemed to be mostly staffed by Royal Marines, there was a Scandinavian field hospital set up on the ground floor, a company from 1RRF, and the RLC had taken over some of the upper floors.

The RLC detachment operated the bulk fuel installation that was located in a field opposite the hotel to the south. This area had huge rubber storage bladders dug into the ground. Alongside was a landing pad that was used as a FARP for helicopters. The usual Hesco protection, sandbags and razor wire were set up all around the hotel perimeter, but the FARP was in the open field to the south. A sandbagged OP was erected to provide protection for the helicopters, as they were at their most vulnerable when refuelling. Once inside, it provided excellent observation of the surrounding area and offered very good protection, but attempts to man it were abandoned as the access was totally exposed and attracted the attentions of local would-be snipers. In the car park were dozens of white-painted vehicles of every description. Danish SISU armoured ambulances were parked outside the hospital, along with some smaller Mercedes jeeps. Close to them in parade like rows were the Saxons from 1RRF and around the perimeter in blob order were the bulk fuel tankers and Land Rovers of the RLC.

The refuelling point for tankers was in the open at the edge of the car park. One evening as it was getting dark we were fired upon while the Loggie tried to undo the padlock on the diesel pump. Me and the UBRE driver took cover beside a nearby parked Saxon while we tried to locate the source. Across from the fuel bladders I saw flashes in the back garden of a house and checked it out through my SUSAT. About seventy-five metres away a man in combats was firing a pistol at us. He seemed to be suffering from a stoppage after each shot as he kept cocking the weapon, but there was no mistaking where he was aiming. At that range he would be very lucky to hit us, so we stayed in cover and kept him under observation until he ran out of ammo and ran off. It might seem strange that we didn't return fire, but as the rounds were not falling all around us we were restricted under the UN Rules of Engagement and couldn't retaliate. In the British Army we knew how to check fire and not retaliate wildly, unlike the Yanks who saw shooting up the world as a constitutional right. As a badged marksman I knew that I could have dropped him with a single shot at that range, even in poor light, so he was lucky he was such a crap shot. Besides, I didn't want to spend the next week being interrogated by the Monkeys and making endless statements if I had opened fire.

When the excitement had died down, we went back over to the UBRE, our thoughts already back to getting the refuelling over with and having a hot shower. We watched as the loggie picked himself off the ground and smiled at each other. He had taken cover under the UBRE; not exactly the one of the safest places to be under fire.

When we got back to the Brick Factory I called in at the CP and reported the incident to Zero. I was told not to worry as it was probably celebratory fire. I tried to explain to the duty watchkeeper that it was a deliberate act, but he didn't even bother to log it. I walked away thinking that it would take a casualty before anyone would take it seriously. Probably the machine-gun and grenade attacks on A Company and the French a few weeks previously were being called celebratory as well!

One of the many groups of visitors we had stay at the Brick Factory was a Recce platoon from the French Foreign Legion. They were pulled back from the front line on Mount Igman to get a bit of R&R. They were given an area to park their vehicles and some empty tents adjacent to B Company. As you would expect with the Legion, they were made up of all nationalities. The officers were French, but the men were mostly East European – from Romania, Russia, Georgia and Ukraine – with a few from England, Germany and Scandinavia. There was even a fearsome little Tamil Tiger from Sri Lanka. It didn't take long for two of the Legionnaires to be recognised as being Brits on the run from the LI, and confirmation of their names was quickly sought after. I was on duty in the CP when a captain from the Legion presented the list of personnel to the duty watchkeeper.

'But all of these names are in French!' exclaimed the confused Rupert, expecting to see a Smith and Jones somewhere in the list.

'*Oui, Monsieur*, what else would you expect?' smiled the Legionnaire. 'My men are all French. I can arrange for you to see zere documents if you so wish, but of course zat could take some time.' With that he casually saluted and left.

The watchkeeper looked at the list, shook his head and muttered 'Bloody French!' then got on with the all-important job of guarding the key to the officers' toilets.

It was interesting to observe the Legion at close hand. They paraded for inspection every morning and were always immaculately turned out despite the ever-present damp and mud. Then they would spend the day carrying out maintenance on their green-and-buff camouflaged AMX 10 RC wheeled tanks and VBL armoured jeeps. In the evenings, apart from sentries on their vehicles, they mounted a guard on their own tents, in case anyone had a notion to desert during the night. On top of this, they also took turns with B Company in providing the base guard. It was reassuring to see the hard men of the Legion flinch just like us when bursts of celebratory fire flew overhead. They were a friendly bunch, and despite the hard regime of the Legion seemed happy with their lot. We were glad to have them with us.

In the Rebro we finally got the heater fitted, and it made a world of difference. We were able to dry out our damp clothes properly and it made working in the Rebro much more comfortable. The mud on the floor of the wagon dried enough to be swept up, and at last I was able to dry out my constantly damp boots. An added bonus was the installation of a SCRA radio set, so that we could get access to the Ptarmigan digital network. This enabled secure comms from the CP, but more importantly, the Royal Signals techie who fitted it gave me the number to dial for phone calls home. I think my sister thought the worst when she got a call from the military switchboard in Woolwich, asking her would she accept a connection from Bosnia!

All Army units are on the military phone network, so I managed a few chats with some of the lads back in my old company, just to catch up on what was happening while I was away. It was great for morale and I didn't overdo the free phone calls myself, but word soon got out and I let a few of the lads make a call. It made a great difference to them as the welfare facilities enjoyed back at Division, Brigade and Vitez were not mirrored closer to the front. Mentions of the generosity of BT and other major British institutions might have made good reading in the tabloids back home, but the phones and gifts never made it to the 'Poor Bloody Infantry' who were at the sharp end of things.

On the communications front there was a period of a few days where we were subjected to jamming by an unknown source. All former Eastern Bloc countries trained extensively in electronic countermeasures and surveillance, so it wasn't surprising that we were being listened to. We hadn't made it hard for someone to listen in by changing frequencies and it was only a matter of time before someone got bored and tried to interrupt comms. The JNA would have had whole regiments dedicated to electronic warfare and it was reasonable to assume it was the BSA or their mates in the JNA that were jamming us. The first time I noticed it was when we were subjected to ten minutes of ethnic Slav accordion music. It could have been a bored squaddie pissing around but not for that length of time. A few hours later it happened again, but this time for half an hour. It was impossible to get through on the net, so I called Zero on the Ptarmigan and gave them a Jamrep. It was annoying but instead of changing frequencies, it was decided to ignore it in the hope it would stop. If it didn't, we would have to go into our normal operating mode of changing frequencies every twelve hours. That might cause problems with the Serbs who would accuse us of being secretive again, and we seemed to be bending over backwards to appease them. It happened a few more times that night, both for about twenty minutes each, and again over the next few days until it finally stopped. It was just another way for the Serbs to try and frustrate us and it didn't work, but it showed that they were willing to try anything at least once.

Near the end of B Company's stint as QRF they lost half of their men to food poisoning, or more precisely the shits! It seemed that the lads were filling up their BVs with non-potable water from tanks supplying the toilets and we must have had a particularly bad delivery that day. A few lads panicked that they might be getting 'spaghetti arse', but after a day of watching dozens of red-faced squaddies rushing through the mud to the toilets it died down and was forgotten about.

Back in the main building, the RE were finishing off the repairs to the ovens. I arranged for a look around and was amazed at what I found. In the chambers that led to the chimney, the RE had put out some tables and chairs and had fixed up a fireplace. Where the chambers met, a bar was in the process of being finished off, but the biggest surprise was the TV and satellite dish sent over from Germany, which they were in the process of tuning in. That evening I was invited to the grand opening of the RE bar, dubbed the Kiseljak Cavern, and had my first beer since arriving in the Brick Factory. There were a few lads from B Company and a few from the Legion, but mainly it was full of Engineers. Inside the ovens the curved bare brickwork and a low ceiling resembled a wine cellar and could have been mistaken for a trendy city wine bar. It was lovely and warm and not before long everyone was in T-shirt order. I sipped at my beer, and with the gathered Engineers watched Southampton v Aston Villa live on Sky Sports.

The effect on morale was amazing, and even though I didn't particularly like any of the teams playing, I was captivated by every pass, every tackle, and every stupid comment from Andy Gray. It was a moment to forget the hardships of being on active service and in particular the hostile climate. I didn't even notice that the local beer we were drinking had a picture of Jesus on the label until I went and got another at half-time. I swear I wasn't drunk, but I felt like it when I left the bar after the match. The ground outside was very icy and in the dark was quite precarious. I seemed to slip and slide more than usual but made it to the Rebro OK. Back inside I checked the batteries, set my alarm for my 4 a.m. stag and got into my doss bag. I went to sleep a very happy bunny.

After two hard weeks on Igman, A Company was relieved by B Company, with C Company taking over as QRF. If I thought that it would be the same as having the other two companies around I was sadly mistaken. I was stagging on in the CP when C Company arrived. My first introduction to them was when I finished and walked back to the Rebro. The HQ Warriors, ØB and ØC, had driven across the raised pallet path and had flattened the marker pickets. Instead of a dry and clearly marked path there was a tangled mess of timber, mud, steel and orange mine tape. Two of the guide ropes for the eight-metre masts had been snapped and the antennas were leaning to one side. The Sigs Det Commander, a lance-corporal known as 'The Prick', was arranging the two Warriors and parking them up close to the building. It took him about half an hour and when he finished I asked him what the fuck was he doing?

He looked at the mayhem all around him and seemed pleased with his efforts. I mentioned that C Company was supposed to be QRF and he had just parked in a cul-de-sac, with their backs facing the way out. He screamed that he was in charge and it was nothing to do with me. I had heard talk of him before and was told that he was a dickhead, but I suppose the proof of the pudding is in the eating. Strangely he put out antenna on eight-metre masts to help communicate with the Rebro that was less than ten metres away. At that range he could have got through using a paper clip stuck to the back of his radio!

I was quite prepared to leave him be, but after he had finished with the crews of C Company's HQ The Prick came over and told me that from then on I was under his command, and this had come direct from the RSWO. I knew that this was total bollocks, as I was a battalion asset and was under the control the RSO and his comms plan, but stranger things have happened in the Army so I called the RSWO on the Ptarmigan and asked him to verify the situation.

As I expected, the RSWO wasn't too happy that his name had been used to back up an illegal order and told me to ignore him. So, with The Prick still thinking that he was king of the jungle, I carried on as normal.

Some time later, as I was filling up from the UBRE, I had a surprise visitor. It was Private Boxhall-Hunt, one of the lads from the Paras. He told me that The Prick had told him to stag on with me until C Company moved up to Igman. I welcomed Box to the Rebro, and he stowed his kit. He stretched out on the spare bench seat, had a good look around at the spacious interior, then looked at me with an approving grin and said, 'Lovely!'

Box wasn't always a private. In fact just before he joined us in Germany he was a corporal, but as is life in the Paras, he got busted for being a little too aggressive. But that wasn't really the story with Box. He was highly intelligent, laid back, and had a great sense of humour. He wasn't bothered about being a private and in a strange regiment; he was there for the adventure. He was tall, confident and with his accent you might have mistaken him for a Rupert. In fact he went to school with the RSO. The Prick had probably felt threatened about his presence and got rid of him at the first opportunity. I didn't mind the help; in fact it did me a big favour. Box wasn't trained on the 432 but quickly learned the basics, and we got on very well. For Box it was a chance to get away from the constant bragging and moaning of his Det Commander, even though it was only for two weeks. For me it meant that I could take a break from constantly monitoring the Rebro and get a few hours to myself. For the first time since I arrived in Kiseljak I slept without worrying if I was being called on the net.

That evening I went with the UBRE driver to the Hotel Kiseljak for a long hot shower. Driving through the town we came upon a small crowd by an old rusty Skoda. There was fresh blood on the pavement and some Croat policemen were chatting to the crowd. We slowed down as we passed but I couldn't see what the commotion was about, but the crowd and the policemen were all laughing and seemed to be having a great time. Back in the Brick Factory CP I found out that a crowd of drunken HVO militiamen had stopped the car and pulled out the two occupants. On discovering that they were Muslims they set about kicking them to death. That was their blood on the pavement. The lads stagging on at the gate saw everything, but were powerless to stop it. Despite the Croat–Muslim peace deal, there were still a lot of hatred and old scores to settle.

It was about time the UN changed to a more forceful mandate so we could intervene and put an end to these petty vendettas. I felt sick and needed a beer so popped into the RE bar. On Sky News we heard that a peace deal had been agreed by the presidents of Croatia, Bosnia and Serbia, and NATO was being lined up to take over from the UN. I noticed that Radovan Karadzic and his BSA weren't mentioned as supporters of the deal.

91

It didn't take long for the folly of C Company's HQ location to be found lacking in military or common sense. In the north of the country, in a town called Velika Kladusa, a Bangladeshi Army base was attacked and overrun by a large BSA force, who confiscated nine BMPs and all of the food and fuel stores. It looked like Karadzic was letting the world know that he wasn't going to give up quietly. On hearing the news of the attack, the QRF stood to. Within ten minutes, all of C Company's Warriors were lined up outside the base ready to move. This also included the whole of the French Foreign Legion recce troop who insisted on not being left behind, something that the OC of C Company warmly welcomed. Unfortunately that same quick reaction was not carried out by the HQ element of C Company. Apart from wasting time taking down the masts, it took half an hour for the OCs and 2I/C's Warriors, ØB and ØC, to back out of the cul-de-sac and join the rest of the company outside the Brick Factory. C Company's OC was not impressed.

From the RE CP I heard that the alert state had been raised as the Serb attack might have been a feint to divert our attentions from a bigger Serb offensive around Sarajevo. The Dayton Peace Accord might have just been agreed, but it wasn't signed, and there was good reason to believe that the Serbs would mount one final push to take as much land as they could before official boundaries were redrawn. With the QRF about to leave, the base was unguarded, so the Royal Engineers gave me an arc of the perimeter to cover, roughly one-quarter of the base. I set up the jimpy, loaded a belt of 200 rounds, put on the headset and stood to. The remainder of the base was protected by a dozen Royal Engineers, our only back-up the handful of cooks who were getting dinner ready. I looked across my arc of fire and started to feel very exposed and vulnerable.

While the QRF were eager to be given the order to move out, General Smith was being told by the UN to refrain from taking any action. Again, positive and quick action against the Serbs by the units of UNPROFOR was prevented by the hierarchy of the UN, who didn't have the backbone to sort out the Serbs, even when caught in the act. A few hours after the QRF massed outside the Brick Factory the order to stand down was given. It was a big disappointment to the British and French soldiers who waited for the go-ahead on the main street of Kiseljak.

Back inside the Brick Factory, the QRF parked up and switched off their vehicles. The only difference from before the call-out was the location of C Company's HQ. After a deep and penetrating bollocking, The Prick was told to park in the open, with as much space as possible between them and any obstacle. Box was grinning like a naughty

92

schoolboy when he came back, and couldn't wait to tell me the intimate details of The Prick's mighty clusterfuck.

From then on, The Prick was unbearable to be around, which meant that in the Rebro we had many visitors from the crews of ØB and ØC, who came over to get away from being picked on to do the most idiotic chore or listen to him suck up to the Company 2I/C. I also got some visits from the Sigs Platoon in Main, who stopped at the Rebros every week to deliver any mail or supplies that were needed. I asked one of the corporals for the low-down on The Prick. He told me that he was loathed within the Sigs Platoon back in Germany, and the only way to stop somebody from lynching him was to get rid of him by giving him a company detachment to run. The general feeling was that the added responsibility would change him for the better. Somehow, I don't think the experiment was working out.

Chapter 8

Mount Igman and the Front Line

As I now had Box to help out, I got stuck into my personal admin, and that meant I could at last sort out my tooth. I made a call to Zero and spoke to Corporal Hamish MacFarlane (a dour Yorkshireman despite his monicker) at Main and got permission to go up to Mount Igman to see the RADC dentist. I knew that a convoy left the Hotel Kiseljak for Igman every morning and managed to blag a lift in an RE Spartan. The RE Troop Commander was happy to help out, and I helped him by providing top cover for the tail end Charlie. Before we moved out, the Troop Commander told the assembled drivers and crews that we would need to be wary as there had been rioting in Hadzici, a BSA-controlled village west of Igman that we were going to travel through. The previous day's convoys had been stoned by what appeared to be an organised crowd and BSA armour was reported moving into the area. 2LI anti-tank positions had been set up with pairs of Milan posts overlooking the town but it was the only route up to the front line, so we had to brass it out.

As a final point he reminded us not to throw sweets to the kids that hung about on street corners. You cannot help but feel for those poor young mites as they suffered from the depravations of war. When you see them the first reaction is to throw them some sweets from a 24-hour rat pack, or even a whole box. Unfortunately it tended to create a surge of bodies as the half-starved kids, blinded by the thought of chocolate and candies, scrambled for anything they could grab. A few kids had died under the wheels of UN trucks as they ignored the dangers of the passing vehicles. We all felt some compassion as we drove by but in this case it really was cruel to be kind.

We travelled along Route Swan towards Sarajevo under dark clouds, but the snow that had been forecast for the last few days was holding off. Despite this it was bitterly cold. For the first time in theatre I used my white cold-weather mask to keep my face from getting frostbite and my US Army driving goggles to stop my eyes from freezing over. We stopped a k outside Hadzici for brew and to wait for a returning convoy to clear the mountain road.

Once the muddy white convoy had passed, we moved off and headed towards the tower of the town's mosque. The town was devastated and the mosque seemed to have taken the brunt of the damage. The townspeople were hanging around, as if waiting to be told what to do. We drove by without incident and after leaving the town behind us started our assent of Mount Igman. Halfway up and just as the snow got really deep we were met by the MT Platoon's newest toy. The BV 206 articulated snow vehicle that was normally used in the Arctic regions of Norway was now being eagerly driven by drivers who a few days previously had been white with fear as their vehicles slipped along close to the edges of the mountain tracks.

As we got crawled up the rest of the mountain, it started to snow heavily. Now and then I spotted the wrecks of some of the ill-fated aid convoy trucks stuck in the trees halfway down the slopes between the tracks. In places it was a near vertical drop. The road, if you can call it that, was covered in ice, and in places the Spartan's winter track slipped and struggled to get any grip as we clawed our way up. If we lost momentum now we might end up sliding backwards and over the edge. Back in August, on their way to deliver a US-sponsored peace plan to the Bosnian government, an APC carrying three American diplomats plunged off the mountain killing all on board. As I watched the BV 206s snake their way up the mountain with ease I willed the Spartan to keep going.

Closer to the top where the track started to level out we saw the BiH trench systems and gun emplacements that overlooked the BSA positions. They reminded me of the German trenches in the film *Cross of Iron*. Lined with tree trunks, the trenches were intersected by bunkers made from more tree trunks. Now and then I spotted some Soviet-style camouflage netting and a few strands of rusting barbed wire, but mainly they were covered by the canopy of the fir trees that grew all over the mountain. Smoke poured from makeshift tin chimneys that protruded from every bunker, and I could smell the distinctive smoke from the damp timber that was being burned that gave the BiH the smallest of comfort in the bitter conditions. The BiH looked filthy, old and tired, but defiant. A few waved as we passed, as though we were fellow conspirators in their battle to defeat the Serbs. I didn't wave back, it was too bloody cold and, besides, I had one hand on the pistol grip of my rifle and the other was gripping the hatch rim to stop me being shaken about too much.

Once we had got to the top, we had to pass through two French checkpoints to get to Tac. The French Task Force Bravo was based in the Hotel Igman, while the Brits of Task Force Alpha were five hundred metres away in the recently completed Corimec base closer to the front line named after the LI battle honour Sevastopol. I checked in with Tac and then headed off to the Hotel Igman where the RADC Det was located. The French Cavalry soldiers at the barrier at the hotel let me through after I flashed them my UN ID card, and I followed the first-aid signs into the basement.

Here, set up in tents in the damp and half-light of the car park and plant areas, was a major field hospital, ready to treat the casualties from the expected push on Sarajevo. Passing wards and operating theatres, I found a small tented area that was unmistakably British Army. Twelve-by-twelve tents were set up with the flaps immaculately rolled back, and storage boxes were neatly stacked against a wall. Inside, a good-looking female nurse directed me to the dentist, who grinned mischievously and showed me to the dentist chair.

After the briefest of inspections the dentist gave me the good news. My tooth had become infected and had to come out. It didn't give up easily, and with the help of a knee on my chest and his arm in my mouth he managed to wrench it out. Even under local anaesthetic it hurt like hell and the nurse quickly stuffed what felt like a field dressing into the cavity to stop the bleeding. The dentist looked at the offending tooth under a lamp and seemed pleased with his efforts. I was glad that someone was happy because even though the nurse was stroking my hand and reminding me of my enforced vow of celibacy, I felt like shit.

Back at Tac I found an empty space by the door in the Sigs Platoon room and rested until the anaesthetic wore off. I had missed the return trip with the Royal Engineers, so after a very boring few hours waiting for the numbness to wear off I went looking for a lift back the next day. Luckily, the MTO was visiting his boys on Op Water Babe and would be able to fit me in for the trip back to Vitez in the morning.

Outside it might have been below zero, but the air was so fresh it was like a drug. I wandered around, taking a look at the ski jump from the Winter Olympics of 1984. I also headed out towards the front line, but as it got darker I could feel the temperature dropping rapidly, so I went back to the warmth of Tac and met up with Jamie Ross again.

Jamie was still on Op Water Babe and was staying on Igman overnight before returning to Sarajevo in the morning. Jamie looked awful. He had a few days' growth on his face and his combats were filthy. His face was pale and he had bags under his eyes. All of this didn't exactly enhance his boyish good looks. While we went to get some scoff, Jamie told me about his adventures so far. On Op Water Babe, Jamie and the other drivers from MT would pick up water from a brewery close to the airport and bring it up to the troops on Igman. It sounded simple, but when you added getting up before dawn, the drive across the confrontation line, snipers, snowstorms, mines, getting stopped at every checkpoint, black ice, riots, BSA armour movements, the terrifying drive up and down the steep mountain track and finishing the day after dark you could forgive him for his appearance. Jamie wasn't quite himself, and tried to remain cheerful while he recounted his story, but the strain of the job was immense and it took a lot of strength, physical and mental, to carry on without a break. After scoff Jamie and the rest of the MT lads went off to sort out their trucks and get their heads down for some desperately needed sleep.

Back in the Sigs Platoon room Pete Wass was about to go on stag and let me use his camp bed and tried to get some sleep myself. The room was crammed full to bursting and there was no room to move between the beds. There were so many people coming and going their wet boots made the floor permanently wet. The stench of unwashed bodies and cigarette smoke made my eyes water, so I pulled the hood of my doss bag tight and closed my eyes. The conditions were so overcrowded it was a wonder anyone got any sleep. I tell you, after experiencing army accommodation on ops I would say that prisons are definitely not overcrowded! In the morning I was up and packed before daylight. Tac had the same problems with hot water, so after another cold wash and a bit of breakfast I met up with the MTO.

There was just about enough room in the back of his 90 to squeeze in, and the driver had to push the back door against the weight of kit to shut it. I couldn't see out of the back as the window was covered in mud, and there was so much kit piled up near the front so I couldn't see where we were going. It could have been a comfortable trip, lying back and trying to snooze, but the 90 didn't have snow chains on and slipped quite alarmingly as the MTO's driver tried to keep from tobogganing down the mountain. I looked for the door handle but it was covered by a Bergan. If we did start to roll off the edge there would be no way I could exit quickly, and would have to wait for REME to turn up with a can opener to get me out! Also, the MTO couldn't help but mention how alert the BiH were in their trenches, that Milan were tracking BSA tanks, and that crowds were gathering in the suburbs of Sarajevo again. It was nice for the MTO to give me a running commentary but I would have preferred if he didn't!

Once past the French, BSA and BIH checkpoints we settled into a steady and more comfortable drive, which finally resulted in a cessation of the commentary. Instead of the local events, the MTO talked about the political situation, how the peace deal was working out. I asked him about MT's job so far and his voice filled with pride as he chatted about his 'boys'' achievements. As the MTO's nickname suggested, Knuckles was one of the battalion's hard men who had come up from the ranks. He was still a fearsome figure, but on that journey back the way he talked about his platoon showed that he had a compassionate side to his personality as well.

Chapter 9

The Wanderer Returns

Back at Kiseljak we stopped at the Brick Factory and I was unpacked from the back of the 90. The MTO was surprised to find that the UBRE driver was co-located with the Rebro and nodded his approval. After a quick welfare chat with the UBRE driver about conditions, food and mail, he said his goodbyes and went off to get the key for the officers' toilets. I walked into the 12 × 12 expecting Box to be fuming about being left on his own. He was lying back against his Bergan on the bench seat with Rebro the kitten purring away in his lap. Box looked up and smiled, welcomed me back and asked me how it went. I apologised about my enforced absence, but Box laughed it off and said it was a bit of a breather to be on his own for a while. There were no problems with the net or the wagon, but would I mind if he could be relieved later so he could go to the Hotel Kiseljak for a shower? It was the least I could do. So I made a brew, pulled up a sandbag and told him all about Mount Igman.

'Lovely,' replied Box. 'About time I packed away my slippers and did some real soldiering!' He grinned, looked up at the roof of the wagon as if dreaming of some daring do, and carried on stroking Rebro.

A few days later I heard in the CP that the French had broken through some of the BSA checkpoints to the west of Sarajevo, near Ilidza and the airport and taken control. It would mean a less hazardous trip up to the top of Mount Igman, but it was still dangerously close to the main BSA troop and armour that still surrounded the besieged city. Over ten thousand Sarajevans had been killed during the siege so far, maybe this Christmas we could stop the slaughter and they would be left in peace.

Life in the Brick Factory during C Company's residency was eventful. The mud in the vehicle park had risen to over half a metre in places, and now and again a cry of help could be heard from the unfortunate squaddies who got stuck trying to take a short cut to their Warriors. Some defence stores arrived from Vitez, and when the working parties prepared to build out a much-needed clean and safe access route around camp they found that when they started the work it wasn't to be built inside the base. Instead of providing a dry route for the company to get to and from the Warriors, a running track was built around the perimeter, *outside* of the barbed wire. The Royal Engineers were speechless. For them it was a blatant waste of resources and they couldn't believe that something wasn't being done to improve the working conditions of the men.

Once completed it was announced that a race was to be held. So C Company, and anyone else in the Brick Factory who wanted to (apart from the Royal Marines in the hotel – they didn't want any non-Army types stealing their glory!), changed into their running gear and were taken by lorry to the start about five miles away. Being on ten minutes' notice to move and so far away in PT kit wasn't a smart idea, but it wasn't going to stop the race.

With armoured protection, the contenders ran along the wet and muddy lanes and roads towards the final few laps of the newly constructed perimeter track. I watched the finish along with some disgusted Royal Engineers, who thought that a clear walkway for the infantry within the camp should have had priority. Many of the lads slipped and fell as the track became muddier with each passing squaddie. I don't know how many injuries were suffered because of that race, but I did see a few lads hobbling about over the next few days.

After completing the race, the sweaty squaddies walked back across the sea of mud, had a cold shower, changed into dirty combats and packed away their muddy running gear. Just the prep you need when you are about to deploy to a front line on a mountain in sub-zero temperatures. Well, at least the SNCOs and officers had a hot shower.

After the race, the lads in the company got on with the job in hand, the event quickly forgotten with the move-up to the front line on their minds. Unsurprisingly, after all the effort and materials used, it was the only race ever held there.

The Prick was still a pain in the arse, but thankfully he didn't interfere too much and left me and Box pretty much alone. The weather was closing in and getting a lot colder now. I didn't need a thermometer to tell me how cold it was; I could feel it with every shiver. In the mornings the base was always covered with a white frosting of snow and ice. It was funny to watch squaddies walk over the mud thinking that the ice would hold them, only for them to suddenly sink up to their knees into the freezing cold muddy slime. Despairing shouts of 'Bollocks!' and 'Aw fook!' could be heard all around the base.

In the Rebro, to stop the heat from getting out of the tent we started to skip breakfast. It didn't take long for me to realise that the kero heater could be used for making toast, so the three of us would sit in the wagon, drinking tea and scoffing delicious hot buttered toast, while in the background the net chattered away like a Geordie version of talk radio. It was nice to be able to relax in the mornings and wait until the weather was less harsh before going outside. After breakfast I would get out and clean away any fresh snow from the path and check the guide ropes for the antenna masts. Vehicle maintenance and refuelling was carried out in the evening just before the shower run so I spent a little time as possible reeking of diesel. That left stagging on, personal admin and a few precious hours of free time. In the last week of C Company's stint as QRF it wasn't all routine though. We had a few moments of high drama when the guard was called during suspected break-ins.

After dark and the customary celebratory fire, men were spotted slipping through gaps in the barbed wire. The armed guard, supplemented by handfuls of keen off-duty squaddies, searched the perimeter, vehicle parks and storage areas in the hope of catching someone. For an hour or so there would be excited shouts, but no one was ever caught. Whoever it was, they were very good and got away, and in the morning missing items were reported and replaced. The intruders were lucky not to get seen or caught. The Royal Fusiliers shot and killed a prowler who turned out to be a mujahadin. It wasn't the same mujahadin who defeated the Russians in Afghanistan, just foreign Muslim fighters, but they had a tough reputation for fighting against the enemy. The mujahadin put out a fatwa on all British soldiers after that, but it was just a frightener. Even so, we tended to make ready when they were in the vicinity.

Other nocturnal visitors were just as mysterious as our intruders but at least they were on our side. Small groups of Special Forces would come and go, using the Brick Factory as a temporary base. We didn't have to be told who they were, their advanced years and non-standard kit was a big give-away. I assumed they were General Smith's JCOs, and it was nice to know they were around. I don't think they were here to sort out our intruder problem, but there were never any incidents when they were around. In the CP we listened to the BBC World Service as the Serbian General Ratko Mladic vowed to resist the Dayton Peace Accord. Maybe the arrival of Special Forces in Kiseljak was a sign of things to come.

I was sorry to see Box leave when C Company moved up to Mount

Igman, but I was glad that A Company came back. It was the first week in December and I was resigned to the fact that I might be spending Christmas here. At least the base had a decent bar where we could celebrate. No one knew what would happen when the warring factions actually signed the peace agreement but we did know that the winter was going to be a bad one.

Chapter 10

Vitez School, GDs and the Riots in Sarajevo

Two days later, without warning, I was relieved and taken back to Vitez. So after thirty-one days on H21H I returned to find out what my next job would be. I thought that it would be a return to the Regimental Aid Post, or maybe a stint at Main. At Vitez School I met the RSWO who thanked me for the job done in Kiseljak. I was given the afternoon off to sort out my admin and report for work at 08:00 hours in the morning. A whole day off would have been nice but it was better than nothing. My first priority was to get a bunk in the accommodation lines so I found out which ones were being used by the Sigs Platoon and found an empty space. Then I cadged a lift to the garage to try to locate my laundry.

Echelon was busier than a month ago, and a lot muddier. Even though it wasn't half as bad as the Brick Factory, I noticed a few of the SNCOs wearing bright-green gardening wellies. I found the Sigs colourboy going through lists of kit in his stores. He looked at my grubby appearance and tutted. I asked him if he had seen my washing bag and he got one of his gophers to fetch it. Apparently it had been doing the rounds but never actually found its way to me, so Colour Serjeant Carney decided to look after it until I turned up. I felt like mentioning sarcastically that he must have known that I was stuck on a Rebro without a change of clothes but he could be a difficult character to get on with at times so I let it go. And besides, I would need him to be nice to me if I needed any more goodies like pencil batteries for my Walkman.

Back at the school I had a tepid shower and changed into a clean set of combats. It felt wonderful to be so clean all over. The combats were wrinkled where they had been dried in the mesh laundry bag, but no one had an iron and in the school no one seemed to care, as long as you took care of your kit and personal hygiene. After scoff I had a few beers in the bar where I caught up with the latest news. The good thing about being an infantry signaller was that you were close to the decision makers and overheard a lot of info, so the lads in the platoon filled me in before we got the watered-down official version.

The takeover of operations by NATO was top of the list, and it looked like we were going to move away from the front line at Sarajevo. The chance to get to grips with the BSA and show them what a professional army could do was slipping by fast. Even though our maximum effort was still on Mount Igman, plans were already being prepared to leave it under French control. The Bosnian government in Sarajevo was sceptical about the Brits leaving, as they considered the French as Serb collaborators. On top of this, the Serbs were still creating civil unrest in the suburbs outside Sarajevo, and there was confirmed sniper activity on the infamous Sniper Alley. Ethnic cleansing was reported in a town in northern Bosnia called Banja Luka, but as bad as the situation still was, one subject dominated above all. The Yanks were coming!

As part of the Dayton Peace Accord, the United States would contribute to the new peace implementation force. The first thing on our minds wasn't the increase in manpower that they would bring, but friendly fire, or Blue on Blue. We all knew of the Yanks' abysmal record of shooting up their own side, and ours, and we began to realise that it might not be the Serbs that inflicted casualties, but our own side. Then it was about how the Yanks always turned up after the Brits did all the hard work and took all of the glory. It would be interesting to see the Hollywood version of events in years to come.

We were used to strange orders coming down from Higher, but a new one in particular was about to be ignored by almost all of BRITFOR. We were told by the UN to stop waving at kids in the street who waved at us. It was a ridiculous order and the Brits simply refused point blank. It was supposed to have upset the Serbs who saw UNPROFOR waving at those poor starving Muslim kids and saw it as sympathising with their enemy. We did sympathise, but with all the poor mites, regardless of where they prayed. We were constantly reminded before we went out on patrol or escort duty but after a few weeks our superiors just gave up trying to stop us.

A few of the lads who were stuck in Main wanted to know what it was like on a Rebro, so I swung the lamp and told them how it went. No one was surprised with the theatricals from The Prick, and wondered how anyone hadn't fragged him by now! The instances of celebratory fire produced a few concerned looks, but the fact that I was left on my own for most of the time was the biggest surprise. I told them it wasn't too bad but the isolation from the platoon meant that you were forgotten about in the scheme of things. I hadn't received any mail yet and getting my washing back was a nightmare. It was good to chat about things, so after stretching the 'two can rule' a little I headed back to the accommodation. Inside the cabin there wasn't a heater and it was like a fridge, but wrapping myself up in my doss bag soon had me away in dreamland.

The next day I put my doss bag in for cleaning and reported for work at Main. The signallers were coping well so I ended up doing GDs. This is just like being a labourer and involves carrying out all types of menial jobs. We collected vehicles from REME; test-drove them, cleaned them and tested the sigs installation. We resupplied a Rebro way out in the sticks to the south-west, almost getting stuck in some deep snowdrifts that covered the approach roads. We had an unusual version of the 432 in the Signals Platoon and used it for convoy escorts and resupplies like this. In the middle of the mortar hatches it had a cupola with an L37 fitted. We never had the manpower to put a bod inside to operate it and didn't know if it was any good, but at least it looked the part.

The most labour-intensive and risky job we did was track bashing. We fitted winter track to the remaining armoured vehicles in the platoon and it was badly needed. Even on the relatively flat roads around Vitez and Kiseljak a tracked vehicle could find itself slipping on the compacted icy roads, but moving around Mount Igman winter track was a must. Back in the heat of the German summer, track bashing was a thankless task, but here in the midst of a freezing Bosnian winter it was a bloody nightmare. Our hands were so cold we couldn't feel our fingers and we didn't notice the accompanying cuts and bruises until long afterwards, and lying on the wet muddy ground meant an uncomfortable few hours under our coveralls. When the track bashing was finished you could easily spot the slackers in this supposed team effort, standing there with their hands in the pockets of their nice clean coveralls, while the rest of us stood there bruised, bloody, damp and shivering.

The next morning I was told to get ready to move up to Igman to collect a 432. We had to bring it back for REME to give it the once-over before it was used on another task. It was another cold and wet day, with traces of sleet in the air, so on top of my combats and body armour I wore my Gore-Tex rain suit to keep out the wet. I joined up with Bobby Belshaw in a Spartan. He was commander and I got in beside him in the right-side crew position. Bobby was wearing one of the newly issued Canadian tank suits and had an arctic smock over the top. There were a few four-tonners and Land Rovers in our convoy as we still had to supply Tac and the forward company, but because of the Serb rioting in Ilidza we had a large escort of Warriors.

Over the last week all of the convoys moving through Ilidza had been stoned and subjected to attempts to stop them. Now there were reports of barricades and movement of BSA armour. The British Army had experience in Northern Ireland of crowds being used as a cover to keep the Army occupied while the IRA sniped or bombed them. This time, though, the Serbs orchestrating the unrest had a much bigger armoury and we couldn't afford to become a static target. Overlooking Ilidza the Anti Tank Platoon was dug in and observing the BSA movements through their MIRA sights, while in Kiseljak the QRF was on standby. We heard that barricades had been left across the road in Ilidza so we led with half-a-dozen Warriors, with pairs of Warriors in the middle and at the rear. Our orders were to travel on radio silence so when the four-tonner in front moved off, we followed.

From Vitez to Kiseljak we travelled with about one hundred metres between vehicles and at about 40kph. It started to snow but we had pretty good visibility. By the time we got to Kiseljak the snow had turned into a blizzard and our visibility dropped considerably. Just after we passed the Hotel Kiseljak, at a particularly narrow section of Route Swan, we pulled in to let a Vitez-bound French convoy pass and to allow our convoy to close up. When they had passed Bobby unclipped his CPU and jumped down in front of the Spartan to guide the driver out from the icy side of the road, so that we wouldn't slip into the muddy ditch like a fuel tanker in front of us. A pair of Scimitars from the Light Dragoons waited front and back to protect their precious load while they waited for a tow. Even though the tanker had snow chains fitted, it still fell foul of the icy roads. I hoped our four-tonner would fare better.

Back on the road to Sarajevo we had a clear run to Ilidza. All other convoys were on hold waiting for the outcome of ours. We closed the gap and travelled with roughly twenty metres between each vehicle. After we passed Blazuj, the last village before Ilidza, we sped up to 60kph. At this speed we would be harder to hit, and the twenty-metre gap would mean that if a vehicle was hit the ones either side would be spared and would have room to manoeuvre around it, if the ice allowed. I wondered at the reception we might meet in Ilidza and hoped that the sight of the Warriors charging at the head of our heavily armed convoy would make the Serbs think twice about trying to stop us. We couldn't afford to get drawn into a contact in a heavily populated area, but the Bosnian Serbs had to be shown that we wouldn't be bullied either. The Serbs were looking for an excuse to boycott the impending peace deal and civilian casualties from UN overreaction would be just what they needed to give their non-participation some credibility.

I remembered how Jamie Ross looked after a drive through Ilidza, so I rearranged my arctic mitts so that my trigger finger was free and slung my rifle over my body. The hatch was to my right, so using that as a shield I kept an eye-out for anything suspicious. As the snow changed to sleet again, I could see Ilidza about a k ahead, grey and uninviting.

The road into Ilidza was empty apart from a few old and battered Ladas travelling in the opposite direction that struggled under the weight of furniture strapped on the roofs and the fleeing families inside. As we drew close to the drab and dreary Soviet-style apartment blocks that made up this Serb-dominated suburb of Sarajevo, I began to feel nervous. On the net the lead Warrior informed Tac that they could see crowds were forming in the street and some kind of barricade was across the road. The Ulster brogue of our Ops Officer told them to carry on as planned. I could hear the throaty roar of the Warriors' turbines echo louder as they speeded up and raced into the canyons of concrete and brick. The Serb-occupied apartment blocks looked remarkably good after four years of war, with very few bullet or shell holes, and virtually no broken glass. Not really surprising as it was the BSA who surrounded the city, and they wouldn't be shooting at their own. Crowds were already lining the main street, but the weather seemed to have kept the numbers down to a few hundred and not the five hundred plus of the previous day's riots. The combined noise of our convoy reverberated off the sides of the buildings and was quite terrifying for the assembled masses and many involuntarily stepped back away from the kerb and covered their ears. Our convoy seemed to gather even more speed as we went deeper into the city but I know it was an optical illusion. A gap appeared in the crowd as the lead Warrior closed in on them. The aggressive attitude of the battalion and their complete faith in the Warrior was clear as the lead vehicle charged through without slowing down. I wondered if anyone was stupid enough to have stayed blocking the road.

As we passed the bulk of the crowd I felt a thud on the back of my body armour. I turned around and saw a few of the brave young thugs that always seem to turn up at these events throwing bricks. I ducked as another skimmed off the body of the Spartan between me and Bobby. I crouched down to present a smaller target and watched as the rearmost Warrior traversed its turret and pointed its cannon in their direction. The sight of those macho men scarpering into the side streets summed up the

Serb bully boys to me. Brave in the face of weakness and cowardly when confronted by strength. I kept looking at the crowd as we drove away from them. A few men in combat jackets, jeans and sheepskin hats were remonstrating with the crowd, shaking their arms and pointing at us. It looked like the hardliners who had organised the demonstration were not best pleased with the crowd's efforts this morning. We had passed through Ilidza without incident, but we still had to return later on that day.

When we neared the airport we turned away from Sarajevo at a BSA checkpoint and started up the road to Mount Igman. The snow had started again, and so we switched our attention to another dangerous foe – the mountain. I put my rifle back into the Spartan and held onto the sides of the hatch as we drove up towards the UN lines. Bobby pointed over to a small field where at first glance there seemed to be a BSA mortar line. As we got closer we could see it was a decoy, made from drainage pipes and planks of wood. The BSA, highly trained and supported by the JNA, were masters at deception and used all sorts of decoys to distract the attention of NATO jets from the real thing. The bomb craters in the field showed it had worked here. On the mountain road facing Ilidza I saw the reassuring sight of the Milan Platoon firing posts. I looked back into Ilidza and saw that they were in a very good position to cover us. I couldn't see the BSA armour, but I knew that if they ventured out into the open they couldn't hide from the MIRA sights on the Milan missile system.

The rest of the climb was made in a growing blizzard. The Spartan slowed down to a safer speed but wasn't as bad as when I came up the other side of the mountain with the Royal Engineers. The winter track made a big difference with the additional spiked edges and we didn't slip as much. The BiH trenches looked deserted, but the wisps of wood smoke indicated their presence. At Tac we separated from the convoy and parked up close to the RSM's Warrior that was on solitary guard at the front of the base.

I looked at Bobby and noticed the icicles hanging from his helmet, goggles and boom mike. The DPM fabric on his helmet was almost white and on the shoulders of his smock was a covering of thick ice. He looked like he had just conquered Everest. As we passed the windows of the Corimecs, I looked at my reflection and saw that I looked the same. Now I knew that I looked as cold as I felt. Moving around and removing our personal kit from the back of the Spartan soon had the ice breaking and falling off, but our movements were slow and clumsy. Taking our gloves off in the cookhouse gave us instant chilblains, but despite the pain we grabbed a brew from the tea urn and gulped down the sweet liquid in an attempt to revive us. It took me about an hour and a few more brews to get any semblance of warmth back into my body. Bobby was luckier in his tank suit and it was only his extremities that were cold. I *had* to get one when we returned. While we waited for the return journey, we took off our outer layers to give them a chance to dry off before the return journey. I was amazed at the consequence of the severe cold, especially the effect of the added wind-chill factor had on those of us that were exposed for hours on end in the turrets and standing in hatches, and bloody glad we didn't have to deal with the expected riots or a BSA ambush.

After lunch we collected the 432 and loaded our kit. We gave it a first parade, started it up and left it running while we filled up our thermal mugs with more sweet scalding tea. We found out from one of the signallers in Tac that the situation in Ilidza had worsened again and that dismounted troops were preventing any barricades from being put out. I asked why we couldn't use the back road down the mountain but the powers that be wanted a show of strength and that meant all traffic had to go back through Ilidza. Lovely! When we mounted up I gave the working parts on the jimpy a squirt of gun oil and made sure the link was free from snags. I unlocked the machine-gun ring on the hatch and swung the jimpy around 360 degrees. Satisfied that everything was working OK I carried out a comms check with the driver and waited as our small convoy formed up. As usual the haste to get ready was followed by a long wait in the snow and cold. Hurry up and wait, one of the biggest moans in the Army. A bit of consideration about the sub-zero temperatures would have been nice, but we were used to being fucked around, it was an infantryman's lot, so we put up with it, hoping that it wouldn't be for too long.

After waiting for close on an hour we finally moved off. In the lead was the Spartan, followed by a four-tonner, a Land Rover, and our 432 bringing up the rear. Both my driver and I were freezing cold when we moved off, and it would only get worse. The only comfort we could look forward to was that the 432 was a slow old beast and the wind-chill factor would have less of an effect on us. Under dark forbidding clouds we trundled back down the mountain road towards Ilidza. If the thought of driving through a volatile crowd wasn't bad enough, we quickly noticed the winter track didn't work that well going downhill. In fact, at times it didn't work at all. The 432's fifteen tonnes slipped dangerously close to the edge as we rounded the bends, giving us a few hairy moments as we waited for the mass of steel to scrape to a stop before we crawled away to safety. Looking down over the edge I could see the rusting wrecks of civilian cars that hadn't made it still stuck in the trees. I let out a huge sigh of relief when we reached the level road near the base of the mountain.

Ilidza looked drearier than earlier. In the late-afternoon light the blocks of flats cast dark shadows across the street. There were no streetlights and what light we did see in the windows of the apartment blocks flickered weak and yellow. As if to match the mood of Ilidza, the locals looked like extras in a B horror movie. Grey was in fashion and Serbians were setting the trends. The crowds were still hanging around looking for trouble but were restricted to shouting and waving a few placards. The dismounted squaddies kept close to their Warriors and stood in the doorways of the permanently closed shops. Groups of thugs stood with BSA military policemen, probably plotting their next move, but the weather was the winner today. The crowds had started to drift back to their cold and dark homes.

When we left Ilidza behind us, we opened up the spacing between the vehicles to about two hundred metres and settled down to a long and freezing drive back to Vitez. It didn't take long before night covered the countryside with total darkness. About half an hour out of Ilidza I noticed the lazy green arc of tracer in the distance to the west. Some poor bugger was getting it and I was glad it wasn't me. For the rest of the way back to Vitez the road was quiet; even the net was silent. For what seemed like an eternity we followed the faint glow of the red rear lights of the Land Rover way ahead of us, often losing sight of them as they turned a bend, and to appear again when we managed to catch up. It was gone midnight when we finally got back to the school, and after parking up, last parade and a visit to the armoury, I crashed out on my bunk, shivering and hungry.

I awoke the next day, still shivering and hungry, and dying for a slash. It was early so I managed to get a lukewarm shower before breakfast. My combats were still damp so I strung up a temporary clothes-line and hung them up to dry and changed into my last clean set. Priority for the day was to get a tank suit, so I collared Fred on the way to Main and arranged to pick one up later that day. After breakfast I enquired about getting a heater for the cabin I was in, only to be told by the bloke running the accommodation that they all had heaters in and I couldn't have another. From the lads in Main I found out that the REMFs from the Royal Sigs, AGC and RLC had a tendency to take them from the unoccupied infantry cabins to improve their own conditions. Their 'I'm all right Jack attitude' really pissed us off so me and a few of the 2LI lads who were living in ice boxes went looking for any cabins with two or more heaters. Most of the cabins were locked, but a few doors were ajar where one or more of the occupants were taking a shower. So taking advantage of their absence we liberated a few heaters from their oven-like quarters. As the keys for our doors had conveniently gone missing we got some bolts and padlocks from Ech and provided our own locks. We spent the rest of the day cleaning and carrying out crew jobs on the 432 we had brought back from Igman.

That evening we returned to warm rooms and dried out clothes. It was just what we needed after working outside in below-zero conditions and no more than we deserved. But as always, the Poor Bloody Infantry had to fend for itself.

The Royal Green Jackets

Proud to be Riflemen

The author on the 1993 recruiting poster for the Royal Green Jackets. The ghostly figure of a 'Chosen Man' of the 95th Rifles represents the spirit of a Rifleman looking over the members of the present-day regiment.

Vitez, central Bosnia, 1995. The region saw some of the bitterest fighting, with all factions fighting each other. Note that most of the timber from windows, doors and roofs has long since been removed by survivors for firewood.

A French VAB leaving Vitez School - our escort to Kiseljak.

ISO troop accommodation at Vitez School. It was fine on a UK building site, but the ISOs were like fridges in the harsh Bosnian winter.

A Company 2LI arrive at the Brick Factory, Kiseljak. The sudden change in weather was a shock for the troops who were not dressed for the arctic conditions. The cold weather driving visors were yet to be issued and winter track was not fitted to the armoured vehicles. The steel post seen in between the turret hatches is to prevent decapitation by steel wires or fishing line.

The Brick Factory, Kiseljak, 2 November 1995. This was the location for the QRF of Task Force Alpha, the Royal Engineers and the 2LI Rebro H21H.

Two days later. It was the first day of the worst winter in fifty years and 2LI were not yet operational.

H21C Rebro beside the Royal Engineers Command Post at the Brick Factory. The extended flaps at the back of the tent were intended as a wind break so we could keep what heat we had inside.

Saxons from 1RRF outside the Hotel Kiseljak. The Saxon might have been under-armed, under-powered and extremely ugly, but was surprisingly mobile in the Bosnian winter, especially with snow chains added to the wheels.

The Scandinavian Field Hospital at the Hotel Kiseljak.

French Foreign Legion recce troop at the rear of the Brick Factory. The Southern European camouflage from their Corsican base suited the muddy surroundings, but like every other vehicle in the task force stood out in the snow.

Convoy to Mount Igman. The four-tonner had skidded onto the grass verge to let a speeding French convoy pass. There was just enough room. Vehicle commanders had to dismount to check for mines and guide the drivers safely back onto the road.

The Hotel Igman. Once a striking symbol of the Winter Olympics of 1984, it was now a bombed-out ruin and its basements were home to the French Task Force Bravo.

Tactical Headquarters Task Force Alpha, Sevastopol Camp, Mount Igman. The RSM's Warrior can be seen hull down as a lone sentry. The CO's Warrior is behind it under cover, and above that on the Corimec cabins is the dome of the Inmarsat telephone.

Convoy from 2LI entering Ilidza, Sarajevo. The waiting crowds were stunned into inactivity when the expected UN convoy of trucks turned out to be British Army Warriors.

The Comms Recce into no-man's land in the mountains to the west of Mrkonjić Grad.
The deep snow made movement difficult and hid the track. To minimise casualties from
mines, our Sultan CVRT led the way.

The Rebro H21H. The hunting tower and the eight-metre masts are in the background.
Mags, our stray Golden Labrador, is waiting for some scraps at the rear of the Spartan.

The inside of the Serb bunker that we lived in over Christmas 1995. In the centre is a kero heater, and to the right two men from the protection party are asleep. It might have afforded us protection, but we suffered from sub-zero temperatures.

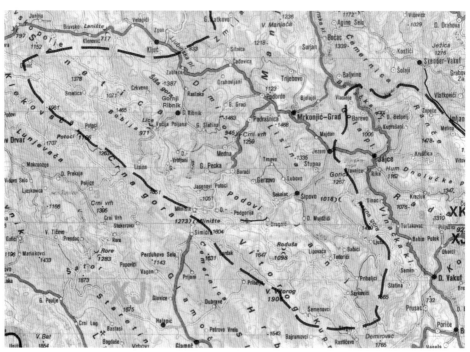

The Anvil. The blue dashed line indicates the Confrontation Line. Above the line was the new Republica Srpska, and below was the Muslim-Croat Federation. In reality, Serbs, Muslims and Croats lived all over the region and would need to be repatriated and protected while crossing the inter entity boundary to their own communities.

Rebro resupply run. The narrow mountain tracks made passing difficult, especially as the twisting nature of the tracks gave you little warning of oncoming traffic. The gunner of the lead Warrior has dismounted to ensure the vehicle doesn't get too close to the edge.

The sheer drop on the sides of mountain tracks as seen by the author when commanding a Warrior. If the Warrior slipped, there would have been no time to get out.

A wrecked M36 tank destroyer used by the HVO. This variant of the ubiquitous Sherman tank was one of hundreds of Allied vehicles that survived the Second World War and found its way to the then friendly Yugoslavia. It was victorious against superior Nazi tanks but was stopped by a hand held Soviet-designed RPG. The soldier fishing in the background can be seen hiding his face, a common practice amongst people who had reason to believe they might be wanted for war crimes.

A Dutch checkpoint on the Confrontation Line. The Dutch didn't take chances with protection and positioned a Leopard 1 tank at either end as a deterrent to the warring factions. The bombed-out houses close by were used by IFOR troops as platoon HQs.

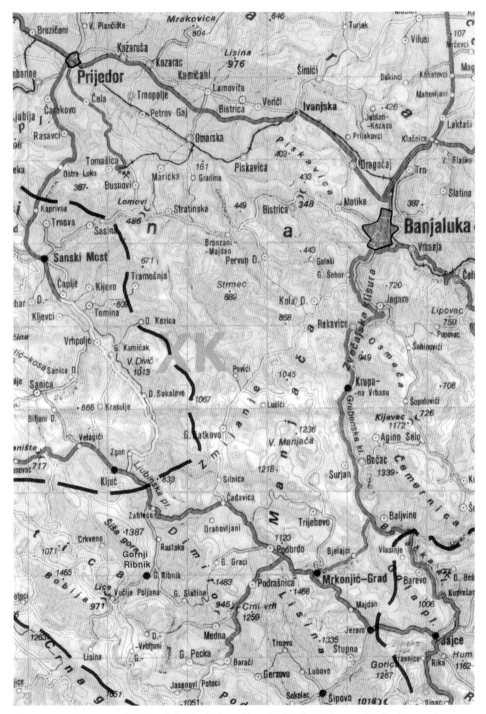

The Area of Responsibility of the 2nd Battalion the Light Infantry Battle Group January to April 1996. It was mountainous, covered dozens of crossing points and had one of the highest concentrations of mines in Bosnia. Each light blue square represents ten square kilometres, showing the hundreds of square kilometres we had to police.

H21D, first location. It was too exposed and the crew worked in terrible conditions. On resupply runs we would find the crew huddled up against the heater. Rations and water would freeze inside the tent and high winds buffeted them keeping them awake at night. Roaming BSA troops and the odd hand-grenade going off didn't help either.

In contrast to the British Army, the Canadians had a far superior Rebro set-up in terms of comfort and newer equipment.

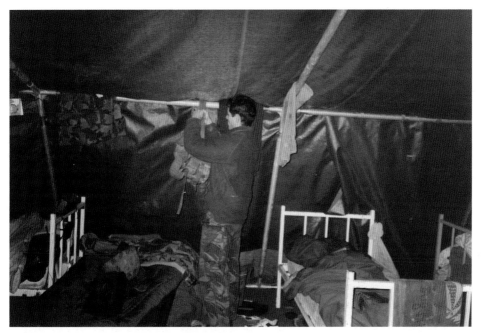

The Signal Platoon tent inside the Metal Factory, Banja Luka. The additional hessian insulation can be seen inside the frame. The beds are a mix of US camp-beds and steel-framed beds that we were told were from an abandoned mental hospital.

What it was all about - refugees returning home.

A Royal Artillery OP Warrior after driving over a doubled-up anti-tank mine. The crew survived with a few cuts and bruises.

BSA Electronic Warfare trucks at the Lisina Radar Complex north-west of Banja Luka, listening in to IFOR radio traffic. Initially the Serb authorities claimed that the trucks were providing a local TV service, but a lack of a transmission signal proved the equipment was for intelligence gathering and was removed.

An AS90 self-propelled gun from 127 Battery, 26 Regiment Royal Artillery. The guns were fully programmed with fire missions in case the Peace Accord failed and the Serbs resorted to military action. A full pallet of shells can be seen to its rear.

The Sultan CVRT used on the Rebro H21L at the end of an operation to look for Bosnian Serb Army anti-aircraft guns. The flue from a wood burning stove can be seen sticking out of the back of the tent.

The radio set-up in the Ops Room in the Metal Factory, Banja Luka. Unlike Hollywood versions of operations centres, with banks of computers and flashing lights, the reality is that radio installations are either spare sets or unbolted from their vehicles. The power is supplied by heavy-duty vehicle batteries attached to a small petrol generator. The connections were complex but we were able to run HF and VHF nets going up to Brigade and down to the companies, as well as Inmarsat, SCRA and the CO's Satcom.

The eight-metre mast and broadband antenna for H21L. The location of an antenna is vital and sometimes means erecting it in a place with difficult access. On this occasion the soldier to the left lost his footing and slid down, resulting in a broken leg.

The second location of the Rebro H21D. This time it was closer to the Lisina Radar Complex but was still exposed to the elements on the side of the peak. The side gate to the complex can be seen on the left. This was the start of a white-out that lasted three days.

L/Cpl Roger Moore, L/Cpl Dave Belshaw and Private Mac McGee on board a C130 Hercules on our departure from Banja Luka airfield. Once airborne the realisation that we were finally going home meant that many just passed out through sheer relief.

The author in the entrance lobby of Paddy Murphy's, a few days after arriving back in Paderborn, Germany. Apparently, as a Royal Green Jacket, the sign didn't apply to me!

Chapter 11

The Peace Accord and the Comms Recce

I had been back in Vitez for nearly a week when the RSWO threw the platoon a fastball. As part of the impending peace deal the battalion was to move to another Area of Responsibility. NATO was taking over from the UN and the British Army would be taking over responsibility for the north-west of the country. Recces were already underway looking for suitable locations but it wasn't going to be easy. The BSA had recently suffered a heavy defeat in the Krajina by the combined HVO and BiH armies. The fighting was supposed to be over, but there were reports of hostility in pockets throughout the region, as revenge for the Serb occupation still raged on. Ethnic cleansing was still being reported by the UNHCR and other NGOs, and one of the towns in the centre, Mrkonjić Grad, was full of HVO rounding up the remaining non-Croats and torching the town. The RSWO looked at me and Private Bullock.

'Consider this a Warning Order. You two be packed and ready to move out tomorrow after we bring back Hotel Two One Delta.' That was a now redundant Rebro. He looked at his notepad. 'We need to have a network of Rebros up and running in the north-west of Bosnia for when the UN hand over to NATO. We are going up country on a comms recce to establish one near a town called Mrkonjić Grad. We'll be the first troops in this area and it might get nasty.'

He went on to say that the platoon had been tasked to provide comms from Sarajevo to Bihac, about 300k, across mountains and in the middle of one of the coldest winters Bosnia had seen in decades. We would need to maintain control of all elements of the battalion and its supporting units on one net as they moved from Tac on Mount Igman up to the north-west of Bosnia. According to the Royal Signals, who are the authority on military communications, we would require a minimum of twelve Rebros to cover that distance. We had only the manpower and spare radio sets for five stations, plus the detachment in Echelon. It was an ominous task and had never been attempted before in peacetime, let alone on operations.

'We'll be taking the 432 "H" brought down from Igman, the Sultan and a Rover. We have to have the Rebro operational in a couple of days.' He looked at us and stroked his moustache. 'See KD for your kit requirements and hand in all your non-essential stuff to be stored away. You won't be coming back to Vitez.' The RSWO walked off and left KD to talk kit.

KD explained that all of the kit coming back from H21D would be taken, as well as taking as much fuel, food and water as it would be possible to carry. We would have about three or four hours to check the kit from H21D for defects and then we would be off. The site for the Rebro was on a mountain, so we scrounged a kero heater and a few jerrycans of kerosene. We needed some water and rations, so we drove over to the garage and picked up a pallet of water cartons and the rations. The Support Company CQMS gave us some dreaded ten-man ration packs, full of tinned odds and sods. We told him we were going to deploy on a mountain and cooking tinned food would be a problem. He was sympathetic but was short on 24-hour boil-in-the-bag rat packs and the Recce Platoon had priority. He must have felt sorry for us because he relented and gave us some buckshee opened 24-hour rat packs in a black bin-liner. From the Sigs stores I stocked up on AA and SP batteries and even managed to get a spare kero heater.

As I was getting ready to leave I met one of Jamie Ross's friends from MT. We had a quick chat about what we were up to and when he heard that I was going up country he asked me if I could do with a US camp-bed. Bloody right I could. As we went over to the REME workshop he told me how they happened to get them. A local Canadian unit was getting ready to leave Bosnia and had been packing away all of its stores. A four-tonner from the MT platoon just happened to be visiting their base and the crew saw the shiny new camp-beds all stacked up and waiting for a Canadian lorry to load onto. The MT lads thought they would be obliging and decided to spare them the hassle of sending them back to the land of the moose, so they loaded them up in double-quick time and buggered off back to the garage. Now the ones that weren't handed out were 'stored' in the roof space above the REME workshop. The MT lad climbed into the hatch and a minute later handed down a few lovely new US camp-beds still in their wrappers. Nice one!

That night we all met in the bar and heard the latest news from Battalion HQ from the lads just off stag. The Bosnian, Croat and Serb

116

leaders were in Paris thrashing out the final details of who got which piece of bombed-out real estate in Bosnia. 2LI had sent a platoon to Mrkonjić Grad to recce the town and secure a base. Reports coming back were not good. The town was ablaze and gunfire could be heard and tracer seen all around. The whole area where the town was, known to us as the Anvil, was to be handed back to the Serbs, and the Croats were extremely pissed off about it. The British Army was sending thousands more men to help the already overstretched units in theatre and NATO had landed the first of its troops in Sarajevo Airport, including some Yanks. That news brought a few concerned looks, but no one went rushing off to put on his body armour. Not yet anyway.

I awoke early and was packed ready to leave before breakfast. Myself and Private Bullock had a larger than normal breakfast as it would be the last time we would have fresh food for God knew how long. I pondered over the suitability of Bully for the task. He was a career private who suffered from delusions of adequacy. In the short time I knew him he failed to impress me and seemed determined to do the minimum stay in the Army. He was a bit of a barrack-room lawyer and a pretty bad one at that. He loved coming up with reasons why he shouldn't do any work and spent more effort on getting out of work than it would have taken to actually do it. On our own on a Rebro in hostile territory, I doubted he would be much help and this made me realise that I would be doing most of the work. I considered talking to the RSWO about replacing him but I knew it would be pointless. We were drastically short-handed and it had to be someone. I just hoped he knew how to handle a 432. We collected our kit and cleaned our bed spaces. I gave the key to the padlock on my cabin to KD so he could hand it on to whoever needed it. In the vehicle park we loaded up the Sultan with our rations, water and fuel, plus any other kit we werc bringing along. Once we had finished everything we collected our weapons from the Armoury ISO container. KD gave us an extra thousand rounds of 5.56mm for our rifles, four thousand 7.62mm link for the vehicle mounted jimpy, two Schermuly flares and two smoke grenades. After I had signed for it all KD looked at me and said, 'If you get into any bother, don't worry about accounting for the ammo. Blatt away and stay alive. It's bandit country where you are going and until the battalion moves up country you'll be on your own.' He looked genuinely concerned. 'Stay safe and get back to the platoon. Any questions?'

It sounded a dodgy enough task and KD sounded a bit edgy, so I didn't hesitate in asking for some defence stores. I requested trip flares, razor wire, steel pickets, monkey, heavy-duty gloves, wire cutters, mine prods and empty sand bags. KD agreed we should have them. The bad news was that all the defence stores were up at Igman and there wasn't enough time to get any before we left. So while we waited in the car park for H21D to arrive my mind kept going over the problems we might face. We would be on a mountain, in the middle of the worst Balkan winter in fifty years, in an area where NATO would be trying to separate the Serbs and Croats from fighting over ground that they had been fighting over for centuries. We would be alone, in the middle of nowhere, days and maybe weeks before the battalion or any other Brit unit would be there in force. Normally a Rebro would follow the forward elements of a formation so that comms could be maintained back to the slower-moving HQ and Echelon. It would be afforded a high degree of protection by those units and supporting arms, but this time we would be going before the main body. I went over to the school to the Int Section to see if they had any info that would be useful.

It was a quick visit: nothing that I didn't learn from the lads in Main. Apparently we were not expecting to move so soon and they were still collating intelligence from Brigade before they could issue it. What they did know was that the area we were reccying had a high probability of being mined. So it was just like the rest of the country then. Back at the Sultan I listened to the net as reports from Mrkonjić Grad came in with news that the town was burning and gunfire was still being heard all over the area. It wasn't encouraging news.

By ten o'clock we had the Sultan packed with all of our kit, jerrycans of fuel and water, ammo and stores. H21D should have been back now but we heard that it was being delayed by a sudden snowstorm. So we waited in the hope that they wouldn't be too long. My feet were so cold I couldn't feel them any more and dribbles of snot were forming stalactites on my nose. We stood behind the Sultan to get some relief from the icy wind that was blowing across the car park, but the protection it gave was minimal. At midday, Serjeant Walters came back from Main with the news that H21D was finally on the way back, so we went to lunch in shifts and got ready for a quick handover.

The wind seemed to stop as the 432 from H21D came into the car park. As soon as it stopped about a dozen of us rushed to unload it and sort out the kit. We had it laid out ready to check it when the Serjeant Major Thirlwell, the RSWO, came along and told us just to repack everything as quick as we could as we should have left hours ago. So another manic ten minutes followed as we hauled the kit into our 432 and the Sultan. Once packed, the lads that were not going on the recce went off and left us to get a final brief from the RSWO. I told Bully to start up the 432 to get the engine warmed up.

'Err, I can't do that.' He looked at me and shrugged his shoulders. 'I haven't got a 432 ticket.' Private Bullock, after years in a specialist platoon in an armoured battalion, had managed to avoid getting a 432 qualification. So even though I was the Rebro commander, I had to drive the bloody thing as well.

The RSWO didn't have time to go through the formal orders process, so gave us the basics. The plan was to drive up to Mrkonjić Grad before last light and stay with a platoon in the town. In the morning we would move out and recce a sight for the Rebro. It was simple enough. The Order of March was the Rover with the Serjeant Major and Serjeant Hodgson, the Sultan and then our 432. The RSWO reminded us of the dangers that lay ahead. We wouldn't stop until Mrkonjić Grad and remember the actions-on if we were bumped were the same as usual – get into the armour and bug out. We were a small force and we didn't have the fire-power or numbers for any heroics.

'Don't forget, they don't want us there. The Croats are extremely pissed off that they have to hand over the land they have just won back from the Serbs, and they just might take out their frustrations on us!' He took off his beret and put on his helmet. He looked at the five of us and nodded: 'Let's go.'

I put my body armour on over my new tank suit and climbed into the driver's seat of the 432 and started the engine. I placed my webbing and rifle on the engine cowling and put on my headset. I connected the headset to the driver's box and called Bully on the intercom. 'OK, Bully?'

'Hang on, my webbing's caught up!' I looked behind me and saw his larger than normal bulk struggle to get into the commander's hatch.

'Take your bloody webbing off and leave it next to mine.' I couldn't believe that I had to state the obvious and hoped that he would improve his drills very quickly. After our engines had warmed up and the temperature gauges moved out of the black we moved off and away from Vitez. It was cold but at least the slow speed of the 432 was keeping the wind-chill factor down. We settled down to a long and boring drive along the first leg of the move, through the towns with a large Brit presence. We travelled north-west on Route Diamond towards Travnik and then on Route Emerald to Bugojno. From there we headed due north on Route Opal to Dornji Vakuf. It was quiet enough. A few white-painted UN convoys passed us by, but it wasn't too long before the skies darkened and the roads emptied. Once past Dornji Vakuf we left behind the relative safety of friendly troops and were on our own. I told Bully to stay alert and keep an eye out for any trouble. I felt vulnerable as a driver, not having the ability to see all around me. I had to trust my vehicle commander and hoped to fuck he was switched on.

The surrounding countryside was dark and gloomy under the cloud cover. The 432 was noisy but I knew that the sound wouldn't travel far, though it still made me feel conspicuous. I would have liked to turn off the driving lights but it was SOPs and we were not supposed to be tactical. It was as if we were playing into the hands of an unseen enemy by advertising our presence. I concentrated on the red rear lights of the Sultan ahead. They were moving faster than us and we began to lose sight of them on bends in the road. All of our vehicles were filthy, covered in a brown film of mud and dust. The black and green camouflage was barely discernable except at close range, and as we had deliberately not cleaned the lenses of the lights this dulled down their effective coverage. The red glow on the back of the Sultan disappeared as it rounded a bend, and it seemed to take ages for me to spot them again. The road started to snake even more and it seemed that the Sultan had disappeared. For about ten minutes we were all alone, and then I saw the faint red glow reappear again. It was reassuring and made me feel like I wasn't alone out there. A single vehicle at night was an easy target. I looked left and right into the countryside and my mind started to imagine killing groups ready to initiate an ambush. My only link to the relative safety of our convoy was the tiny specs of red light ahead. I could see them disappear into the darkness again when the explosion rocked the 432.

'What the fuck was that?!' I screamed over the intercom at Bully. There was no reply. My vision was clouded by smoke and steam so I couldn't see what was going on. My first thoughts were that we had been hit by an RPG as we were rocked sideways. Was it an ambush? I couldn't hear any small arms fire. My first reaction was to get the fuck out of there. I pushed the accelerator fully but the engine died on me. I called out to Bully.

'You OK? Are you hurt?' There was no reply. I still couldn't see anything through my goggles and my headset was quiet, so I unstrapped myself, grabbed my webbing and rifle and de-bussed. I glanced back at the commander's space behind me, but it was empty. The normal drill in a contact if the vehicle was disabled was to exit through the back and keep low, but we were stuffed full of kit so that ruled that out. That left jumping out of the front. It was exposed but I didn't want to hang around, so I launched myself over the front and landed in a heap on the ground. I scrambled over to the side of the road by a telegraph pole and glanced back at the wagon. There was a huge white cloud billowing from the top but no sign of Bully. I stood up and lifted up my driving goggles. I scanned the other side of the road, my rifle at my shoulder, but there was no sign of activity.

'What are you doing?' came a voice from beside me. I turned around and saw Bully standing there with a stupid grin on his face.

'I thought we'd been hit. There was a fook-off bang and we stopped dead, so I jumped out.' I looked at him. His helmet was missing and he had no rifle or webbing. Smoke and steam was still pouring from the wagon but I couldn't see any external damage. I checked the tracks and under the wagon. Not a mark. That left only one other possibility: the engine had blown up. There was no sign of the Sultan or Rover coming back, or any other vehicle on the road. I needed to get in touch with the RSWO and let him know what had happened. I left Bully standing on the road grinning like an idiot and climbed up over the front, reached inside and pulled the red toggle to activate the engine extinguisher. Then I clipped the CPU onto my headset and called the RSWO.

'Hello Hotel Two One Alpha, this is Hotel Two One Charlie, over.' I waited about ten seconds before calling again. I tried half a dozen times but there was no reply. Mobile comms are always more difficult and we were in hilly terrain as well. It was a long shot but I tried Main.

'Hello Zero, this is Hotel Two One Charlie, over.'

'Hello Hotel Two One Charlie, this is Zero. Send, over.' The signal was weak but readable. it was a relief to get through. I told them our 432 had packed up and to call Two One Alpha and let him know. I heard them send out the call, and even though I didn't hear a reply, Zero acknowledged them and told me they had turned around. All we could do was wait.

So while Bully made his own cloud of steam by pissing up against the side of the 432, I had a walk around to see if we had any company. There were a few bombed-out houses a few hundred metres back, but apart from that we were in the open with fields on both sides. The sides of the road were made up of small snow-covered embankments with emaciated hedging forming the fields' boundaries. There were hundreds of spent 7.62 short casings lying in the snow at the side of the road. In the dim glow of our headlights they looked like glistening golden ingots, but nobody was any richer for them. I looked into the countryside but it was too dark to make out anything, so I walked back to the 432 and waited.

It took the Rover and Sultan half an hour to get back to us. The RSWO was fuming and told us to start unloading. A replacement vehicle was on its way and we needed to get moving as soon as it arrived. The RSWO looked at the 432. Steam was still rising from the engine covers but there was no smoke now. Bully tried to make a joke of it, but the RSWO shot him a glance that said, 'Keep that up and I'll skull fuck you!' We unloaded the kit from the back in record time.

The replacement vehicle arrived about two hours after we stopped. It was a testament to the platoon that it got there so quickly. It was the RSO's Spartan and it was accompanied by a REME 434 recovery wagon. We transferred the kit into the smaller Spartan and the bits we couldn't stuff in went into the Sultan. The RSWO looked at his watch and told us to prepare to move. We were behind schedule and should have been there by now. It was getting dark now. We were probably the first UN convoy to travel at night in years and we weren't exactly heavily armed or substantial in numbers. The only good news was that Bully had to go back with the 432. I climbed in the cupola and connected my headset to the CPU. My driver was Private Joey Jordan, a young Yorkshire lad.

'You OK, Joey?' I asked as I made myself comfortable.

'Fook no. I was getting into my pit when I was told to come here.' He didn't sound too happy. 'What the fook happened?'

'Sorry, Joey. I'll fill you in on the move.' I took off my webbing and placed it with my rifle next to Joey's kit. I double-clicked the pressel switch and got a thumbs-up from the commander of the Sultan. We all moved off into the darkness, leaving behind REME who were still attaching a tow bar to the 432. The Spartan was much quicker than the 432 and we had no trouble keeping up with the other two vehicles. The downside was that the wind-chill factor was much worse. I turned the cupola to the left and leaned against the hatch, put on my arctic mitts and told Joey about the little bit of excitement that forced him from his bed. He laughed when I told him I thought we had been bumped, but I don't suppose an engine had blown up on him before, especially in a war zone. I started to feel the cold and began to shiver. It was a relief to be back on the road and moving again. At one point my whole body shuddered and I could feel a trickle of cold sweat run down the small of my back. My body was relaxing after the excitement of the last few hours and the relief felt like a drug running through my body. I looked into the unwelcoming countryside and wondered if anything else was going to happen while we ventured away from the safety of the battalion.

Chapter 12

Hotel Two One Charlie, the Mountain Rebro

After the stand-off with the Croats at the checkpoint, an incident that has already been described at the start off this book, we drove for about twenty minutes before hitting the suburbs of Mrkonjić Grad. The smell of burning was getting stronger and in the distance I could see the flickering of naked flames from some of the torched buildings and houses. To the north there were green lines of tracer floating across the night sky.

When we entered the town I didn't need the beam of our headlights to tell us that the town was in ruins. Flames danced in windows and smoke drifted across the road. The town was deserted and not even a stray dog was seen or heard. We slowed down as we approached two Warriors from A Company that were standing as sentinels outside the town's old bus garage. We turned off the road and went in through the main gate. The advance platoon had arrived earlier and was reccying for a place for the Battalion HQ to set up in when it moved. We all gathered round as a SNCO told us the score about the locality. The buildings were out of bounds as the first patrols had discovered dozens of booby-traps. Some were designed to bc tripped when someone picked up a discarded AK47 or other piece of desirable military kit, or more horribly when a child picked up a toy. Mines were everywhere and even linked to some booby-traps to cause a chain reaction. The tracer we saw and the gunfire we heard was the local opposing factions finishing off business. They had moved to the outskirts of the town when the first Warriors arrived and were still there. Basically, the whole town was out of bounds until the Engineers declared areas safe, so we would have to stay put and sleep out. There was a sweet smell of burning, almost like a barbeque that drifted on the wind. Some of the bodies found burning were animal, some looked human. The smell started to make us feel queasy.

To my surprise I met Jamie Ross again. He was here with a few four-tonners carrying fuel, ammo and stores for the forward platoon. After he had parked up he was used on the clearance patrols that found the booby-traps and charred remains. He was looking better than when I saw him on Op Water Babe, but the scenes he had witnessed had made him appear withdrawn and distant.

It was close to midnight and very dark, but we needed some kind of shelter from the elements and for us to get away from the smell of burning flesh, so we piled our personal kit by the vehicles and set up a 12×12 tent next to the gable end of the main garage building. Years of practice doing this tactically in the field with no lights meant that it was second nature to us and we had it up in minutes. We parked the vehicles all around to act as a protective wall and brought our kit inside. In no time we had a brew going but the smells outside had taken away our hunger. The dirty odour from my doss bag never smelt so good as I pulled the hood tight and drifted off into a fitful sleep.

We awoke at daylight and packed away our kit. Thoughts of burning bodies were forgotten so we had a boil-in-the-bag breakfast and a brew. The first few minutes out of the doss bag quickly woke us up and we wrapped up again. We put our body armour back on – a habit we were used to, plus we were conscious of our new surroundings. It was like wearing the heaviest body-warmer in the world, but we reasoned if it stopped bullets it would stop the wind as well! After breakfast we packed away the tent and waited by the wagons ready for the next phase of our mission.

The RSWO seemed happier after a few hours' sleep and called us together. He had carried out a map recce back in Vitez and had worked out that we should get good comms on the top of a mountain about 5k to the west of the town. The area was likely to be covered in minefields and there were still reports of small skirmishes between the HVO and BSA, but we were limited in our choice of location and had to risk it. He had our complete attention as he told us to keep strict convoy discipline with no less than twenty metres between each vehicle. If the lead vehicle hit a mine then at least the next one would be spared. Under no circumstances were we to veer from the track, no matter what happened. Actions-on were as per SOPs and if we had to de-bus for any reason, stay in the vehicle tracks. There were no questions so we mounted up and moved out of the bus garage.

In daylight we could clearly see the extent of the damage to the town, which had been hidden by the darkness as we entered last night. The devastation was complete and there wasn't a building unaffected by the fighting or the Croat withdrawal. Bomb, shell and bullet damage was ever present and was now joined by smouldering timber rafters and window frames. Inside the ruins we could see the charred remains of the possessions of the townspeople. The town was still empty of life. It was an alien landscape that reminded me of photos of the siege of Stalingrad during World War Two. It was hard to believe that it was only a few hours' drive from the normality and stability of the European Union, and for me it strengthened the reasons why we needed to be here.

Leaving the town, we headed west along a main road until we came to our turn-off for the mountain. We slowed down and turned onto a track that was covered in deep snowdrifts. We waited while the Rover waded into the snow and followed behind at a snail's pace. As we progressed along the track the trees lining our route started to get denser and closer to the track. We continued along for a few hundred metres until we came to a fork in the track. It was impossible to guess which one was the right one as they continued parallel to each other until they were lost in the white-out of the snow-covered trees. We stopped and RSWO walked back to the Sultan and chatted with the commander and walked back to the Rover. He then drove a small track on the left used by tree fellers and let the Sultan overtake us. He then drove back and slotted into the middle of our formation and we continued up the mountain. He was obviously worried about mines and let the more armoured Sultan take the lead.

Our pace picked up slightly due to the fact that the Sultan was better at cutting a path through the ever-deepening snowdrifts. At times the tracks completely disappeared but it ploughed on regardless. We knew that the tracks and roads were relatively free of mines in Bosnia. That way the warring factions could control the enemy by denying them ground, channelling them into ambushes or killing grounds. That didn't mean that the withdrawing Serbs hadn't mined this particular track, and I bet the driver of the Sultan was thinking that as well. It takes a special kind of courage to carry on regardless of a known threat, especially mines, and I was full of admiration for that.

At the base of the mountain there was a small village, very much like an Alpine village scene that you might see on a Christmas card. It, too, had suffered from the recent fighting, but still retained some beauty. Like all of the other towns and villages in this region it was deserted. It looked like it was once a nice place to live. The houses were all built close to the track, and you could clearly see inside the open windows. It was a sad sight. Dinner tables were still set and beds were made. Some rooms had pop or football posters on the walls and cuddly toys on shelves, just like any kid's room back home. In the gardens, clothes still hung limply from washing-lines. I guessed that the owners had left in a hurry when the HVO overran the area.

A little way past the village we started the climb up the mountain track. The snow wasn't as deep here, but the track was barely the width of one vehicle. As usual with all the mountain roads and tracks we had encountered in Bosnia, we had the additional worry of a sheer drop to one side. At one bend there was a small waterfall that had frozen and had spread a large sheet of ice all over the road. We had a nervous few minutes as we started to slide towards the edge as we drove over it, but Joey dropped a gear and let the winter track bite and pull us forward. It was a relief to everyone when we finally left the track and pulled into a small clearing close to the summit of the mountain.

It was about the size of two tennis courts and on all sides we were surrounded by snow-covered fir trees. There were two gaps where two other tracks converged at the summit, but apart from that we were completely enclosed by the dense forest. To our surprise there was a timber hut sitting about ten metres in the air on timber poles, like a guard tower from a World War Two POW film. It looked completely out of place, as its field of view was completely obstructed by the trees. I guessed it was a hunting tower for wolves, bears or whatever else roamed the mountains here. We dismounted and looked around. I took off my helmet and cold-weather mask and breathed in the heady smell of fresh pine. Close by the track that we had driven up and dug into the ground was a bunker. The quickest FIBUA clearance ever showed it was safe, but around the sides were scattered some empty light green ammo boxes. We gathered back at the Sultan and waited while the RSWO tried to get in touch with Vitez. After ten minutes of asking for a radio check and getting no reply the RSWO stopped and checked the map to look for another location. We were in the right place but comms had failed. It was a huge disappointment, especially after our recent endeavours, so while he thought of our next move he told us to get a brew on to try and warm up. Night-times were going be a bastard.

I climbed up onto the engine covers of the Sultan to sit on the lovely warm metal grill. I have always hated having a cold arse and this was heaven. I noticed the commander's headset and thought I would try to call Vitez. One thing I had learned was that infantry signals are not a precise science; it was more of an art. Atmospheric conditions, cold, snow, terrain all played a part, and the most important factor in signalling was a pig-headed determination not to give up. I put on the headset and called Zero.

126

Nothing. Echelon was a bit closer so I tried them. Still nothing. I tried Ech again and got a faint and garbled reply that sounded as if it had a Geordie accent. We were operating from a vehicle whip antenna but would need to put up some broadbands. I looked around and knew it was the trees that were blocking our transmission. I tried one more time. To compensate for not having a broadband antenna up, I turned the power dial on the 353 up to fifty watts. Power means distance, but it had a downside – the enemy can hear you. Military signals operate on low power and short distances for security. That's why when we operated over extensive ranges we change frequencies and sent the signal on via a Rebro. Fifty watts was only supposed to be used in an emergency but I guess this was one. I tried again.

'Hello Hotel Four Two, this is Hotel Two One Charlie, radio check, over.' I held my breath while I waited for a reply.

'Hello Hotel Two One Charlie, this is Hotel Four Two, OK, over.' It was clear as a bell. I called over to the RSWO and told him we were through to Ech. He looked up and came over. I handed him the headset and he gave Ech a Sitrep. We didn't wait to be told and started to get the Rebro ready by unpacking the Sultan and Spartan. After he had finished talking to Ech, the RSWO came over and took control of things. He wanted to be away as soon as possible and set about giving us orders. The Spartan would be too small to live out of, so as the area was considered 'hot' we were told to use the bunker as living quarters. It would give us a high degree of protection from mortars and small arms fire, much more than our canvas 12×12 tent. Two eight-metre masts with broadband antennas were set up close together on the watchtower and connected to the Spartan. According to the Signals Pamphlets the two antennas were so close together they would interfere with each other's signals, but we had no problems whatsoever and maintained comms over one of the biggest and most difficult sectors in the battalion's AOR. A temporary POL point was set up under the watchtower, and the rest of the kit was stowed away in the bunker. We even had a chemical toilet set up in the watchtower to give us a bit of privacy and, besides, with the propensity of mines Bosnia wasn't the ideal place to carry out a shovel recce!

Once we were set up, we got through to Zero and told them we were now up and running and that the RSWO's party would be returning soon. The RSWO looked around the area and seemed satisfied with the set-up. He asked if I needed anything and without hesitation I said yes – a protection party. He asked me why, so I mentioned the local situation, the lack of defence stores and the fact that the on-duty signaller would be in the wagon while the off-duty one would be in the bunker. That would leave the Rebro totally compromised if anyone turned up. He agreed with my assessment and said he would call in at the bus garage in Mrkonjić Grad to see if the advance platoon could spare anyone. He wished us good luck and got into the Rover. I watched the Rover and Sultan as they disappeared back down the mountain. I felt vulnerable but put on a brave face and told Joey to stag on while I sorted out our personal kit in the bunker. Joey didn't need to be asked to stay inside the wagon. Just like me he wasn't too happy being left alone in no-man's land.

It was freezing cold inside the bunker and very dark. I took a candle from my Bergan and lit it to give me some light. We both had a US camp-bed, so I set them up at the back of the bunker and put our Bergans and holdalls on top. I got our two kero heaters and got them going to see if they would be of any help. I hung up my poncho over the opening to help keep some heat in and the wind out.

Back at the Spartan I packed the 12×12 on the top and covered everything with the vehicle tarp, leaving the L37 uncovered, just in case we needed it. I stood back and looked at the Rebro. We were very exposed in the middle of the clearing and we had driven in as far as we could. I know we were supposed to be visible, with the UN markings clearly defined, but I was worried that without a barbed-wire defence we would be vulnerable to the attentions of any passing baddies and I wanted to give us a chance of avoiding that. I wanted to screen the Rebro from the road, so I went over to the edge of the tree-line and cut down some smaller firs and bought them back to the Rebro. I placed them around the Spartan to camouflage us and took another look. It wasn't perfect but if anyone passed by we would be hidden from view, and that could be enough.

I had finished our admin and was having a brew when we heard some Rovers coming up the track. The RSWO must have arranged the protection and sure enough we were given a Fire Team of four men from the platoon in the bus garage, commanded by a lance jack. I briefed him on the set-up and showed him the bunker. He was delighted that we were at least in a shelter, as he thought they would be having a rough time under the stars. We agreed that he would help us on radio stag, while his lads would do sentry duties. Basically we would work in pairs, four on and eight off, which would give a good rotation and enable us to get some sleep. As there would be two on duty and four off we decided on a hot bunk system, where the bloke just off stag wouldn't have to sort out his bed space and disrupt those asleep, and use the sleeping bag of the one going on stag. That meant we had four sleeping spaces set up at the back of the bunker as far away from the opening as possible. I told the sentries not to stray from the Rebro or the bunker as we had yet to carry out a clearance patrol and it was too dark to do one now.

We got some scoff going and agreed to start the stag system at six. We opened a ten-man rat pack and sorted out all of the goodies. The ten-man rat pack was probably a good idea when it was first designed in the days of the Cold War, but there was no reason why we should have to put up with the bland and poor-quality food in them now. First of all we opened the tins with chocolate bars in and distributed them between us. That was the good stuff sorted out. Then we poured the tins of mince and macedoine into a pot from the number one cookset and boiled them. The mince was greasy and full of white fatty bits, and it looked just like dog food. It was a messy job separating it from the meat (or was it soya?) so we just spooned it in. The macedoine was mixed vegetables in water. I didn't have a clue why it was called that. Maybe it was the process of boiling the taste out of diced veg and putting them in a tin of stinky water. To add a bit of flavour to it we added some powdered beef drink, tomato soup powder, black pepper and some Tabasco sauce that one of the lads had, then we added some crushed biscuits brown to bulk it up a bit. It didn't look or taste too clever but it was hot and filled a hole. We scoffed it down quickly but it still got cold before we got halfway through. Afterwards we had a brew with some biscuits brown and some plasticky cheese 'possessed'.

I took the first stag, and gave my orders to the sentry. I relieved Joey on the net and got settled into the back of the Spartan. I packed away a brew kit, some biscuits AB and some tins of boiled sweets next to the cartons of milk. I sat back and surveyed all around me. The inside of the Spartan was tiny in comparison to a 432 but everything was neat and tidy, and there was more than enough room for one or two men to work inside in comfort. I sat back and sipped at my brew. The batteries were full and the net was quiet. My feet were freezing and I couldn't feel my toes so I took off my boots to rub some life back into them. I don't think my wet socks were helping keep the cold out. I checked my boots. They were soaking inside and rivulets of water ran out when I held them upside down. My poxy BCH were leaking even in the snow. I left them off to dry and put my socks on the radio to dry off. I looked at my wrinkly feet and decided to cut my toenails. And there was me thinking it was going to be a boring stag.

After I had done that I opened my daysack and pulled out my word search. I only had two more to do, so I decided to leave them for when it really got boring. So I decided to read the last few chapters of *Sharpe's*

Eagle. I had another two books with me, so I wasn't worried that finishing it would leave me with nothing to read. Reading was a great morale-boost and made those long and cold night-time stags more bearable. When off duty and tucked up inside my doss bag trying to keep warm, I would listen to my Walkman. I had some mix tapes and some compilations. The northern soul, disco and jazz funk I listened to helped stop the boredom of just lying there for a few hours and reminded me of much warmer times sweating and dancing at weekenders and all-nighters. Memories of another lifetime.

A few hours after the stag had started, the sentry knocked on the door. I turned off the inside lights and opened the door. He said it was Baltic outside and could he come inside for a few minutes to warm up. I looked around the clearing. It was snowing lightly and was pitch black. Visibility was down to about ten metres and after that everything became a blur. I asked to look through his night-sight to check the area but he didn't have one. He told me none of the protection party did as they had left them behind in their Warrior. I was annoyed with their lack of foresight, but it was too late to worry about it now and it was a long walk back down the mountain to Mrkonjić Grad. It was deathly silent outside and we would be able to hear the snow crunching if anyone came close. He said he couldn't feel his feet or hands and was shivering. It was important to keep the sentry alert and outside, but it could be dangerous if we kept him outside for too long in those conditions. I weighed up the situation and decided to let him in. He came inside while I made him a quick brew. Just as he promised, he went back outside after ten minutes.

After another hour out in the snow the sentry knocked on the door again. I turned off the light and opened the door. He was shaking and stuttered as he asked me if I could cover for him while he went into the bunker and put on some more warm kit. I told him it was fine but to wait until I put my boots back on. So while he walked off into the bunker I sat by the back door listening to the loudspeaker and looking into the blackness that surrounded the Rebro site.

God, it was freezing. The cold began to seep through my combats straight away. Like the sentry, I was wearing standard-issue kit. It was designed for a more temperate climate and definitely not for the arctic conditions we were experiencing. The temperature had dropped rapidly since dusk and would only get worse. It didn't look good for the sentry.

He came back fifteen minutes later and we swapped over. He told me he had put on everything he could find, including his incredibly sexy Army-issue long johns. Under his helmet like a badly fitting balaclava

130

was his cap comforter, and around his neck was a football scarf, a bit like Private Pike in *Dad's Army*. He asked me if I minded. I told him that up here, away from the Razzman, I couldn't give a toss if it was a feather boa as long as he was warm, but maybe he should tuck the scarf inside his combat jacket before he carried on.

I felt for him. As a rifleman I had done my share of stagging on in all types of weather, and knew how morale-sapping it could be. He understood that though, and as harsh as it sounds it was the way things are done in the Army. One day, if he didn't PVR, he would be ordering his men to go outside in inhospitable conditions or even in the face of enemy fire. Because he had been there himself he would have a better understanding of his actions. I could have been all matey and let him stay inside the Rebro, but that went against all of my training and common sense. I was responsible primarily for maintaining comms on the Rebro, then for the men under my command, and last of all for my own welfare. The units relying on my Rebro for comms operated with the knowledge that help was only a radio call away. The lads asleep in the bunker rested safe in the knowledge that the sentry was there keeping an eye-out for them, and in return the sentry and me could rest safely in the knowledge that our relief would be looking out for us. If that system broke down we would be useless as a fighting unit, and that was drilled into every infantry soldier since the first days in training.

When I finished my stag I had a chat with the lance jack who was relieving me. We discussed the plight of the sentries and agreed that we had to let them inside the wagon for ten or fifteen minutes every hour to warm up. It might not be much but it would stop them from getting hypothermia. And besides, it was unlikely that anyone would be foolish enough to be wandering around at night on the top of a mountain in those temperatures. We could have solved a lot of problems with the advanced warning trip flares would have given but it was pointless worrying about that now.

It was cold inside the bunker and the kero heaters were struggling to keep the chill out of the air. I turned on my mini Maglite and found the empty bed space. The sentry was already inside his doss bag trying to warm up. I took off my webbing, body armour, helmet and gloves and left them at the foot of the camp-bed. I changed my wet boots and socks and put my spare boots on. I kept my rifle with me and got into the doss bag along with my wet boots to try and dry them out. It was still a bit warm from the previous occupier and I quickly fell into a dark and dreamless sleep.

I awoke the next morning with a wet bivvy bag stuck to my face. I looked around with my mini Maglite but the inside of the bunker was dry, so it must have been the condensation from my breathing. I could feel the freezing cold outside and would have loved to stay inside my warm doss bag, but I had to check out how things were going. I got out and stretched my body. It was dark but I didn't want to pull back the poncho covering the door as it would let what warmth we had out. I lit another candle so I could see what I was doing and got myself ready. My other boots were still damp, but I took off my dry pair and after putting on my Gore-Tex socks put my damp ones back on. It was a tight fit but I got them on. I looked at my watch. It was coming up to half five in the morning.

It was a lovely bright but bloody cold morning on the mountain. Fresh snow overnight had covered the vehicle tracks from yesterday and had deepened the snow. At first glace I couldn't see the Rebro. The sentry was having a fag and a brew at the back door.

I opened the door and looked in at Joey. The inside of the wagon was soaking wet. The seals on all of the hatches were fucked and melting snow was dripping everywhere. All the kit was wet and the floor was awash with a muddy brown liquid. Joey was freezing but had managed to stay fairly dry by sitting as close as possible to the back door. I had no choice but to cover the whole of the wagon with the vehicle tarpaulin, even the L37. It would be the only way we could survive the weeks ahead in the sub-zero temperatures if we didn't want to catch pneumonia.

Apart from the wet everything was working fine, but we would have to fill up with petrol soon as the tanks were low and the batteries needed charging again. The net had been quiet but it was starting to get a bit busier as the battalion prepared to move.

I tried to make a brew before I went on stag but the BV was empty. It was now that we found out that all the water jerrycans had frozen solid. One had even popped the lid off. I got the sentry to help me put them all into the bunker to thaw out. I know the bunker was cold but at least it might stop them from freezing. I kept one by the radios to let it thaw out quickly, but that took hours and I resorted to using my water bottle from my webbing.

After my stag I stayed outside. I filled the tanks with petrol, checked the antennas and while I was up in the watchtower had a dump in the chemical toilet. It was a horrible sensation sitting there while the cold gradually made my legs turn purple and made my dick shrink and disappear. The toilet was just a plastic drum with a toilet seat on it. We didn't have any chemicals but put black bin-liners inside to hold the number twos that had been put on hold for days on end by a diet of compo. We didn't need to worry about the smell as our deposits froze straight away, so we decided to burn the bag along with the rest of our rubbish as soon as it got half full.

As I walked back to the Rebro I heard some noises in the forest. Both me and the sentry scanned the area with our SUSATs but we couldn't spot anything except lumps of snow falling from the branches of the fir trees. It was the probable source of the noise but just in case I told the lance jack we were going to have a look around and carry out a clearance patrol.

Normally we would have carried out a clearance patrol as soon as we set up, but by the time the protection party turned up it was too dark to risk the mines. It would have been standard procedure go out into the trees between fifty to one hundred metres on a clearance patrol and circle around our location, but the mine threat meant that we had to keep it much closer. We walked in the direction where we heard the sound and stopped by the edge of the trees. We scanned the forest for a few minutes then listened for a few more, not moving or making a sound. We then walked around the tree line in a clockwise direction, stopping periodically to look and listen. At the track openings we ventured as far as the snow would let us. It was impossible to walk through it when it was nuts high, and the thought of a few toe tappers scattered around made us think about every step. It was only when we were completing the patrol that I spotted something out of the ordinary.

I was looking through my SUSAT when I spotted a flash of yellowy green. It was out of place in the dark green of the fir trees and white of the snow. I signalled to the sentry to kneel down while I looked again. To the north of our position and about fifty metres away a camouflaged figure was standing next to another bunker. I couldn't make out what he was doing but he wasn't one of ours, so I motioned for the sentry to follow me as we tried to get a closer look. A gap in the trees indicated a path so we tried to follow it. It was almost impossible as we soon found ourselves up to our nuts in snow again. We stopped and scanned the area again. There was definitely someone there and I could make out some smaller boxes and what looked like a camouflage net. I left the sentry to cover me while I went forward for a closer look.

I moved to the right to so the sentry could have a clear view ahead and pushed forward. Every few metres I stopped and looked through my SUSAT. It was a tense few minutes and I could feel my heart racing. I kneeled down and looked again. On the top of the bunker was a covering of fir branches and snow, and hanging from the side was a camouflage net.

I watched for a few minutes and began to pick out some more man-made shapes through the mass of branches and snow. I was going to move forward again when the figure came into view. My heart jumped and I froze. I could clearly see the pattern of his JNA camouflaged jump suit as he stopped in a clearing a short way from the bunker. He seemed unaware of my presence and was putting something over his shoulder when I heard the unmistakable sound of the Spartan's engine starting up. He looked up, obviously startled by the unexpected sound and for a few seconds seemed to ponder over his options, then scarpered.

I tried to run forward but fell into a dip in the path and disappeared up to my neck in snow. I struggled to stand up and knew it was pointless in going forward, so we returned to the Rebro. I told the lance jack that we had sighted an unfriendly in a nearby encampment and we needed to recce it a bit sharpish. I left the sentry there to listen to the net while we went to investigate our new neighbours. We cocked our weapons and moved off. We weren't supposed to have a round up the spout in case of an ND, but everyone in close proximity to the warring factions did it. In our case we did it because we were going towards a known sighting in a deeply wooded area and anyone who has trained on a CQB range knows that split-second reactions make the difference between getting medals or a nice white headstone.

We followed the same route that the sentry and I took a few minutes earlier. We kept close to the edge of the treeline to keep out of the deep snow and stopped at the edge of the clearing. We searched the area through our SUSATS and when we were satisfied we were on our own we closed in on the second bunker. It was built the same as the one we were using but was surrounded by empty wooden ammo boxes. A quick look in the bunker showed it was clear and we continued around the clearing. The area wasn't as big as the one where we had set up the Rebro but unlike ours it was almost entirely surrounded by trees. It was this reason why we hadn't spotted it, but now we had we needed to know why it was still being used.

I checked out the direction the figure had fled and followed the tracks in the snow as they disappeared into the trees. I noticed some red paint marks on the lower part of the trunks of the trees, and closer in I could see they ran parallel and indicated a path through a minefield. We were told that the area was probably mined before we left Vitez and this confirmed the guesswork.

We continued to search the area, treading carefully and listening for any strange noises or sudden movements. The boxes I spotted had

134

markings showing they contained 82mm mortar rounds. We checked for booby-traps and carefully opened the lid of the top box. The rounds were primed ready for use. I closed the lid and we carried on with our search. Close to the entrance of the bunker was a wooden box full of PMR anti-personnel mines. The pineapple-shaped casings, wooden stakes, explosive charges and wire reels were all inside. In the centre of the clearing we found three mortar base plates and support legs but the barrels were missing, probably what our visitor had returned for. Next to the bunker was a cooking area with old pots, pans, cups, and even a few boxes of JNA rations. Finally we gave the bunker a more thorough check. It was full of grey blankets, brightly coloured civvy sleeping bags, and various bits of clothing and kit. It was obvious that this mortar line had recently been used and it didn't look good for our Rebro sharing the same location. From the evidence it was a BSA set up and I was concerned that the Serbs might want their kit back so we went back to report in to Zero.

Back at the Rebro I got up on the net and informed Zero of our discovery. They acknowledged my report and told me they would send someone up to us. I heard the Ulster accent of Captain Gillanders, our Ops Officer on attachment from the Royal Irish Regiment, acknowledge as well.

I left the lance jack on stag and told the sentry to concentrate his attention on the treeline to the north. There was nothing else I could do but get on with our normal routine, so I went back to the bunker and lit the cooker while I sorted out some breakfast. There wasn't much choice, so it would have to be the Boy Scouts' favourite of sausage and beans. I opened a tin of sausages and struggled to get them out. In the cold of the bunker the fat surrounding them had frozen solid, so I had to burn the outside of the tin to melt it enough to free them. I boiled the beans and fried the sausages on the lid of the cooker. It tasted much better than last night's meal but got cold far too quickly to enjoy it. That pretty much summed up the cooking on H21C. The only decent grub was our boil-in-the-bag rations but they didn't last long. I kept six boxes back for emergencies but it was so cold up here our bodies needed more calories to burn to keep us warm. That meant we were using up our rations quicker than we had anticipated.

It snowed on and off all morning, and I did any odd jobs that needed sorting. My feet felt like they were getting blisters so I checked them out as well. My Gore-Tex socks were the problem. They might have been good at keeping out moisture but they creased when I put my boots on and those creases had been rubbing against my skin causing huge red welts to appear. I didn't need the discomfort of blisters so had no choice but to take off the Gore-Tex socks and go into a routine of changing my boots every day.

I hadn't had a wash in a few days so I boiled up the BVs, filled the plastic basin with some steaming water and had a strip wash at the front of the Spartan. Stripping off my top clothes gave me the shiver so much it made holding a wet bar of soap very difficult. My hands couldn't keep still and it kept jumping around like a live fish. After a very swift wash I put my clothes back on before I shaved. I really needed a wet shave to get at some of the more stubborn bristles that the battery shaver didn't get but I knew that because I was now shivering uncontrollably I would cut my face to pieces so I decided to wait until the weather picked up. From the state of things I guessed that would be in a few months time! The feeling of having a good wash really picked me up, but it was so uncomfortable I doubted it would be a regular occurrence on the mountain.

The afternoon stag was a bit of a non-event. The only thing that got my attention was that I noticed the batteries needed to be charged more often than they did in Kiseljak. Joey had run the engine when he took over and I had to do the same just after I got on stag. With the limited amount of traffic we should have kept the charge for longer, but the extreme cold must have been sapping at the batteries more than we expected. I calculated the fuel use and estimated we had enough for another five days. We had about the same supply of food and water. I got on the net and gave Ech my Logsitrep. I told the duty signaller we needed a resupply in four days to give us a day's margin of error. We also got some good news that the battalion was ready to move. We wouldn't be alone for much longer.

I handed over the Rebro to the lance jack and got some scoff. It was too cold and dark to hang around outside so I went into the bunker and got into my doss bag. I listened to my Walkman for an hour and nodded off to sleep. I was fast asleep when I was awoken by a strange noise. At the same time a member of the protection party came in to wake me. I came to my senses immediately and realised what the sound was before he told me. The rhythmic da-da-da-da-da of machine-gun fire was sounding off in the night air. I scrambled out of my doss bag and picked up my kit. Outside the bunker I stopped for a few seconds to listen to the gunfire then ran over to the Rebro. Everyone was there and I stopped next to the lance jack. There was a pause in the firing and then a prolonged burst. It was loud, clear and even though we couldn't see anything it was obvious by the intensity it was very close by. I listened to the sound of it. It was deeper than a jimpy and had a high rate of fire. That ruled out the larger

20mm or 30mm anti-aircraft cannons, so we agreed that it was probably a heavy machine gun, a 12.7mm, common with all ex Eastern Bloc forces.

I looked at the lance jack and told him to pair off his protection party and go left and right of the Spartan and wait there. I got inside the Spartan and closed the door. Joey was manning the net in darkness. I asked him if he had called it in, but he said no, he was waiting for me. I picked up a map and with the aid of my Maglite looked at our location. I asked Joey if any of our callsigns were under contact, but he said no, the net was quiet. Judging the likely position of the HMG and the lack of any visual signs like tracer meant that it was firing downwards and the only logical target was a small village called Podrašnica to the east of the mountain. The area was controlled by the Croats so it was likely that it was the BSA. It could be a unit out to harass the HVO or locals before they left the area completely or the vanguard of a larger force. Whatever it was it could mean bad news for us. I picked up the spare handset and called Zero.

It wasn't a sighting report or a contact report, and still we were not using Batco, so I had to be guarded with what I said. I told Zero that we had sustained HMG fire between one and two hundred metres east of our location and the direction of fire. I let them work out the target.

I was surprised when a Rupert got up on the net and told me not to worry as it was probably celebratory fire. I was dumbfounded. How could he come to that conclusion over 100k away? Maybe he was looking at the bottom of his tea cup when I called! I got back on the net and told him he was wrong. I was worried that apart from giving some poor sods a bad time the culprits would attract the attention of some of the opposing faction forces that were still at large in our area. We were on a junction with two other tracks and anyone coming up to sort out the HMG might think we were the enemy and give us the good news instead. I was glad that I had camouflaged the Spartan but it would never stand up to a really close inspection. I listened as Zero came back and told us the same celebratory fire nonsense. It was as if our safety was an inconvenience. I threw the handset down in disbelief and left the Rebro to talk to the lance jack.

He was standing to the front of the Spartan and was shaking with the cold and probably a little apprehension as well. He wasn't the only one. I discussed the situation and he swore to himself when I told him of Zero's reply. We looked in the direction of the gunfire and listened as another burst echoed all around. We came to the same conclusion that if we were compromised we would have to react to whatever materialised. We couldn't withdraw into the woods because of the mine threat so we would have to either stay and fight or withdraw along one of the tracks. We had no choice but to stay put and wait this one out. I stayed by the back door of the Spartan, leaving Joey inside on the net. If the shit hit the fan I would pull back the tarp and he could operate the L37.

The firing continued on and off for another half-hour and then stopped. I thought I could hear the cough of an engine but I wasn't sure. I was straining my hearing for the slightest hint of anything unusual, and the occasional lump of snow falling from the fir branches in the woods wasn't helping our nerves much. A 12.7 is a monster of a machine gun and it would have been nigh impossible to drag it up to the top of the mountain in this weather without transport. Almost all Eastern Bloc APCs and AFVs had a 12.7 mounted in some fashion, as well as some of the locally produced steel-clad bodge jobs that the BiH militia were so proud of.

We waited for another hour in silence but nothing had come up the track towards us. I needed to find out what was going on, otherwise we would freeze to death, so I went forward with the sentry and recced the track. It was pitch black but the track was clearly visible between the dark of the trees. I stopped still in sight of the protection party and listened. At that altitude the air was clear and I could smell faint traces of cordite and exhaust fumes that lingered around in the thin mountain air. I waited for ten minutes but there was no sign or sound of anything, so I went back and reviewed our situation with the lance jack. We had been outside for nearly two hours and I didn't need to see the lads as I could hear their teeth chattering. The lads risked getting hypothermia if they stayed out much longer so I stood them down. I was due on stag so I stayed up. I covered for the sentry for fifteen minutes while he grabbed a brew and warmed up in the Rebro with Joey, and then went inside myself to thaw out.

I wondered what Main was up to failing to respond positively to my radio message. There was a very good possibility that we could have been compromised but they ignored me without verifying the facts. It was a chilling reminder of how vulnerable we were on the Rebro.

At ten the lance jack relieved me and we talked about the night's excitement. He wasn't happy at all about the way Zero had fobbed us off.

'Fook this for a game of soldiers, Les. You can keep the fookin' Rebro. I can't wait to get back down to my fookin' platoon. They don't give a fook about us up here!' He was pissed off and I couldn't blame him. Main could have at least acknowledged the message but instead decided to leave us alone and see how the events played out. It was getting light so I took a walk down the track with the sentry and see what I could find.

The snow on the track was up to our knees and it was very difficult to wade through. At least the effort warmed me up. After about ten minutes I reached a bend in the track. I looked back at the Rebro. It was hidden by a bank of rock and trees. I carried on down the track and after another ten minutes of hard work stopped at a spot where the snow had been disturbed. Even though there had been constant snowfall it was obvious from the twin furrows that some kind of vehicle had been here recently. The sentry bent down and pulled something from the snow. He held it up and showed it to me. I looked at it in the palm of my gloved hand. It was a big, shiny, new bullet casing, and on the bottom next to some Cyrillic symbols was the number 12.7. I lifted it up to my nose and sniffed at the open end. The unmistakable smell of freshly ignited cordite confirmed what we already knew. The sentry searched around in the snow and found hundreds of them. I looked over the edge of the track and saw dozens more lying on fir branches. I pocketed a handful and we headed back to the Rebro.

Back inside I showed the empty cases to the lance jack. He stared at it for a few moments.

'I'd like to meet that fookin' Rupert and shove this up his arse and see how he celebrates!' said the unimpressed Junior NCO. 'In Northern Ireland I never heard a shot fired in anger in six months but I knew that my arse was covered. In Boz you get to see and hear gunfire every other bloody day, and being up here on our jack is bloody scary. I never thought I'd say it but I'd swap Boz with that bog anytime!' I left him there to brood over the situation and keep an eye on things. I went back to the bunker for some scoff and to get my head down for a few hours. That day the Bosnian Peace Accord was signed in Paris.

The weather started to get worse. The clouds closed in the temperature dropped yet again. It was now constantly below zero during the day, and God knows what it was at night. We were freezing our balls off up there and it wasn't getting any better. The conditions were atrocious and the snow was getting deeper and deeper. We ran out of kero for the heaters and at night it became so cold in our doss bags we couldn't sleep and so just stayed there, listening to Walkmans or chatting, leaving sleep to the less cold daylight hours. On the day of the resupply we had the worst snowfall yet and some bad news from Ech.

The wagons attempting to get up the mountain to us got bogged down on the lower slopes and they had to reschedule for the next day. I checked our supplies. We had enough food for today and we still had the emergency 24-hour packs. To make matters worse the lads had run out of ciggies and were starting to get really narky. Water wasn't a problem, when we could defrost it, but we were desperately short of petrol. The cold was severely affecting the charge of the batteries and we needed to keep running the engine more often. We had half a tank of petrol and enough for one more refill. On the net we heard that the battalion was ready to move away from its commitment to support the French around Sarajevo and that meant more radio traffic. I hoped we would get a break in the weather.

That day we had a couple of visitors. Two stray dogs, a black and a Golden labrador sniffed us out and after the lads gave them a bit of compo they decided to stay. The lads immediately took to them and named them Rebro and Mags respectively. I suppose with the amount of stray pets wandering all over Bosnia it was no wonder there were dozens of new pets wherever the UN set up camp.

The next morning the sun broke through intermittent cloud cover. It had stopped snowing but still threatened more. Our resupply had tried again but couldn't get past the snow. We cooked the last of our food and I issued the 24-hour rat packs. We carried on as normal but we knew that we couldn't survive on the mountain without food for our bodies to burn. That afternoon as it started to get dark I got a message saying that the resupply would try again tomorrow. I spoke to Joey and the lance jack in the Spartan and discussed our options. It boiled down to two things, the Rebro and the men. By the next afternoon, if the resup failed to appear, the lance jack would lead the protection party and Joey back down the mountain. The protection party was due to be relieved anyway. I would stay until the Spartan ran out of petrol and the batteries died. I would then unplug the radio sets and change the frequency dials, hide the L37, then lock up and head down the mountain to meet up with the first British unit I could find. I got back on the net and told Zero the basics of my plan and in reply got a simple 'Roger, out!'

It was a long and freezing cold night. In the morning we awoke with empty bellies and no more food. We heard that the resup was trying again but was still having difficulties. We made loads of brews to try to compensate for having no food and even used up the powdered cow to make hot sweet milk drinks. The lads had their Bergans packed and were ready to move by midday. We decided that as it started to get dark around four o'clock they would have move off before one if they were going to make the journey in daylight. They weren't looking forward to a TAB down the mountain but it should give them time to get down and meet up with the resup party at the bottom before it got dark.

I was getting ready to move my Bergan over to the Rebro when I heard an excited shout from the sentry. I rushed outside the bunker to see what the commotion was and heard the unmistakable sound of a Land Rover. I searched the track and was thankful when I saw a snow-covered little 90 appear round the bend in the track. It was revving like mad and the back slipped and swerved as it struggled to make headway. Of all the vehicles that could have made it I should have guessed it would be a Land Rover. We all watched as it stopped on the track between us and the Serb mortar line. Steam was rising from the chain-covered wheels and bonnet, but the engine purred perfectly as it waited there like an obedient gun dog.

The resupply party looked a bit shaken by the struggle to get up the mountain but were met with smiles and backslaps by the relieved protection party. Joey was even gladder to see them as he was given a handful of mail from his fiancée and most importantly a carton of 200 Silk Cut from the Sigs colourboy! More bodies fell out of the 90 and came over. They were part of the relief for the protection party and they began unloading some of our supplies. We were told that the rest were in a Warrior near the bottom of the mountain and the Rover would run a relay back and forth until we had been resupplied. While this went on me and Joey grabbed something to eat and listened as we were filled in on the latest developments.

The Peace Agreement might have been signed but some of the hardline Serbs begrudged it and sent a few mortar rounds into Sarajevo to emphasise the point. Transfer of authority from the UN to NATO was on for December 20th and the battalion was on the process of changing its AOR. An Advance Party was on its way to Mrkonjić Grad to look for a location for the Battle Group HQ. For morale, CSE shows were being held on Igman, in Kiseljak and Vitez. Sheila Ferguson, one of the Three Degrees, was the star, but I somehow doubted that she would make a personal appearance on our Rebro.

After a few shuttle runs back and forth from the Warrior we had all of our resupply and the protection party had swapped over. The resup party made their farewells and promised not to leave it so late next time. I watched the 90 as it disappeared down the track and turned to look at the new protection party. They didn't look too impressed with their new location. I introduced myself to the commander whom I recognised immediately. He was a lance corporal who was one of the PTIs who had run us ragged in the build-up to deployment. I showed them to the bunker and they dumped their kit. They were all wearing new Matterhorn Gore-Tex-lined boots, and the battalion was being issued them because the issue boots were too cold and were not waterproof. I was annoyed that me and Joey had been left out and made a mental note to remind the Sigs colourboy the next time I spoke to him on the net. We put one lad straight on stag and while the others put the stores away I showed the PTI around our set-up and the Serb mortar line. We agreed to keep the same stag system, as it had worked well, and I told him about the problems we had with the cold at night and unwelcome visitors. The good thing was that all of them had brought an IWS with them. He seemed thoughtful as we walked back to the Rebro and didn't say much.

I looked in on Joey who was manning the net. He looked upset but I could see he was just getting a bit emotional as he read his mail. It was a week to go until Christmas and he was a thousand miles from his fiancée in Leeds. Letters from home, blueys and even an old local newspaper meant so much to a squaddie separated from their partner, family and friends. They might make them homesick and wish they were far from the horrors and dreadful conditions in Bosnia, but they would feel a great deal worse if they didn't get any. We did get some good news, though. We would get our Christmas mail and a few beers to celebrate on Christmas Eve.

A few days later we had a visit from some SNCOs who inspected the mortar line and abruptly left. I was hoping one of them was an ATO but when they returned to their 110 I saw they all wore the rifle green berets of the LI and not the RLC navy blue that Felix would have worn. I hoped they would tell us what they intended to do with all that loose ordnance but the cold probably got to them and they hurried away.

The next morning I was back on stag and settled back to another four hours of listening to the net and trying to keep warm. I had finished my book and looked in my daysack for another one to start. I pulled out a dog-eared copy of one of my favourite books, Spike Milligan's *Rommel? – Gunner Who?* I made myself a brew and started to read the first chapter. Even though I had read the book a few times I couldn't help giggling to myself – Spike's exploits in North Africa during World War Two could easily have happened in today's Army. If the sentry outside was listening he might have thought I was losing it! It was in this book that I had first come across the term PBI. As a Gunner, Spike had commented on the men in the front line who had to put up with the worst conditions of the Allied armies. The 'Poor Bloody Infantry' wasn't one of the descriptions of the heroic British Tommy that I read about in comics like *Warlord* and *Victor* that I had grown up with, and it made me wonder why they were nicknamed that. I understood now – I was one of them!

The faces in the relief protection party might have been different but the routine remained the same. Eat, sleep, freeze and stag on. The 2LI Battle Group Advance Party had moved to a town called Sanski Most and christened the location the 'Mud Factory'. It didn't sound too clever. It was still freezing cold and the snow was still falling. The food was still as bad as usual but at least we now had plenty of it. We were resupplied after another few days and began to stockpile fuel, water and even more of those bloody awful ten-man ration packs. It was a shame that the fire at Donnington didn't reach the store with those in!

Chapter 13

D-Day, Peace and the Transfer
of Authority to NATO

On December 20th the Transfer of Authority to NATO took place signalling the changeover from peacekeeping to peace enforcing. This would mean a change in the ROE and basically meant we could use lethal force to protect ourselves, property and those in our protection. It was a gloves-off approach and heralded a change in the way we were allowed to operate. Many restraints had been placed on the warring factions and we were expected to police the situation. Lethal force was authorised to ensure all conditions were met, especially as many of the armed gangs operating in the area were ignoring their own government's orders. The area we were in was nicknamed the Anvil, due to its shape on the map formed by the Inter Entity Boundary Line, or Confrontation Line as it was known by the troops. It was to be handed back to the Serbs and the local HVO warlords were not very happy about this. American forces were beginning to pour into the north-east of the country overland from Hungary and Croatia, and the various contributing countries were moving to their respective sectors.

2LI changed from Task Force Alpha to the 2LI Battle Group. A Company moved to Mrkonjić Grad and were joined by Main and B Company for an overnight stop. The next day Main moved to Sanski Most and B Company took over the crossing point at White Fang, between Sanski Most and Prijedor. C Company had to stay behind on Igman until the French replaced them. Instead we were given X Company from 1RRF, who moved to Coralici, north of Bihac. We now came under command of the 4th Armoured Brigade, the famous Desert Rats, who also had the 1RRF Battle Group under command. The battalion's Warriors were constantly on the go restoring freedom of movement every time a bored or vindictive militiaman on a checkpoint tried to stop an IFOR vehicle. On the net we heard of a RE Rover that blew up on a land-mine, but thankfully there were no serious casualties.

One of the things about Army life is the long periods of boredom that are broken by short intense periods of excitement. I was stagging on one evening and going through bouts of reading, boredom, polishing my boots, more boredom, and trying to keep warm. There was a blizzard blowing about outside and the sentry had just left me after warming up with a mug of hot chocolate. I was contemplating whether to have some biscuits brown with marge and cheese possessed or heat up a tin of fruit pudding when I heard a commotion on the net.

A 2LI soldier had suffered a gunshot wound to the head but was still alive and needed an emergency Casevac. A request had gone into Brigade for a helicopter, and the ambulance had been called out from the RAP. An all-callsigns message had been sent out to keep the net clear for emergency traffic. I checked the battery levels and signal strengths. They were fine, so I put on my headset and sat back to listen as the crisis unfolded.

The ambulance and medics soon reached the casualty but his condition was critical. I could hear them keep asking Zero where the helicopter was. The reply wasn't good. The blizzard was getting worse and the Crabs were refusing to fly. The medics confirmed the critical condition the casualty was in but were told to wait out. It was a long wait. The net went deathly quiet as if the gods knew what was in store for the poor unfortunate victim.

It was at times like these that all the other callsigns listening in felt really useless. We couldn't do anything and had to wait expectantly while the events were played out like a tragic radio play. The medics kept asking for an update but Zero kept telling them to wait. It was beginning to look hopeless when a strange voice came over the air waves.

'Hello Zero, this is Junglie One, over.' I sat up expectantly. It was a Royal Navy callsign used by the black-and-white striped Sea King Commando Carriers.

'Hello Zero, this is Junglie One, acknowledge, over.' Apart from the pilot the net stayed silent. What was Zero up to? If I could hear them, so should Zero. The pilot in Junglie One called again but the net stayed silent. I checked the radios and batteries but they were still OK. Something was wrong but I couldn't figure it out. I heard the medics get on the net and ask for an update. The red light on the forward 353 meant that comms were good but they couldn't hear each other. Then Junglie One called again and I spotted the reason why they were not talking. The red light was glowing on the set providing my link to Hotel Two One

India. The Sea King had been given the frequency for the forward leg of the network and was still too far away to talk to Zero directly. I could hear him because I was between them, but that signal was only being sent back to Vitez and Igman and they wouldn't answer for Zero. There was only one option so I thumbed the pressel switch in my hand.

'Hello Junglie One, this is Hotel Two One Charlie, through me over.' I would have to take the message and relay it to Zero.

'Hello Hotel Two One Charlie, this is Junglie One.' The pilot sounded relieved to have got through to someone. 'Tell Zero weather conditions are too bad and we cannot make the casualty's location. The ambulance will have to meet us in Mrkonjić Grad, over.' The pilot sounded anxious to get the job over with. I passed on the message to Zero and began a hectic few minutes of relaying messages back and forth between Junglie One and Zero.

The pilot told me that he was about to turn around as he wasn't getting any replies and was risking the lives of his crew by flying in white-out conditions. I could understand as it was blowing a gale outside the Rebro and our visibility was down to about ten metres. He didn't have the comfort of air traffic control or brightly lit streets guiding him along; it was pure navigational ability and flying by the seat of his pants. He told us he would risk it as far as Mrkonjić Grad and the ambulance would have to meet him there. At first Zero was reluctant but after consulting with the MO he agreed and the ambulance was sent south to Mrkonjić Grad. I could sense the relief in the pilot's voice when he acknowledged the reply from Zero.

On the ground the ambulance crew drove through the blizzard in double-quick time and met up with the waiting Sea King. Once airborne, the pilot of Sea King got back on the net to confirm he had the casualty on board and to say thanks to me for helping out. I was pleased to get the compliment but I was just doing my job and was glad the poor sod that had been shot in the head now had a chance of surviving.

I took off my headset and sat back. The net became quiet again and I thought about what had just happened. It was lucky I realised the problem with the frequencies. It was a sobering thought and illustrated the need to monitor the net at all times. I hoped Junglie One arrived back safely and got him to a hospital in time. There was a knock on the door and I turned the light off. I let the sentry in and he stamped his Matterhorns on the floor to get his circulation going.

'Any news?' He sounded edgy and I guessed it was the lonely stag outside in the pitch black and freezing cold. I didn't want to give him anything to distract his attention when he went back outside, so I told him it was all quiet on the Western Front. He seemed happy with that and made himself a brew.

The next day the weather cleared up and the snow stopped. It was the calm after the storm. It was still very cold on the mountain, especially at night, but it made our job a bit easier. It didn't stop the privates moaning about everything, but that's life in the Army. We were all pissed off that we were away from home for Christmas but it was harder for the younger privates. We had no access to phones, and being stuck on a mountain away from the battalion meant we didn't get mail as often as those below. It was out of sight, out of mind. On Christmas Eve we were all up and about very early, waiting expectantly for a visit from Ech with our mail and parcels from home and the promised few beers.

We waited all morning and all afternoon. It was getting dark when Ech told us the visit would be tomorrow. It seemed that it wasn't the weather this time; the post was late getting up country. The men were upset and rightly so, but Joey took it worse than the others. He was a quiet lad, but the endless hours of stagging on alone had probably given him too much time to mope about being away from his beloved.

I took over from him at midnight. It was quiet on the net and gave me time to reflect on what we had achieved since we had arrived in Bosnia. The battalion had stood firm in the face of adversity, sniping, rioting, piss-poor facilities, higher politics and the appalling weather. We had provided the front-line troops on Igman and had moved halfway across the country to take over an unfamiliar area to enforce a fragile peace agreement. Not many units could have achieved what we did in such a short period. The sentry came inside the Spartan for a warm-up and I wished him a merry Christmas. I got out and stretched my legs. I looked up at the clear night sky. There wasn't a cloud to be seen and there was a blanket of thousands of shining stars covering the mountain. The people of Bosnia hadn't celebrated Christmas for three years, and it was possible now, mainly to the hard work and self-sacrifice of the soldiers from all nationalities who had risked their lives to help them. I wondered how many more would die to keep the peace.

In the morning I was relieved by the PTI, shivering and still half-asleep. We wished each other a merry Christmas, and I went into the bunker to get some sleep. I was up at midday and made myself something to eat. As a special treat I had a corned-beef hash boil-in-the-bag instead of the usual compo. Not exactly a roast with all the trimmings, but it was better than spooning into a tin of cold greasy bacon burgers. Everyone was up and congregated by the Spartan. We were cold, so we lit a fire in a concrete sewerage ring that for some strange reason was sitting in the middle of the clearing. We chopped up some dead trees and added some petrol to get it going. I also remembered to throw in the shit bag from the chemical toilet and all the other rubbish that we had accumulated over the last two weeks. Joey started up the Spartan to charge the batteries and drowned any chat that managed to pass as conversation.

The lads were not in a good mood. We would normally have moved away so we could hear each other but they didn't bother. They just stood there, staring into the flames, probably thinking of Christmases past. They were so lost in their own thoughts that they didn't notice the two Land-Rovers pull into the clearing. The looks on their faces changed instantly when they realised we hadn't been forgotten. We had loads of mail and parcels, and they had brought up a few newspapers so we could catch up on the news and the all-so-important football scores.

I had mail from friends and family and a parcel from my sister. Inside she had put some Christmas decorations and a thermal long-sleeved vest. From my cousin Mark I received a small bottle of Smirnoff vodka. He must have guessed we needed cheering up! The atmosphere had changed in an instant. Joey turned off the engine and all around you could hear loud chat and laughter. Everyone was smiling and sharing news from home. An added bonus was the Norwegian containers that had our Christmas dinner of turkey, roast spuds and veg. The smell was gorgeous and it tasted even better. It had been nearly three weeks since I had eaten fresh food and I devoured it greedily, not even thinking about the impending bowel movements after weeks of all that compo! We were in such a good mood that we didn't even complain when they handed out two 330ml cans of beer each instead of the usual 500ml that the EFI sold. We had been up on the mountain for so long we didn't care what size they were. It was like the scene at the end of the film *Ice Cold in Alex* when John Mills sank a glass of Carlsberg in one. We downed the first one as soon as we opened it, and for some the second as well.

Our DPM Santa and his helpers couldn't stay long and had to get off the mountain before dark, so we said our goodbyes and watched them disappear down the mountain track. I hung a gold and red 'Merry Christmas' sign on the side of the Spartan and we all gathered around the fire again. Someone put on a Roy 'Chubby' Brown tape, which soon had us laughing out loud and cheered us up no end. We were still in a festive mood after the tape finished so I decided to open the vodka. Between six of us it didn't go far, but mixed with some orange screech it made a lovely nightcap.

It was dark when I started my stag. The fire was dying out, and the lads waited until it got too cold then disappeared to the bunker. Once I had settled in I read my mail and Christmas cards. Everyone at home was wishing me well, but there wasn't much real news. One of my mates, Garry, had sent me a few West Ham fanzines called *Over Land and Sea*. It was great reading the critical comments full of slagging and Cockney wit. I am sure I was still grinning like an idiot when I went to sleep that night.

On Boxing Day we heard that C Company was finally released from Ops on Mount Igman. MT handed over the BV 206s, and B Company had possibly discovered a mass grave at their location. Based in a disused mine outside Sanski Most, we heard reports of hundreds of bodies in the mineshaft. Another crossing point on the Confrontation Line, Bondi Beach, was opened to allow Displaced Persons to cross into areas occupied by their respective ethnic communities.

The following day, C Company finally arrived in Banja Luka, but under Opcom 1RRF, while A Company, along with our protection party, moved to Coralici with X Company 1RRF. The battalion was desperately short of men, and as we supposedly controlled the immediate area now it was decided we would be safe from any threat. Considering the activity we had encountered and the munitions lying around up here we didn't feel that safe, but we were promised that a QRF from Mrkonjić Grad could reach us in minutes in the event of an emergency. I wondered who the bright spark who calculated that was!

We didn't have too long to worry about things. A few days later the Sigs Platoon came up to us with a 432 and we swapped over with them. The RSO needed his company car back so Joey and me were ordered to take the Spartan back down to Main. The UN number plates on the escort Warriors had been taken off and the logos on the sides of the vehicles had been painted over with the large white letters I-F-O-R, brightly displaying our new designation. Even brighter was the orange Day-Glo marker panel that was tied over the mortar hatches, intended to let the Yanks know who they were shooting at. I was intrigued with the choice of name we were now operating under, which I found out was pronounced i-for and stood for Implementation Force. We were now on Operation Resolute Rat, partly named after the badge of the 4th Armoured Brigade, but the 'Rat' part was dropped after it was realised that it was also the Serbo-Croat word for war! The UN badge had been removed from the lads' brassards and the 20 Armoured Brigade badge had been removed from their combat jackets. We quickly packed our kit away and tagged onto the back of our escort.

We followed the Warriors carefully down the mountain and through the village at the bottom. It was still deserted and covered with snow. I wondered if the owners would ever return. I hoped so; after all, that was why we were here. We drove by Mrkonjić Grad and drove north to Sanski Most. The road was wet with slush but we made good progress. The region of north-west Bosnia was more mountainous than I expected and wondered how we had ever managed to communicate over such awful signalling terrain. We passed a few closed HVO and BiH checkpoints, made redundant by the peace agreement, and passed a Warrior manning an IFOR checkpoint on the Confrontation Line.

Sanski Most was a small town in north-western Bosnia. It was to remain a Croat area as part of the Peace Accord but had suffered from the Serb occupation and then again when the Croats retook it a few months back. Our new location was the Mud Factory, so called because of the ever-present mud. It was late when we arrived so we parked up and got something to eat. The vehicle park was in about half a metre of thick, liquid mud. We parked as close to the building as possible and waded up to a building where the cooks had set up. We had an unbelievable meal of steak and chips cooked on a number-five cookset on the back of a trailer, followed by a superb cheesecake made from crushed compo oatmeal blocks. I know I keep mentioning it but I was full of admiration for these cooks who operated in extremely primitive conditions but served up first-class fare.

The next morning we were told we were moving to another town further north. It was supposed to have been to a hotel but at the last moment negotiations with the owner broke down because he thought he could get more money from the UN. We packed our kit and went over to the vehicle park. The mud had frozen over night and now the vehicles were stuck fast. It was no wonder we had to move. A few drivers tried to drive their way out of it but it just resulted in screams from the transmissions and the smell of burning clutch plates. Small fires were lit under the tracks to defrost the mud and you could see the drivers holding their boots in the flames to try and warm up their frozen feet. While we waited we had a breakfast of egg, bacon, tomatoes and a fried slice. The cooks were doing wonders again and it made up slightly for the shitty location and hanging around in the freezing cold.

It was mid-morning by the time we had the Sigs Platoon vehicles free enough to move. We moved off in a mixed convoy of Scimitars, four-tonners, 432s and our Spartan. It was a slow drive as we had to wait for the geriatric 432s but it gave us time to take in our new AOR. Just like Mrkonjić Grad, Vitez and the villages around Sarajevo, the landscape was bleak and littered with ruined houses, but we saw more wrecked APCs and tanks than before, evidence of the recent fighting.

We passed another IFOR checkpoint and headed further north into Serb-held territory. The wind-chill was starting to make the trip uncomfortable and to help I traversed the cupola so the hatch faced forward. An hour after leaving Sanski Most found us on the outskirts of a town called Dornji Ljubija. It was a predominantly Serb town and as we entered we could see that it had barely suffered during the war. Serb police stood next to a navy-blue painted BOV-M at a disused checkpoint. They looked bored but the dark look in their eyes reminded me of their Croat counterparts, nasty and vicious.

We pulled up outside a small factory and unloaded our kit. In a junior school opposite us B Squadron of the Light Dragoons, who were back under our Opcom, set up shop. There wasn't much space to park but after a bit of shunting we managed to get in between the RSM's Warrior and a back wall. Our accommodation was an open-plan workshop full of rows of sewing machines. It was a textile factory but quickly became known by everyone as the Sewing Machine Factory. I put up my camp-bed between two sewing machines and laid out my kit. We then helped finish the set-up of Main using one of the general offices on the second floor. Once we were set up, we sorted out a stag system. Due to the numbers of men on leave and on the Rebros we had more duties than normal. The RSWO's need for multi-skilled platoon members was being tested to the full.

The Sewing Machine Factory was a clean if congested location. We stagged on in a warm office and slept in a warmish building. We didn't have showers but at least we had proper toilets and hot water and even had cooked meals in the old staff canteen. After spending most of the tour so far in the field it was luxury I could get used to.

I was in the Ops Room helping run some cables around the back of the desks. Also there was a watchkeeper and signaller. The RSWO came in to check the set-up and was beaming from ear to ear. I was finishing up when he came over and told us of a visit he had earlier by a lieutenant colonel from the Royal Signals. The signals world had heard of our record-breaking Rebro chain from Mount Igman to Coralici and the Royal Signals couldn't believe we had managed it with such limited resources. After all, if the Royal Signals said it can't be done, then we must have been embellishing the truth. So a Lt Colonel from the Royal Signals, visited the HQ of the 2LI Battle Group to set matters straight. He was polite but simply refused to believe we had achieved the impossible, but the RSWO politely explained the set-up and showed it to him on a map.

The Royal Signals gentleman still claimed it was impossible but after listening to the clear comms from Mount Igman to Bihac he reluctantly agreed we had achieved something special. He thanked the RSWO for his time and left. We didn't hear any more from the Royal Signals, so I guess we had proved to them that our operation, though fantastic in its composition, actually worked. It was an outstanding accomplishment. No wonder the RSWO looked like the cat that got the cream!

It was a fairly busy time in Main with most of the reports and returns coming in at the same time so that the various callsigns could get ready for the New Year celebrations. I stagged on from six till ten and was looking forward to our own little celebration. We had a few crates of pivo hidden under a camp-bed and we laid out the extension lead for a portable stereo belonging to one of the lads. By half ten we had all gathered around the sewing machines and passed the time by joking and slagging until most of the lads were there, waiting for the cue to open another bottle and bring in the New Year.

At midnight we raised our beers and cheered as a few photo flashes went off. We shook hands and slapped each other on the back. We raised our bottles again and said a toast to all the lads who were still stagging on and then we started a series of toasts to everyone and anyone. Even the Provost Serjeant got a toast! After about ten minutes we sat down and carried on with our celebrating. We let off steam and laughed at some of the stories that were doing the rounds. Private Smith still hadn't washed since he arrived in theatre and was becoming a bio hazard and of Private Jones who got his dick stuck to the frozen Chobam armour on his Warrior when he went for a slash at night! I knew the first story had some merit but the second sounded like a wind-up. Everyone who passed by got a cheer and we even cheered the OC HQ Company who came over to quieten us down.

At half twelve someone had the bright idea that we should celebrate the New Year again at one, as that was when it would be midnight in the UK. We all agreed that it was a great idea, so we took out another crate of pivo and handed around the bottles. So at midnight GMT we raised our bottles again and cheered!

The OC HQ Company wasn't impressed and came over again to see what the commotion was. He couldn't fault our reasoning, so let us carry on for a while. He even took a few photos. By half one we had had enough and started to drift off to our own beds. The lights were turned down and the room went quiet. We weren't drunk, no one had more than three or four bottles of pivo, but we were tired and some of us had started to get a bit emotional. I lay back on my camp-bed and closed my eyes. There might be peace but it was still the most dangerous place in Europe. The situation between the warring factions and the abundance of ordnance was still a major concern. That was why we were still needed, and the law of averages in those circumstances meant that there would be a few lads who would never see home again. That might have been my last New Year's celebration, and I wondered how many more lads were thinking that this night. I would have given anything to have been able to phone home right then.

Chapter 14

IFOR and the Fragile Peace of 1996

New Year's Day 1996 was no different from the days that went before. We still had a very crucial job to do and we couldn't afford any slip-ups because of lapses in concentration. The stag list meant that I was to be on duty at midday and at eight so I managed to have a strip wash at the sink in the toilets and change into my last clean set of combats.

In Main, I made myself a brew and settled into the routine of receiving reports and returns from the companies and sending them up to Brigade. A new face was Captain Johnny Bowron, who had joined us as adjutant after a staff course back in England. He was bright and cheery, but then again he hadn't been living in freezing shit-holes for the last two months! It was good to have a happy face around and he was always trying to crack jokes. I wondered how long that would last. With the TOA we had a new area to get familiar with. I started to learn the new route names and nicknames of the checkpoints on the Confrontation Line. Names like Black Dog, White Fang, Malibu Corner and Bondi Beach. I also found out that a convoy carrying goodies donated by the great British public intended for us had gone missing. The RLC had 'misplaced' two steel ISO containers destined for 2LI and couldn't find them. It seemed to me that the blokes running our combat service support in theatre were only interested in supporting themselves. It was no use wondering about them so I just got on with the job.

I was back on stag at sparrow's fart again. I didn't have time for a wash or shave and looked a right mess. A few of the officers gave me funny looks but I was too tired to care. Most of the Signal Platoon looked the same and we were getting very little time off to sort ourselves out. I was off at ten and grabbed the last of the breakfast and a brew. I didn't know when I would be called on next, so I quickly grabbed my wash kit and disappeared into the toilets for twenty minutes to freshen up.

Not long after I was lying on my camp-bed listening to my Walkman when I was dicked to go back to Mrkonjić Grad to pick up the laundry. We took a Land Rover and a VPK and sped off in order to get to Ech in time for scoff. The SOPs for vehicle movement hadn't changed since the TOA and the VPK was considered our armour, though its fibreglass panels were nowhere near as armoured as a Spartan or 432. It was nice and warm in the VPK and I relaxed a little, even though it was a little top-heavy and leaned a bit too much on the bends.

At some of the checkpoints I noticed that Hesco bastions were being put in place to create a kind of chicane to give the lads some protection and force vehicles to slow down. At others, the lads had to rely on their vehicles and a raised hand. At 2LI locations a Warrior would provide security and protection, and at 1RRF locations it was the less menacing Saxon. The Dutch were not taking any chances and had parked Leopard 1 tanks next to their checkpoints. Along the main routes we saw patrols of Scimitars, but they were so dirty I couldn't tell if they were our Recce Platoon or the Light Dragoons. Above, a few Lynx darted in and out of the low cloud cover and disappeared in a northerly direction. Their TOW missile pods hung menacingly from their sides ready to respond quickly to any attacks upon NATO.

We picked up the laundry, spares and anything else intended for the platoon. After lunch we headed back to the Sewing Machine Factory. This time the road was even busier, with convoys of trucks, engineer vehicles moving up country, and a pair of Scimitars from the Light Dragoons who raced past us, showering our Rovers with muddy slush.

That night I was on drag stag from midnight to six a.m. When I was relieved I got straight into my doss bag, looking forward to a decent kip. It seemed that I had just nodded off to sleep when I was woken up by Fred. I looked at my watch: it had just gone seven o'clock.

I was told to get up and join the convoy that were going to Brigade to get the fill gun charged for the encrypted 353. I told Fred that I had just got off drag stag, but he said it was tough as there was no one else.

I got up and changed into my kit. I was starving but there was no time for breakfast so we would have to get something at Brigade. I went outside where the same Land Rover and VPK were waiting. I found a space by the driver in the 90 and clipped my rifle into the holder in between the seats and threw my doss bag in the back. I was still sleepy but I quickly woke up when I found out that the heater was U/S. I was not a happy bunny!

We headed south on a very icy Route Phoenix. It was bloody cold and I

156

had to stamp my feet to get the blood flowing, which really bugged the driver. We passed by the IFOR checkpoints and continued south towards Mrkonjić Grad. We stopped to pick up their fill gun and to have a slash, and then carried on to Sipovo. We arrived at Brigade just in time for lunch.

While the fill gun was being charged the two drivers and I had a look around the Brigade location. There were dozens of new Corimec cabins including sleeping accommodation and shower blocks with copious supplies of hot water. Next time we would have to bring our wash kits. It seemed that Brigade in their efforts to provide basic and warm accommodation to the troops made sure they were OK first. It was a typical REMF attitude and really alienated the infantry on the front line. I know that our tough training and ability to operate and survive in harsh conditions was a big factor in why we were the best infantry in the world, but it didn't mean that we wanted to be treated better than anyone else in the army – equal would have been nice.

On the way back to the Rovers we noticed a US Army Humvee. It was the first time we had seen one close up, so we had a good look around it. It was a beast of a 4 × 4, but we were surprised to see that despite being almost twice the size of a Land Rover it was still only a four-seater. It also didn't have a Day-Glo orange panel on the roof to identify it as one of ours from the air. Maybe the US Air Force had given up shooting their own.

There was some personal kit in the back, but to our amazement an M4 Colt Commando lay on the front passenger seat. We would never be without our personal weapon and never leave it lying around, but then again it was the Yanks. One of our less scrupulous privates wanted to take the M4 as a souvenir, but before he could get the door open we spotted the owner coming back and moved away. He was a black major and one of the biggest soldiers I had ever seen, a bit like Arnold Schwarzenegger in *Predator*. The Yank didn't seem to notice us skulking around and after throwing a big bundle of maps and files got in and drove off towards the main entrance. We watched as he drove out of the base and disappeared without an escort. Instead of learning from the UN's hard earned experience it looked like the Yanks would be learning the hard way.

We left as soon as we had the guns filled and made our way back to Mrkonjić Grad to make it in time for dinner. While we were there I tried to get a pair of Matterhorn boots but the Support Company stores had only been given a certain amount of each size and they had no eights left. I asked for the next size up or down but the colourboy refused to give me boots that were the wrong size as he would be held responsible if they caused any medical problems. A conscientious CQMS was a rare animal but he had a point.

For those of us in Main it was a very busy period. Even though more troops had been promised for the British contingent, we still only had two infantry battalions and four cavalry squadrons in the British AOR to man the checkpoints, carry out patrols and enforce the peace. We had the back-up of engineers, signals and artillery, but the vast majority of the British manpower was in logistics and staff. It sounded good that we had over ten thousand personnel attached to IFOR, but only about 20 per cent were actually involved in policing the British AOR. A few thousand were Royal Navy and RAF that were supporting ops from bases and ships outside the Balkans. We had an area roughly the size of Kent to look after and a Confrontation Line the length of the M2. We were severely overstretched on the ground and often carried out jobs with vastly reduced numbers that ideally should have been done by other units.

That evening I was dicked to stag on at the main entrance to the factory. For me it wasn't unexpected but it was annoying all the same, as sleep would have to wait for another day. Unfortunately for some of the guard it was a major change in the way they had worked in theatre, and probably anywhere else. There were six of us and all JNCOs. A Signal Platoon full screw was guard commander and an AGC full screw was 2I/C. The rest of us were made up of me, another signaller, our Intelligence Corps analyst and a RAMC medic. None of us would normally be employed as security for Main as we had dedicated roles, but it highlighted the acute shortage of manpower we had, especially with leave well under way. Those of us in the Signal Platoon took it in our stride; we were well used to being messed around and knew the futility of arguing. Jack, our Int Corps analyst, didn't mind too much and quite enjoyed the chance to do something else and break up the repetitiveness of his job, but the AGC clerk thought this was a complete waste of his highly trained admin skills. The medic, though, complained incessantly, as he was supposed to be a non-combatant and the Geneva Convention didn't allow him to bear arms except to protect himself. He was told to take off his Red Cross armband, stop whinging and get outside and protect himself. He got no sympathy from us and after an hour outside in the freezing cold wasn't able to moan any more, which made us all much happier.

We did an hour outside then three off. That gave us three stags between the four sentries during the twelve hours we were on duty. As usual, the guard commander and 2I/C didn't actually stag on, but that didn't do anything to appease the clerk.

Normal UN SOPs for foot patrols and sentries were to hold our rifles in a non-aggressive manner; that is, with the barrels pointing down but still firmly held by the pistol grip and stock. That was supposed to give off a non-threatening message and prevent the local factions from overreacting. That had changed with the TOA, so now we carried our rifles across our chests. Outside the main building there was an iron railing about twenty-five metres long and in the middle was a gate in front of the main entrance. At the gate there was an old security hut that we now used as our own guard house. It gave a good view of anyone who wanted to enter the factory, but we needed a physical presence outside, so that meant getting cold.

My first stag was at 8 p.m. It was a clear night and there were thousands of stars in the sky. In order to try to keep warm and to stop any boredom setting in I walked up and down the front of the railings. It didn't work though. My feet soon started to tingle with the cold and the short walk back and forth wasn't that mentally stimulating. The town was livelier than most I had seen so far in Bosnia, but it was still quiet compared to back home. Most people still didn't venture out after dark due to the sub-zero temperatures and armed gangs that tended to be a bit unpredictable after a night on the slivovitz – the moonshine spirit that was distilled everywhere in the Balkans.

As we were close to the police station we did get a lot of BSA military policemen passing by. They were always in pairs and were dressed in their new blue, black and white urban camouflage uniforms. They carried folding stock AKs over their backs and wore pistol holsters on shiny leather belts. A few wore small black plastic hand-grenades as well, but why a policeman needed one was beyond me. They would often saunter up to us, then after noticing the sentry they would brace up, pull the peaks of their baseball-style caps down over their eyes and act macho. One even put on a pair of sunglasses to beef up his act – at night! They thought they looked really hard, but to us they just looked like wannabe rappers on the way to a drive-by shooting. Wankers, but dangerous wankers!

During the small hours we were the only ones outside. The streets were empty and silent. I was back on at midnight and the cold had kept the streets empty. I was wearing my arctic mitts and my woolly hat under my helmet and it was still bitterly cold. I extended my walk to include the boundary of the playground of the local school just over the way from the factory. It was the HQ of B Squadron, the Light Dragoons, who were attached to the 2LI Battlegroup. It doubled the distance I walked but it didn't do anything to shorten the time I spent on stag.

I thought back to the time when infantry battalions had Defence Platoons. They were normally made up of the older or medically downgraded members of the battalion who weren't up to the more physical jobs in the Rifle companies but could still soldier on. They would provide defence for the battalion HQ and allow the HQ personnel to do their jobs without the burden of any added duties. Defence cuts, manning control and streamlining had done away with the capability to provide a Defence Platoon, so it was left to those of us who were already overworked and should have been getting adequate rest to be able to perform our jobs efficiently. When we finished I knew that I would be out on the road as well as on radio stag. Sleep deprivation might be tolerable in short bouts, but for prolonged periods it could have dangerous consequences, especially on these roads. I really hoped I wasn't driving tomorrow. I wasn't complaining about doing the job though, well, not too much. If I wanted an easy life and better food I would have joined the RLC or the Crabs. This was an aspect of the job I had done ever since joining up many years ago, and I knew I would be doing it again some time soon.

When my hour was up, I changed over with a now not so happy Jack and went into the warmth of the security hut. As usual with night-time stags, it dragged out. We were tired when we handed over to the regimental provosts at 6 a.m. and went inside for a well-deserved fry-up and caffeine hit to wake us up.

I did drive after the sentry duty but luckily it was in the afternoon after getting a surprisingly undisturbed five hours' kip. It was restricted to picking up and dropping off the interpreters in and around Prijedor. The interpreters were mostly good-looking female Serb university students who lived locally. They were very nice and we got on with them well, but I couldn't get out of my mind that these beauties may have been involved somehow in the ethnic cleansing of the town. Before the war, Prijedor had more Muslims than Serbs, but now it was a Serb-only town. Tens of thousands of Muslims had been displaced or murdered, and it would have been naive to think that these sweet young things had not been part of the mass nationalist hysteria that the BSA gangs were hyped up on. The younger squaddies only saw something that stirred their libido and tried their best to get inside their knickers. Being a bit older and wiser, I looked at them in a different light and kept my distance.

When we got back to the Sewing Machine Factory we handed the Rovers over to one of our LOs who, together with his interpreter and protection, drove off into Serb-held territory to meet with the local commander of the BSA 43rd Brigade. The CO wasn't too happy that the B Company checkpoint at White Fang had come under heavy fire which resulted in a fire-fight when they returned fire. The local BSA Commander had been summonsed to explain why the BSA was firing on IFOR troops. I think the Serb commander was a bit shocked at the ferocity of the response – both physically and verbally. Later on I heard that A Company had come under fire at their new location in the TMP Factory, Bosanska Krupa, 20k south-east of Coralici. Tensions were definitely high.

The next day was the Serb Orthodox Christmas, which resulted in millions of rounds being fired in celebrations that lasted most of the afternoon and evening. In all locations our troops were on a heightened alert, but the Serbs, tanked up on slivovitz and pivo, refrained from celebrating too close to our locations. The next day, while the local Serbs slept off their hangovers, I was warned off to go back to H21C.

Chapter 15

Hotel To One Charlie – Part Two

The weather on Hotel Two One Charlie had changed for the better but it was still very cold. There had been hardly any snowfall and the track up to the top of the mountain was clear and dry. When we reached the clearing I noticed a few changes. Apart from the 432, a 12×12 tent had been put up close by for the accommodation. The bunker we had previously used was now leaking and waterlogged as the snow had thawed and it was constantly dripping water inside. The snow was still deep in and bordering the forests, but in the clearing and along the tracks it had reduced to about a foot deep. Walking around would be much easier and hopefully it would mean dryer feet. The downside was that defence stores were still not present. We should have had the minimum of a barbed-wire perimeter fence by now but in the excitement of the battalion's move the Rebro was still forgotten about.

I was about to say how quiet it was now when I realised that the dogs Mags and Rebro were no longer a fixture of the Rebro. I wondered what had happened to them. Maybe they found their way home or went for a walk in the mined forest and never came back. Or maybe Bully supplemented his diet with a bit of fresh? He did look a lot fatter than when I last saw him!

For my return to H21C I was given Private Benny Benton as my driver/operator. Benny was a cheerful lad from Telford and one of the jokers in the platoon. He was popular with the lads and I got on with him well. He was also one of the brighter members of the platoon and had even invented a new smaller and lighter crew box for connecting headsets to the radios in an APC. It was on trial and he was hoping that it would be accepted. After we formally handed over and everyone drove off, we settled down to organising our kit. We had stopped off in Mrkonjić Grad and stocked up with loads of frozen food, water and milk, which we laid out in the snow to keep fresh. We also took some ten-man boxes, but I hoped we wouldn't need to use much of it as we were promised frequent resupplies.

Inside the 12×12 we organised a fold-away table as our cooking area and put up our US camp-beds on the opposite side. We remoted a loudspeaker and handset to inside the tent and lit the kero heaters. We stowed our kit on our beds and went outside so that I could show Benny around.

First of all were the watchtower, POL point and toilet. Then we looked at the bunker and the mortar line. It was easier to walk around and a lot more equipment was visible now the snow was melting. I noticed more base plates, bits of uniforms and a few helmets. I was surprised that the bombs were still there though, especially as it was policy to dispose of any ordnance we found, particularly this close to a remote location.

We were fully aware of the precarious peace that presided over Bosnia, and despite that a dangerous and unreasonable armed militia were still out there. The Serbs reclaiming the Anvil knew that the HVO or BiH were not content to just let them walk back in without some form of reprisal. What that entailed was anyone's guess, whether it was armed resistance or booby-traps, but we were still exposed and located in an area that had recently been fought over and where we had confirmed activity over the last few weeks. If we now found it easier to get around, then so would the locals. The warring factions were due to withdraw to barracks in two weeks, but many of the men who fought were not from a regular army and didn't always acknowledge the commands of their superiors. Some of the armed gangs operating as Serb or Croat militia were nothing more than gangsters, using the war to increase their own power and wealth, often removing rival gangs in the process as well as carrying out some cleansing for political favours. It was these gangs who we were most concerned about, and now that the protection party wasn't available we were worried about how exposed and unprotected we were. Back at the tent, Benny prepared the jimpy and left it by the entrance. We kept the door of the 432 closed but we didn't lock it in case we needed to get inside in a hurry.

Worrying about our situation wasn't going to improve things, so we got on with the job in hand. We agreed on a stag system of eight on eight off. That would give us plenty of time to sleep and rest, as well as maintain the Rebro and monitor the net. The first night was a bit scary. We kept hearing noises which I could only assume were lumps of snow falling from the branches of the fir trees. We weren't issued with night-sights in the

Signals Platoon so didn't have the luxury of being able to check out the treeline. We didn't get much sleep at night.

Being part of a successful platoon is not just hard work – it relies on teamwork, good command and support. Word soon gets around and people start to copy your methods. An example of that was the arrival of a Royal Artillery Rebro that set up close by. They had heard of our impressive comms record and decided to emulate us by co-locating on the mountain. They had tried a few other locations but couldn't quite manage to get the coverage we had, so they parked up their 90 FFR and set up.

There was a lance bombardier and a gunner and we were glad to have another pair of rifles with us, and instead of the usual rivalry that would have resulted in us telling them to Foxtrot Oscar we welcomed them to our location. After they had established comms they set up their camp. We had expected them to put up a 9 × 9 tent on the back of their 90 FFR, just like I did in my old light-role battalion, but they put up a superb arctic bell tent. It was double lined, had a waterproof base and slept two with all their kit. Inside it was lit by a small gas lamp, which doubled up as a heater. In fact it got so warm they didn't even sleep inside their doss bags! We were jealous and doubly so when we found out it was all issue kit! They even had Thermos flasks and fibre-pile jackets on issue, while we had to do with plastic cups and woolly jumpers. Someone somewhere wasn't doing his job properly. That night, while I was wearing all my kit, and still shivering inside my doss bag trying to get to sleep, I wondered why the Army always let down the men on the front line – the PBI!

Life in the Battle Group wasn't getting any easier for the troops on the ground. The militant and hardline Serbs were trying to destablise the still fragile peace accord. A day didn't seem to go by without someone driving over a mine or rolling their vehicle over an embankment. At night we listened to reports from the checkpoints telling of sniper/celebratory fire. The 2LI checkpoints had the protection of their Warriors, and on one occasion I was on stag listening to the net when I heard the phrase that grabs everyone's attention and sends out alarm signals in their minds – 'Contact, wait out!'

With that one phrase the whole net went quiet. The airways were kept clear so that the callsign and Zero had uninterrupted comms. The B Company platoon at Grey Cat was taking machine-gun fire from some nearby bunkers. There was a pause then Zero came back and told the checkpoint that they had permission to return fire. The Section Commander on the checkpoint didn't need to be told though. He came back with a blunt reply: 'Too late, I've already given them the good news!'

It transpired that the checkpoint was taking direct and sustained machine-gun fire. The Section Commander had no option but to take out the threat. He located the position of the sniper through the Raven night-sights on the turret of the Warrior and fired a two-round burst from the Rarden cannon. The gunfire stopped and they were left in peace. The next day we were informed by Higher that a JCO OP party in a covert hide observed two bodies being taken away by an ambulance. The Fusiliers on Black Dog were not having the same success. They only had a jimpy mounted on their Saxon and it didn't have the accuracy or firepower of the Rarden. They returned fire but it was ineffective and for a few days they suffered from constant sniping. However, help was at hand as Challenger 1 tanks from the QRH were positioned in place of the Saxons. If the warring factions had learned not to mix it with a Warrior, then rocking up for a night's carefree sniping only to find a sixty-tonne monster with a huge 120mm gun pointing at you definitely made them think twice! From then on the checkpoints were a lot safer, and the lads manning them could get on with the job of controlling the movements of locals and weapons across the new inter-entity border.

A few days later we woke up and noticed some fresh footprints over by one of the tracks that led down to the village of Podrašnica. Benny was on stag, as was the Gunner, so me and the Lance Bombardier kitted up and went to investigate. We followed the footprints down the track for a hundred metres and stopped. We could still see the two Rebros but the track was beginning to descend. We checked the area with our SUSATs and saw nothing. We had a quick chat and decided to carry on slowly down the track to ensure the area was clear. About five hundred metres further on, and lower down the mountain, we came across a junction in the track. We stopped and checked again with our SUSATs. The track that joined ours was small and not on the map, and was probably cut out for the woodsmen. A little bit further on I spotted an unusual bump on the ground. We moved forward again and moved up to it. At first it just looked like a rut in the earth, but as we got closer we could see a distinctly human shape partially covered in snow. As we got closer we saw that it wasn't one but two very thin bodies, still dressed in camouflage suits and lying on their backs. They were dressed in JNA camouflage with BSA badges on their arms. Their faces were a bluey white and their skin had shrunk around their facial features. Their arms were tied behind their backs and each had a small neat black hole in the side of their head. I looked at the Lance Bombardier. His face was expressionless and he spoke very quietly.

'The poor fuckers were executed. They were POWs but they still

166

slotted 'em!' He looked away and stared down the track. The dead Serbs had been preserved by the snow and ice. I wondered how many more bodies would be appearing because of the thaw.

I made a note of the grid reference and we carried on down the track. At the bottom was the village, the same one that had been shot up when I was last on H21C. It had suffered badly, worse than any village I had seen in Bosnia. Most houses were in ruins, some just badly shot up, some flattened. As we got closer we saw thousands of pieces of discarded and boxed military kit scattered around. There were hand-grenades, bombs, shells, missiles, bits of webbing, magazines, loose rounds, anti-tank and personnel mines, empty cases of all sizes, body parts, broken AKs, rocket-propelled grenades, dead horses, dogs and a few pigs. The place was a scene of total devastation and stank to high heaven. The Lance Bombardier picked up a Serb flag from the rubble. It had a few bullet holes in it and I could clearly see the Serbian nationalist acronym of four 'c's around an Orthodox cross. Only unity saves the Serb. They obviously weren't that unified here.

We went over to one of the houses to check for recent signs of activity. In the garden were an old metal framed kid's trike and some dolls. A few old Soviet-style helmets lay on the ground as well, but the thing that really caught my eye was the small black plastic PNM-1 anti-personnel mines that were scattered around the front door. The tops were all exposed making them look like discarded shoe-polish tins. They were probably put there hurriedly by the retreating BSA to catch out the advancing HVO. We spotted more black dots like this outside most houses. The insides of the houses probably had some more surprises for whoever ventured inside, but now that the area was being handed back to the Serbs they would be harming or killing their own. It just went to show how indiscriminate mines are.

As we saw no sign of life we returned up the mountain. Back at the Rebro I called in the grid of the dead bodies and mentioned the munitions in the village. Because of the lack of response to the mortar line, I didn't expect any major response. I did hear on the net later on that day that at least one of our Recce patrols had found the bodies and tagged them with mine tape. This was so that the same bodies were not recorded twice and a record of the location would be noted and passed on to the local Serb or Bosnian authorities so that the families could repatriate and bury their dead.

Even though we didn't see anyone on our recce we were still aware that we were exposed when it came to protection. It was the third time I had

had visitors while on this site and we needed to do something to deter them. I went over to the mortar line and picked up the box of PMR anti-personnel mines. We walked about one hundred metres and staked out about half a dozen of each across the track that led off the mountain, and repeated it on the track leading down the other side, but left the road clear as we knew we would get visitors from that direction – our own resupplies. We deliberately exposed the pineapple casings and tripwire so that they would be visible even if it snowed, and staggered them so that there wasn't any room to pass either side. We didn't want to kill or maim anyone, just deter them from getting too close, so we left out the explosive charges. Plus we might have had to bug out that way ourselves. From a few metres away you couldn't tell that the tops were just stuffed with a twig holding the tripwire, and we hoped that would do the job.

The weather remained stable over the next week and allowed us to stay outside in the fresh air for longer than normal. After weeks of going without a proper shower we didn't smell too great, and this, combined with the cooking smells, meant the inside of the tent was starting to ming. It was still freezing at night though, so we took some of the JNA-issue blankets from the mortar line and hung them from the inside of the tent to act as a form of insulation. The two layers on the gunners' bell tent worked, so we tried to copy them. It seemed to work, and even meant that our night-time stags were not done from inside our doss bags but we could sit on one of our fold-away canvas chairs. We still had to be well wrapped up all the same.

It wasn't just the checkpoint duties that were hazardous in nature. A provision of the Peace Accord was that all forces from the warring factions had to remove themselves from areas that were handed over to other factions. In the area of the 2LI Battle Group's AOR we had the problem that a huge area of land under the control of the Muslim–Croat alliance was being handed back to the Serbs. Units of HVO and BiH militia were still in the Anvil and had to make their way back to their own lines. Unfortunately, not everyone was happy about this and tensions were high. Some of the armed gangs had taken control of profitable legal and black-market businesses and were forced to leave most of them behind. There were also legitimate businesses owned by Bosnians or Serbs that were now on the wrong side of the Confrontation Line. This resulted in resentment towards IFOR and they were not that keen to cooperate with us.

As I have mentioned before, we were dangerously thin on the ground. We were still desperately short of assets that could patrol and enforce the Peace Accord, and one of the conditions was about to make that job much

168

harder. On D+30 (19 January 1996) a four-kilometre buffer zone was set up along the Confrontation Line. Called the Zone of Separation, or ZOS, it was a weapons- and troops-free zone that separated the warring factions and prevented them from sniping at each other. To help police it, a new MNB became operational. 2 (Canadian) MNB took responsibility of the area to the west and to help them settle in quickly were given A and B Company 2LI, as well as B Squadron Light Dragoons and half a squadron of Challengers from the Queen's Royal Hussars. To compensate, we were given C Company from the 1RRF Battle Group, as well as 127 Battery RA, who operated the powerful AS90. I had to keep amending our CEI to cope with the changes and it became a mess of scribbled notes.

So the companies and squadrons from the Battle Groups were given AORs, and then they were divided between the platoons and troops. Apart from key points like HQs and checkpoints on the Confrontation Line, the platoons had to patrol vast areas, especially in the ZOS, and show a larger-than-life presence. In order to do this they mounted vehicle and foot patrols. The Warriors and Saxons of the infantry patrolled giving the impression that they were loaded with fully armed troops, while the troops that should have been in the back were patrolling another location on foot.

Overhead, Chinooks with underslung Scimitars flew far and wide dropping off recce patrols. We knew that the various militia groups would record our troop movements, and then forward them on to their own Higher Command. As their command and control was pretty basic we knew that each sighting would be sent to their various commands and assessments of our dispositions would be made without being verified. A recce patrol from 2LI might be recorded in one area, then picked up by Chinooks and flown to another and recorded there. At the same time, Warrior patrols and foot patrols were recorded and passed on. It was in this way that we managed to mislead the various factions and convince them that we had twice the number of assets on the ground than we actually did.

The recce patrols in particular were used extensively as the CVRTs were fast and highly mobile. Like the companies, they, too, were overworked and were carrying out their tasks to the point of exhaustion. A patrol from C Squadron the Light Dragoons investigating faction activity on the Viterog Ridge on the southern edge of the Anvil came across a tree laid out across the track. It was a classic sign of mines but it was sometimes used as a bluff to frustrate the UN and now IFOR. The normal drill was to dismount and carry out a painstaking physical search but the

169

Troop Commander became impatient and decided to call the bluff. As the Spartan drove over the tree it set off a TMM1 which blew the CVRT onto another one. The petrol fuel tanks ruptured and a fire quickly started. A trooper from another vehicle tried to get to the crew but had to be held back by his oppos just as ammo started to cook off. It was a difficult decision for the Troop 2I/C to make but they risked losing more men if they rushed in head first. The area had to be cleared of mines first and the exploding ammo made it suicidal to approach. When the Spartan was finally safe to reach, the crew were dead. I know it's only speculation, but the Dragoons were probably overtired and under immense pressure to complete their allotted tasks, forcing an error in judgement. It was a blow to the Light Dragoons but they were a very professional unit and carried on supporting their Battle Groups wherever and whenever they were required. It highlighted the pressure we were under and the risks we were all taking to ensure the Peace Accord didn't fail.

I looked out of the tent and saw the red paint marks around the edge of the clearing. The snow had melted, reducing the level and making the marks more visible. I shuddered when I remembered taking a clearance patrol past those same trees. Bosnia was a dangerous place to lose concentration.

After two weeks we began to realise that our days on the mountain were numbered. The 2LI Battle Group had moved from the Sewing Machine Factory to a factory in Banja Luka and as a result the comms plan was changing. We were too far away to be of any use now, and to keep a Rebro so close to Mrkonjić Grad would be a luxury we couldn't afford. The Artillery Rebro packed up after ten days on the mountain, and a few days later we were given the order to prepare to move. We packed away everything except the antennas and carried on working inside the 432 until the RSWO came up and formally closed down the site. We took down the antennas and masts and drove away from Hotel Two One Charlie for the last time.

Chapter 16

Banja Luka and the Metal Factory

We drove up to our new Battle Group HQ location as it was getting dark. The countryside was wet and the roads were muddy from the constant military traffic. We drove through the main gates at the back of the Metal Factory and parked the vehicles at the rear of the huge factory building. We unpacked our personal kit and walked into the dark interior. It was like walking into the biggest fridge in the world. It was so cold that we immediately wanted to go back outside. We stopped by a tent and were told it was the Signal Platoon accommodation. There was light coming from the inside so we opened the flap to see who was at home. Sure enough, some of the lads from the platoon were there and we went inside. The tent was made from connecting two 12×12s together and there were a few metal bed frames and US camp-beds scattered around the sides and a table and bench seats in the middle. It was joked that the iron beds came from an abandoned mental home and I could well believe it. Myself and Benny found a spot and set up our camp-beds. While we did this two of our corporals, Jock Downing and Daz Woods, were arguing with each other while trying to light a cast-iron stove that someone had rescued from a bombed-out building. Dave Belshaw was putting on his body armour and webbing. He looked shagged out and didn't even look up when we entered. There were a few lads asleep in their doss bags and another, the ever-smiling Lance Corporal Roger Moore, was putting away his wash kit and hanging up his towel.

It took me about half an hour to get squared away. I asked if anyone could tell me where I could wash up and Roger Moore told me to hang on for a few minutes and he would show me when he went on duty.

Back outside the tent, we walked in the opposite direction to the one we came in by and came up to three toilet cabins at the opposite end of the factory. My eyes were getting used to the dim interior of the hangar-like space and I looked around. There were a dozen rows of tents alongside a huge rusting machine that used to roll steel plate. Along the outside wall to the left were some smaller 12×12 and 9×9 tents that were being used as SNCO and female accommodation. Roger was poking his head into a 9×9 and I saw why he managed to keep smiling while everyone else was getting fed up with the crap accommodation. His AGC wife of less than a year was in there and he was getting a quick hug and kiss before he went to work. Now that's how to go to war!

Roger walked off towards the huge hangar doors at the front of the building and disappeared through a small door to the side. At the front of the factory was a two-storey office set up. Some of the offices on the upper level were being used as officers' accommodation as well as for a RMP detachment. On the lower level I saw the Support Company storeman locking up one of the office doors so they must have set up there.

The toilets were exactly the same as those in the Brick Factory in Kiseljak, too few and no hot water. I was desperate for a shower and a proper shave, so I put up with the cold water and scrubbed away. The floor was wet and muddy from constant use and there was nowhere to hang my clothes so I put them on the sink. After staying under the water for as long as I could bear I got out and dried off. My trousers had fallen onto the floor and now had a wet arse but all my other clothes were dirty and waiting to be washed, so I put them back on and suffered the discomfort. At least I felt a bit better after the wash, and walking back to the tent I got that false feeling of warmth you get after going from one really cold area into a less cold one.

Back in the tent, the fire was blazing away and throwing out heat for about a metre, so there was a gang of the lads crowding around it shoulder to shoulder, with their arms outstretched and rubbing their hands. Mac McGee walked in and gave me a bear hug.

'Les, yer fookin' wanker. Yer dinna get eaten by a grizzly, man!'

I suppose he was pleased to see me, but he was a strong fucker and took the wind out of me. It was time for scoff so after I got my breath back, we grabbed our eating irons and mugs, picked up our rifles and walked over to the cookhouse.

Outside the factory building was another single-storey building that was used as Battalion HQ, and because it had a kitchen and canteen area we used it as our cookhouse. Inside there was a long servery manned by our own cooks, and opposite that was a seating area that could seat a couple of hundred. From the new appearance and quality of materials used in construction I would say that the factory was built in the last ten years and was spared the usual Communist meddling that made everything look like it was old before it was opened. It looked like it had been built by a European construction company, or at least had a European design team, and was much more modern than all the other large industrial buildings I had been in so far in the Former Yugoslavia. We took off our berets and queued up with about a hundred others. I took some very decent chicken curry and poppadums that would instantly unblock my compo-lined innards and followed Mac to a table near the back. A few of the other lads from the Sigs Platoon sat down with us and we caught up on events and gossip.

Foremost in the minds of everyone was the Light Dragoon Spartan that ran over a mine. It wasn't the only one of our vehicles to have run over a mine, but it was the first with fatalities. It had taken three days to be able to get to the bodies. The force of the explosion and the fire had combined to cook off the thousands of rounds of ammo for the jimpy, which meant the medics had to wait until long after the last bang before they could risk entering. The sniping on the checkpoints had stopped and most of the warring factions were on the right side of the ZOS. Finding dead bodies and mass graves was becoming a common occurrence, and our medics had a full-time job examining them after the RE had cleared them for booby-traps. News crews from around the world were covering their discoveries, as well as the prisoner exchanges that were taking place at the various checkpoints along the Confrontation Line. Operations to police the ZOS were also successful. Heavy weapons were stopped trying to cross the IEBL, and foot patrols were stopping armed gangs and individuals from crossing and confiscating their weapons.

In the Signal Platoon we were getting used to operating in a more formal set-up. Main and Tac were combined now and it was getting to be like a Brigade HQ with an abundance of spare Ruperts milling around. Gone was the relaxed but professional attitude of being on operations and in its place was a more regimental approach. We still had two Rebros out in the field, but most of our work was in the Metal Factory. That meant that despite having lads on leave we still had bods to spare, so they were given to whoever needed them. Escorting LOs and interpreters was one job that seemed to get more volunteers than usual, as it was a way of escaping the bullshit of being around the BGHQ. Apart from that there were the usual runs to HQ 4th Armoured Brigade at Sipovo and HQ MND(SW) at Gornji Vakuf, as well as the Rebro resupply runs.

One of our Rebros was on a desolate mountain next to the Serb Lisina

Radar Complex. After the close-run thing on H21C, we took resupplying the Rebros more seriously. Apart from the comms aspect, we had to look after the lads on them.

After arranging transport, we would load up with food, water, fuel, mail and personal supplies like cigs, then take a trip up to the Rebro. It was normally a fairly good run, despite the cold. On one resup we travelled in two Warriors and as we started the climb up the mountain track we ran into a blizzard.

The drivers couldn't see the road, and up in the turret we couldn't either. Visibility was down to a few metres and we couldn't afford to veer off the track because of the mine threat. We slowed down to a crawl and had to guide the driver forward by hanging over the sides of the turret to ensure we didn't get too close to the edge. We tried to stop and wait for better weather, but the moment we stopped the Warrior started to slide backwards. There was no option so we kept going and hoped that we wouldn't bump into the Warrior in front as it slid back into us or into another vehicle on its way down. I'm glad we were speaking on intercom and not on the net because the airwaves would have been the darkest shade of blue!

It was a nerve-wracking ascent and when we reached the Rebro we joined the crew of the lead Warrior inside the 12×12 at the back of the Rebro. The tent was being buffeted by high winds and we helped stack boxes of ten-man ration packs and jerrycans of water on the rubber flaps on the bottom of the canvas to stop the tent flying away. We waited for about two hours for the storm to die out before we ventured outside.

The Warriors were totally covered in snow and the track had disappeared, but the sun had come out and the dark clouds that accompanied the blizzard were drifting away. We mounted up and slowly headed back down the mountain. We passed a Royal Artillery CP for 26 Regiment, and lower down we came across a Canadian Rebro, with two Bison APCs and a tent. One of the Canadians was outside and waved for us to stop. He came over and asked us if we could wait so he could get his camera. We stopped and let him take some snaps, and then he invited us into their Rebro for a coffee.

A British squaddie doesn't need an excuse to stop and chat so we pulled over and went inside. We couldn't believe the difference between our Rebro and theirs. It was set up in the equivalent of two 12×12s, much like our platoon tent back in the Metal Factory. They had wooden pallets for a floor and had four camp-beds with lockers, an eating area with table and chairs, a cooking area with a gas cooker, and for entertainment they had a TV, video and a collection of just released films. It was like a holiday camp compared to any of our set-ups and we started to feel like refugees being offered a kindness by some strangers.

There were four men on the Rebro and two were on stag inside their Bison APCs, while the other two rested and cooked for them. We were given coffee, tea, and, most surprisingly, freshly cooked cheese burgers! We were stunned at the set-up and couldn't help looking around in amazement. The Canadians must have taken this for a look of dismay because one of them then told us he was sorry for the appearance of the tent, and the coconut matting for the floor was on its way. We had to laugh and told him to visit our Rebro at the top of the mountain. He said he would love to visit the Brits as he had Scottish grandparents. I would have loved to see the look on his face as soon as he walked inside the shit-hole that the world's finest infantry were living in!

A few days later the Signal Platoon lads based in the Metal Factory were called together for a brief on what we were going to do for the next few weeks barring any emergencies. It was headed by the RSO, and it was the first time since I had been in Bosnia that I had seen him for more than five minutes. Captain Winston-Davies, or WD as we called him, was tall and was as laid-back as you could be without falling over. He was very affable and everyone liked him. He was sitting on a camp-bed and began by congratulating us on a job well done, but reminded us that we were still only halfway through the tour. He explained the comms plan and how we still had a very important job to do. Next, Serjeant Walters took over and went through our duties for the next week. Basically, we had to cover Rebro resupplies and man the radios and a field telephone network, as well as carry out much needed maintenance to our mixed fleet of vehicles. This would mean two or three duties a day, depending on tasking.

It was decided in the Ops Room we would need two people during the day and one at night. During the day we would stag on the radio for two hours at a time and be available for other duties as directed. On the telephones, as it was less stressful, the stag would be for four hours at a time. At night, from 10 p.m. until 6 a.m. one person would be on 'drag stag', so called because with the lack of activity in the Battle Group it would drag on and on! We would, of course be assisted by a watchkeeper, but sometimes that was more of a hindrance than a help.

KD called out those who were to go out on the Rebros first, then those on radio stag, and then those on the telephone exchange. The resupply runs and escort duties would take their manpower from those not on stag.

I was down to run the telephone exchange for the next week, along with two others, Lance Corporal West and a private.

After we had been dismissed, Westy almost ran over to KD and started grousing that he should be in charge and not me. After all, he had been in the Sigs Platoon longer than me and I was a bin lid! I couldn't believe what I was hearing. Westy was not a signaller but came to the Signal Platoon as a gunner for the 2I/C's Warrior, so he wasn't even able or trained to run a telephone exchange. I had commanded a Sigs Det in my old battalion, commanded Rebros in theatre and had proved my worth to a very demanding RSWO, who wouldn't have used me if I was pants. But KD looked exhausted and was probably too tired to argue, so he relented and changed the duty roster. Westy looked all pleased with himself and sauntered off. KD pulled me aside and said don't worry, let him think that he's in charge but keep an eye on the kit. I was disappointed that KD had let Westy's childish outburst go by but shrugged my shoulders and agreed. After all, they had to work together after I left the battalion. It was just a stag on a telephone exchange and not a ticket back to Paderborn!

Westy came back and gave me a piece of paper with a scrawl that was supposed to represent handwriting. It was my stag times and I noted that he had thoughtfully put himself down for all the midday stags, with me and the private alternating on the others. The next day I went over to the Ops room and sat down by the exchange. The exchange was set up to provide comms throughout the factory complex so that all the sub units and locations like the Guard at the Main Gate could be easily reached, reducing the need for runners. It was a very quiet stag, as there was only one call from the RMP Det for a comms check as they had inadvertently unplugged the D10 and wanted to see if they had put it back with the right polarity.

Westy was on next and sat down in front of the exchange. I told him the state of the kit and showed him the almost empty logbook and walked off. I hadn't even got to the door when Westy called me back. He looked a little embarrassed and waited until everyone was out of earshot. I wasn't expecting an apology for his little tantrum – you rarely get them in the Army – but I was very surprised when he asked me to show him how the exchange worked. I should have walked out and left him to stew, but KD had realised that this would happen and had asked me to look after the kit. I didn't want Westy breaking it because he didn't know how to operate it or make the platoon look stupid, so I sat down next to him and gave him a demonstration just like a good Green Jacket would. I couldn't believe this was the same Westy I had gone drinking with in Paderborn and had classed as a friend. He used to hurry me up when we were getting ready to go out and loved it in the company of the new lads. Now I could see that it was just an act and he probably spent his entire Army career hanging about with different groups and never really making friends.

I left Westy to his new command and went to pick up my wash bag. I cold-showered again and changed into a clean set of combats, something that I tried to do every few days now that I could get my kit washed whenever I needed. That afternoon I was dicked to accompany an LO while he visited one of the local BSA Brigades. I got kitted up and joined the others by a 90 and VPK outside the HQ block. While we waited for the LO I went into the cookhouse and managed to get some horror boxes for lunch. I was detailed to go in the VPK, but not as driver as I hadn't done a conversion course on it. I didn't understand the need really, it might be a bit heavier with all the add-on fibre-glass panels but was still a Land Rover underneath. I gave Zero a radio check and we moved off.

We left the Metal Factory and drove south from Banja Luka towards the ZOS. We stopped at a RRF base at the Krupa Hydroelectric Dam so that the LO could get the latest int on the local BSA units and continued south towards the ZOS. We passed by a few burnt-out and wrecked armoured vehicles. We stopped to look at one in particular. It was a Sherman tank, as used in the D-Day landings. I'm not sure how it ended up here but after surviving World War Two it had finally met its match along the banks of a Bosnian river.

We did a tour of all the local villages near Black Dog and waited by the Rovers while the LO went inside makeshift faction HQs and visited the local Brigade commanders. A brigade to NATO usually meant two or three infantry battalions, with a tank regiment, recce regiment, artillery regiment, engineer, signals and logistics squadrons, commanded by a brigadier, totalling close on three thousand men. In Bosnia, it could be fifty or a hundred men, with little or no supporting arms, commanded by the local warlord who called himself anything from colonel to general. So the presence of three or four brigades in a relatively small area didn't really add up to a major force. That said, two Land-Rovers wasn't exactly a show of strength either, but I suppose having the balls to show up in them was!

We got back to the Metal Factory just in time for me to get some scoff before everything was gone. There was a tall Fusilier waiting just inside the entrance and I recognised him from a course I attended a few years previously in Pirbright. His name was Mem Kavaz and I remembered him because he had an unusual good-luck charm – a fluffy bunny! It was a few

177

years since I had seen him but he recognised me straight away. Together with a lad who wore a bright-blue stable belt we had taken the bunny hostage and held it for ransom. He went berserk looking for it. I asked him what was he doing here and he told me he was his OC's bodyguard and had accompanied him to visit our Ops Officer. We chatted a bit about 1RRF but he was called away by his OC before I could ask if he still had the bunny.

After scoff I sat down with a brew and caught up with a few of the old British newspapers that were lying around. I felt kind of detached when I read about things back home and by the way that Bosnia was being reported. It was as if the reports were talking about another place. You couldn't get the sights, sounds or smell from those single photos or few paragraphs. Some of the stories, especially from the tabloids, were comical and surreal. They had columns of messages sent home from 'our brave lads' but they were all from REMF units in Split or Gornji Vakuf. There were none from those at the sharp end who were fighting to keep the peace. An old copy of the *Sun* showed a Light Infantry squaddie having a wash in a tin bath outside in the snow with a fire lit under it. It was an amusing photo and the squaddie was naked except for his helmet, and probably gave the public at home a good laugh, but what it didn't show was that the lads couldn't get a hot wash and that after agreeing to sit in the staged photo the lad had burned his arse in the process.

The remaining stags on the exchange were a non event and the RSWO soon realised that as there were virtually no calls it could be operated by the Ops Room staff as an extra duty. That gave us a few more bods to carry out the platoon duties and gave us a bit more time off. From a few hours a week to a few hours a night – we were really getting spoiled now!

We had a bar next to the cookhouse run by the EFI – the NAAFI on tour. Here we had a large TV and Sky satellite where we could watch Sky while enjoying the two can rule. The PRI ran the EFI and it was good for morale to be able to get small things like films for cameras and toiletries. You could also get larger items like softie sleeping bags and assault vest webbing, if you had enough money.

We didn't have access to our accounts in Bosnia – you couldn't exactly use a hole in the wall – and we were not expected to carry bundles of cash like a tourist. Instead we could draw money from the AGC. It was a simple system where we could get small sums of Deutchmarks to get a few luxuries or a beer or two. As I had spent most of the tour on Rebros, I never had the chance to withdraw much cash and never really had any on me since we arrived. Even though there wasn't much to spend it on, it still felt nice to have a few bob in your pocket. When not on duty, we spent a lot of time in this makeshift NAAFI, and often it was standing-room only as we watched *The Simpsons*, a film or a live Premiership game.

Back in the Sigs Platoon tent we were told to stop using the iron stove for heating as one had set a neighbouring tent alight. We scrounged three kero heaters and set them up in the middle of the tent. It was fine standing or sitting next to them but once you moved a few centimetres away it became cold again. Temperatures hovered around zero inside the factory during the day and the canvas tents did nothing to keep the heat in. In the next tent one of the Recce Platoon lads had bashed the bag and the piss had frozen on the outside overnight! At the back roller-shutter doors I had noticed a roll of hessian that was normally used for camouflaging wagons. I went out on a raid that evening and brought it back to the tent. Just like the two layers in the tent on H21C, I hoped that by creating an air gap between the canvas and the inside of the tent we could insulate the tent and make conditions better. A team effort had it fitted in half an hour and even though it wasn't perfect, it did make the inside temperature more comfortable. The trouble now was getting enough kerosene for the heaters.

We were told by the MT Platoon lads that ran the POL point that there was none to be had in theatre. It created a lot of anger with the infantry and cavalry units that relied on kero heaters for warmth, but for some reason the RLC were not letting us have any. On one of our trips to Brigade in Sipovo we filled up our Rovers for the return trip and asked for some cans of kerosene. The loggie told us smugly that there wasn't any in theatre and that was that. While we waited for the loggie to fill in the work ticket I nipped around the back and saw some grey-painted jerrycans full of kerosene. I grabbed a few cans and threw them into the back of the Rover before the loggie copped on. As far as I was concerned it was another dirty trick from the REMFs to maintain their lifestyle and fuck us on the front line. They had Corimec accommodation which was insulated and had fitted heaters. They had no need for the kero but kept it to fill their own heaters so they could watch videos wearing shorts and T-shirts, while we worked, rested and slept fully clothed! My co-driver looked shocked that I was taking the kero and asked whether I worried about getting caught. I looked at him and gave him the stock answer that many of the PBI used.

'What can they do? Send me to Bosnia!'

Back in our tent the lads appreciated the gesture and we set about filling the heaters. We saved one of the cans for H21D, and in case anyone decided to liberate our supply when the tent was empty, we hid them from view between the layer of hessian and the tent.

After that anytime we went to Brigade we didn't ask and just took the cans of kero and if anyone told us to stop we would gang up on them and ask if there was a problem. That way we kept the heaters on the Rebros and in our tent burning until the kero officially became available again.

It wasn't the only thing that happened around this time that really pissed us off. The RMP began to set up speed traps along the main routes to catch speeding drivers. Apparently some RMP Rupert safe in Split had decided that as the war was officially over a speed limit needed to be enforced. It was the most ridiculous thing we were told since we were told to stop waving at the kids. Vehicle patrols were still being sniped at intermittently, and the only way to prevent being hit was by driving fast. Slowing down would only increase the likelihood of getting shot.

At the same time as we heard this I met one of the Paras, Stevie Locke, in the cookhouse. We sat down together and he wasn't his usual smiley self. He was just back from a patrol with his platoon and his vehicle was sniped at half a dozen times. He was providing top cover, covering the rear when he heard rounds whizzing over his head. He picked up a headset and told the vehicle commander, but the noise of the turbo-charged engine drowned out the sound of whizzing lead. Stevie counted at least six rounds that were deliberately aimed at his Warrior but luckily none found their target. It wasn't uncommon and he had been sniped at quite a few times since his platoon started patrolling the ZOS. As no one was hit they continued on, but it made them nervous about patrolling certain areas and as a result they tended to drive through them a lot faster than normal. Stevie wasn't in shock, just a little upset at being shot at, and when I mentioned the speed checks he just looked at me as if I was taking the piss. It just went to show that to us on the front line of operations it appeared that some of those in Higher Command were living on another planet.

D+45 (3rd February 1996) saw the withdrawal of all forces from areas that were to be taken over by another faction as part of the Peace Accord. For us, on the whole, it meant the HVO and BiH moving out of areas they had captured from the BSA. It also meant that security was stepped up in all locations as tensions heightened. A very busy few days followed as we had to ensure that former enemies were allowed to travel unhindered.

In the Metal Factory security at this time was provided by C Company and Mortars, but due to the current situation most of them were out keeping an eye on things. That meant that for Signal Platoon we would have to provide bods to help out.

At the Metal Factory we had two access points, both on the same side of the access road. The Main Gate was a road entrance near the back of the complex, while closer to the main road was a Side Gate that had been the old pedestrian entrance. On 5 February, I was down as Guard 2I/C at the Side Gate. With me were five lads from the Paras, while up at the Main Gate the guard was all LI and commanded by a full screw.

The gate wasn't that busy as almost all of our visitors came by road, but we did get a few visitors, mainly locals looking for work. It was a quiet stag and we spent most of the day chatting about our tours so far. Half of them had come straight from a tour in Northern Ireland and were enjoying being Armoured Infantry; something they thought they would never get to do as trained paratroopers. They did moan about the way they were treated though, and it seemed to them that they were doing more than their fair share of the crap duties. I knew how they felt but it was useless to complain – besides, the LI outnumbered us ten to one!

That evening those not on stag started to get their heads down while the rest of us listened to Radio Big, a radio station from Banja Luka. It was as good as any commercial station back home and played some really good music. We munched away on the spam and cheese sandwiches supplied by the cookhouse and drank gallons of tea. It was turning out to be a quiet night but that was all about to change.

Just after midnight I went back to the Sigs Platoon tent to get my doss bag. On the way back I noticed flames rising from the back of the cookhouse. I ran into the guardroom and roused the men telling them to get up as we had a fire at the back of the cookhouse. Leaving two men at the gate, one who was on stag and one to call the ops room on the telephone, I sprinted over to the fire.

Rounding the corner of the building I saw that it was a four-tonner that was ablaze and it was parked a few metres from the building beside a loading bay. Flames and smoke were leaping high into the air and there was a sound of popping and crackling. Four tall red Calor gas cylinders were standing alongside the burning wagon, but my first thoughts were that someone might still be inside it. It was against SOPs, but sometimes the crews slept on board as it was warmer than the accommodation inside the factory. I didn't think about the risks and dashed up the ramp of the loading bay and tried to get as close as the heat would allow. The back was an inferno, but the cab was free of flames. I peered into the inside but it was empty. I turned around to see one of the Paras standing at the bottom of the ramp. It was Private Fluker and I told him to help me move the gas cylinders in case they went up and took the cookhouse with them.

'Bollocks to that!' came the reply as he stayed at the bottom of the ramp. I couldn't blame him but we had people inside the building and we had to get the gas bottles away from the flames. I turned back and as I got closer I noticed that the flames were licking the tops of the bottles. The paint was bubbling and catching alight. I had my NI gloves on and hoped they would be enough to protect me from the flames and heat. I grabbed the protective ring near the valve on the nearest bottle and pulled it away from the flames. The metal of the ring was red hot and I could feel it burning through the gloves. Shit, I hoped it wouldn't blow! The cylinder was heavy but I managed to drag it to the ramp before it became too painful and I had to let it go. It slid down the ramp and stopped at the feet of the nervous looking Para.

'Throw it into the snow by the fence so it can cool down!' I ran back to the next gas bottle and grabbed the ring. The flames were perilously close and licking at my combats. I was sweating and my eyes started stinging as waves of furnace-like heat radiated from the blaze. I dragged it to the ramp and let go.

Private Fluker had moved the first cylinder into a snowdrift and I could see steam rising where the hot metal was being cooled by the snow. I went back again and grabbed the third cylinder. The paint on the ring was alight so I tried to pull it away by the body but that was impossible without putting my face and arms close to the flames. I had no choice but to grab the ring and suffer later. The leather on my gloves singed and my hands stung as I pulled the cylinder away. Fluker was ready for it and stopped it with his boot as it rolled down. My heart was beating like mad when I went back for the last cylinder.

It took all my nerve to go back but I knew it had to be done. One gas bottle exploding could be as bad as four. I forgot about my burnt hands and the intense heat as I grabbed the ring and pulled it away from danger. I rolled it down to Fluker who had been joined by another of the Paras. They laid it in the snow next to the other three cylinders. Happy that at least we wouldn't be blown up, we went up to the back door of the kitchen.

By this time we had been joined by some lads from inside the kitchen, two I recognised as the HQ Company storemen who normally slept in the back. They were laughing and trying to get some fire extinguishers to work. The trouble was they were also trying not to drop the bottles of pivo they were holding. I went over to them and saw that they were steaming drunk. The mongs had been on the piss inside the kitchen while I risked my life checking to see if anyone was still on the lorry and stopping the kitchen from blowing up! I told them to get away from the fire, but they cheered as one of them got his extinguisher to work. He stood there and sprayed the whole contents at the blaze. Apart from the fact that it would have had no effect anyway, he was about two metres too far from the flames and just sprayed it into the wind.

They were becoming a nuisance, so we moved them out of the way. Private Fluker got a fire hose in the corridor to work and started to douse the fire as the Ops Officer and OC HQ Company turned up. It took about ten minutes to put out the fire completely but we kept on soaking the lorry for half an hour to prevent it sparking up again. I told one of the Paras, Private Smith, to stay outside and keep people away from the burnt-out wreck and sent the others back to the Side Gate.

The Ops Officer looked at the now shamefaced piss heads and told them to get out of his sight and report to him first thing. I went into the Ops Room and reported the fire as out and that I was returning to the Side Gate.

I took my gloves off outside and picked up a handful of snow. It stung my hands but after the initial shock started to soothe away the pain. I looked back at the smouldering remains and started to shake. Now that it was over I started to think about what would have happened if one of those gas cylinders had blown. It would have been messy all right.

I carried the snowball over to the sentry and stood there talking to him until I stopped shaking and my hands got too cold. Inside I looked at my hands in the light. Bright-red welts had appeared on my palms and fingertips and were very sore to the touch. The warmth of the room started to make them tingle painfully. My gloves stank of burning and had melted in places, making them deformed and useless. I put them in my pocket and went back outside for another snowball.

After breakfast I went into the RAP and got some cream for my hands and some pain-killers. The RAMC medic said the cream should help prevent my skin from scarring. He asked me if I wanted a sick chit, but I said I would see how things went. I figured that the pain would go pretty soon and I didn't want to make a fuss.

When we handed over at the Side Gate I was told to report to the Monkeys and make a statement. I gave them a detailed account of what happened and the Monkey wrote it down nice and slowly. The written statement was a bit shorter than my verbal description, but it covered the basics. I was too tired to argue the finer details so I signed the bottom and headed off to the Sigs tent to get my head down and forget about everything.

Over the next week the pain in my hands and scarring started to disappear and for a while having a cold shower was a blessing because getting hot water on my hands was extremely painful. I swapped my burnt pair of gloves for a new pair and wore them around for a while to help protect my tender skin. For the first week after the fire I was given the drag stag and after that it was a mix of stagging on in the Ops Room and resupplying the Rebros.

It was a busy time for the Battle Group. The Serb General Djukic was captured by BiH troops on 30 January and handed over to the ICTY. News had finally filtered down to the BSA units on the ground, which raised tensions leading to increased security, especially at small detachments like platoon outposts and Rebros. C Company left for Krupa and we formed a QRF with the 432s from Mortars. At first we thought it was a joke as the 432 was anything but quick, but they were the only spare vehicles we had. In the ZOS, patrols were sent out to verify that the remaining heavy weapons were removed and that the only armed personnel left on either side were policemen. It didn't take the Serbs long to get around this problem, they simply sewed police badges onto their soldiers' uniforms. It was strange to see a platoon-sized police unit where you might only expect the equivalent of a village bobby, and it was difficult to monitor, but having decades of experience policing the troubles in Northern Ireland, the squaddies on the ground coped well.

The peace was holding out, but the Serbs were still coming up with ways to get IFOR to overreact. At the Kosmos electronics plant in Banja Luka radar emissions were detected, but when the ARRC EW inspection team tried to gain access they were turned away. NATO didn't want their combat air patrols to be tracked and took a dim view on this. It also become known that this factory supplied refurbished radars for Iraq after the Gulf War, despite the UN embargo, so we knew the Serbs running the factory couldn't be trusted. Noticeboards started to appear outside BSA bases asking IFOR not to try and liaise under the present climate of poor relations. They didn't like it when the boot was on the other foot!

Then one evening we were queuing up for scoff and watching Sky News when we heard that the IRA had broken their two-year ceasefire and had bombed Canary Wharf on the Isle of Dogs in London. The pictures showed massive damage and there was at least one dead. The squaddies in line with me looked in disbelief at the screen. The Light Infantry had lost dozens of men to the Troubles and had hoped that they would never see a return to violence. They were due to swap with 2RGJ in Ulster and were hoping for an easy tour, full of sports, training courses and a decent family life. It looked like those hopes had just gone up in a mix of glass, steel and smoke. Now they would be back patrolling the streets and living in fear. For me it went deeper than that. London was my home and I had friends and family there. My brother-in-law Frank was a cab driver and Canary Wharf was five minutes from his office. It was a common pick-up and drop-off point. I went to junior school on the Island and used to play on the derelict land that was now part of Canary Wharf. My Aunt Nell, who had survived the Blitz, lived around the corner. It was almost personal. I left the queue and phoned my sister to make sure everyone was OK.

Chapter 17

The Search for the Renegade Anti-Aircraft Guns

I was getting used to the routine in Banja Luka, cleaner uniforms and being able to relax in the evenings for a few hours with a beer, watch a film or a Premiership match, and get a decent night's kip, when the RSWO gave me another rush job. This time it was a four-day mission in support of the Light Dragoons. AAC Lynx patrols in the northern Bosnia had been illuminated by the radar from BSA ZSU-23-4s, highly mobile and potent anti-aircraft self-propelled guns. Despite warnings by NATO to cease all radar searches, the BSA continued to flout the terms of the accord. The Light Dragoons were tasked with locating the rogue ZSUs, so that we could forcibly remove the threat from the area.

Our job was to provide comms while the Light Dragoons charged around the area looking for the bad guys. We left Banja Luka on a wet and blustery day in a three-vehicle convoy of two Warriors as escort and the Rebro crew in a Sultan CVRT. My driver/radio operator was a private called Stevie Sadler, a Middlesbrough lad who I had got on very well with back in Germany. Stevie was a good laugh and couldn't stop chatting and cracking jokes over the intercom all the way to our new location.

It took just over an hour of driving through narrow country lanes and up hills until we found ourselves in a clearing in between two villages. It was in the middle of the area where the ZSUs were operating and ideal for maintaining comms with the Light Dragoons. We immediately set up the Sultan with a 9×9 on the back while the crews from the Warrior found a good spot for the antennas on a hill close by. The clearing was covered in a light-brown stony claylike mud, but the hill behind us was still covered in a metre of snow. It had very steep sides and the crews struggled to get the eight-metre masts up to the top. I took the coaxes from the wagon and climbed up the hill with them. It was a bitch of a climb, and I kept slipping back as I tried to gain a foothold after each step. At the top I managed to pass on the coaxes before I slipped and tobogganed back down on my arse.

It was very rocky under the snow and I had a bad bruise on one of my cheeks that made it quite sore to sit down for many hours. I was fortunate though, because one of the Warrior crewmen came down in the same manner a few minutes later, but this time he ended up with a broken leg. He was carried into the back of a Warrior and had to wait in quite some pain until we had established comms and formally came on air.

After the escort left, Stevie and I set up our living space in the 9×9 and sorted out our kit. We would stag on in the wagon and sleep in the tent. It was cold in the back so we set up an iron stove that we had brought along. We found some branches, chopped them up and dried them out on the engine grille on the front of the Sultan before getting a fire going. It warmed up the tent nicely and made it comfortable to operate in. I was boiling up some water with some boil-in-the-bag rations when Stevie came inside the tent and told me we had a visitor. I looked out the back of the tent and saw a man walking by with an AK47 tucked under his arm.

We didn't want to alarm him so I nodded and he nodded back. He was in his twenties and was wearing a worn JNA combat jacket and jeans. Stevie asked me what we were going to do about it. My first thought was he had come to check us out. He could have lived near by, but he could have been sent by the local BSA unit. Why else would he be carrying an AK? I told Stevie not to worry too much but stay alert just in case he came back with some friends.

With that Stevie got up into the commander's position on the Sultan and cocked the jimpy. He jumped back down and grinned at me,

'Just in case!' I couldn't agree more.

When we were dicked to go on this Rebro, I had asked for protection again. The RSWO told me we didn't have the manpower and, besides, he had only agreed to provide the Rebro if the Light Dragoons protected it. We could hear them on the net now and then but as yet we hadn't seen them. Maybe they would use our location as a base and stay here overnight, which would be better than nothing. I told Stevie to get on the net and let Zero know we had armed locals in the vicinity while I went for a quick clearance patrol.

I didn't go far, as I was on my jack, but it was important to get to know our surroundings in case we were bumped and needed to make a hasty getaway. Like previous patrols I had one up the spout of my rifle, but this time I knew we had an unsavoury-looking character with an AK walking about, so I wanted to have the upper hand if he started blatting off a few 7.62 shorts. To our right was a long and straight path about fifty metres long that led to a fork. The left-hand path led on to a cluster of houses that wasn't on the map; the right-hand one disappeared into the forest. To the left of the Rebro was a bend in the road that led back down to the main dirt track that we came up on. Just below the bend was another collection of houses. I looked down at the houses and noted that despite four years of war not one of them showed any signs of damage. We were in a Serb-dominated area and I guessed that the fighting hadn't reached this far north or that the neighbours were all in the four C's club. There were a few trickles of smoke coming out of the chimneys which showed that they were occupied. I looked around and noticed an old man walking towards me in the trees. He stopped a few metres away and stared at me. He didn't show any sign of panic and I guessed he was coming over to check out the noises our vehicles had made. He was skinny and pale and was smoking a thin roll-up. He wore an old brown boiler suit, high-leg leather boots and a grey fleece hat, but the thing that really caught my eye was the old Russian bolt action rifle he was cradling in his arms. He looked too old to have fought in this war but he might have been issued the rifle to fight the Germans in the Second. He didn't move but kept staring at me. It was unlikely he had ever seen a British soldier before and was probably wondering if I was a Croat or a Muslim. I didn't want him to panic him into a rash action, so I slowly raised my right hand and waved to him. He raised his right hand but instead of a wave he took a pull from his roll-up. I smiled and stepped back, and he did the same, but without the smile. I took it as a sign that he knew I wasn't an old enemy and we both walked away from each other.

Back at the Rebro I told Stevie about the old man and called in the news to Zero. This time Zero acknowledged our message and asked the Light Dragoons to acknowledge as well. I was happy that at last the presence of armed men in the vicinity of our location was taken seriously, especially as relations with the BSA were very low, and hoped that the Dragoons realised the huge risk we were taking for them.

I spent the next few hours chopping firewood and putting it on the engine cover to dry. Stevie stood in the commander's hatch leaning on the jimpy and smoking while he listened to the net on the loudspeaker. It was exhausting work chopping the wet branches and wasn't made easy when the wooden helve snapped in half. With that I decided we had enough wood for tonight, so I cleaned up and packed away ready to take over from Stevie.

I took my seat in the spacious interior of the Sultan and went through my equipment checks. It was getting colder, so Stevie made a brew and filled up the burner. He was fast asleep and snoring contentedly when I called Zero to ask when we should expect the Light Dragoons back. It was a good half-hour before Zero came back and told me that they had already harboured up for the night. I didn't hear anything on the net, so I guessed they had forgotten about us in the excitement of the chase. We were left alone, deep in Serb territory, without protection. I wondered if a Rebro would have been left unprotected in the hills of South Armagh. I doubted it, and Bosnia was a hundred times more dangerous. A burst of machine-gun fire in the distance reinforced my fears.

I got up in the commander's hatch and peered into the darkness. I wondered what was out there. This area had been cleansed of all non-Serbs and there were a lot of people who had something to hide. We knew they were afraid of us finding mass graves or catching those responsible. Even those who had stood by and watched as their neighbour was killed or taken away were worried that they might be named by survivors as conspirators. They didn't know our mission and might think we were part of a coordinated search for war criminals. And from the impromptu recce by AK man I had to assume that the local band of Serb brothers knew we were here. Would they take things into their own hands and disrupt the search by taking out our comms? It was one of the possibilities that were niggling at me.

Another was that the Serbs might try to force IFOR into over-reacting to a small incident and so get the world's media to see NATO as an aggressor of the poor peace-loving Serb peoples. That could happen by taking out a soft target like our Rebro. Maybe the intentional radar tracking by the ZSUs was a ruse to get us out here? We had taken many risks since we arrived in theatre – maybe our luck was running out? It was the fear of the unknown that worried me and made me more than a little frightened about what could happen.

I sat for a few hours in the commander's hatch listening to the net just as Stevie had a few hours earlier. I looked around us. We were by the side of a track and there were woods close by on all sides. If we were bumped they would be on top of us in no time and we would have little chance of reacting. Maybe now wasn't a good time to wonder about *what if*! It was pointless to stay on lookout scaring myself shitless, so by about half one, when the cold became too unbearable and I couldn't feel my fingers, I got inside the wagon and closed the hatch. I took my new NI gloves off and put my hands on the warm casing of one of the 353s. My fingers tingled painfully as the blood started to surge through them once again.

Stevie was up at two and took over on the net. I told him we were still on our jack and he shrugged sleepily. I presumed from his demeanour he was either waiting for his brain to catch up or he wasn't at all surprised. I left him to start the engine while I unrolled my doss bag. I was exhausted and didn't worry about the noise of the exhaust blowing away outside the tent a few feet above me. I closed my eyes and tried to forget about the nocturnal activities of the BSA.

I slept fitfully and woke up at first light. The first thing I did was go outside and take a stroll around the site. Everything looked fine so I went back into the 9 × 9 and put a brew on. I chatted to Stevie about what we should do, as it looked like we would be stuck out here on our own. We decided that it would be best to look non-threatening and carry on as normal. So we started the day by hanging the speaker on the back of the tent and having breakfast al fresco. We were surprised when we spotted a local walking down the track. He was old, small, very skinny and wearing an old and crumpled grey suit. We waved as he passed and he waved back. I looked at my watch; it was coming up to 7 a.m. We had a few more passers-by that day, but later that day while I was trying to chop wood with the broken axe the man in the suit came back. He stopped and watched as I struggled with the heavy blade and stumpy handle. He came over and spoke to me in Serbo-Croat. I said '*Dobro dan*' ('Good day') and after looking in my small green Nirex orders book said, '*Zdravo, ja sam Englez.*' He grinned at my attempt to say 'Hello, I am English' and carried on talking. It was my first real go at talking in Serbo-Croat and it was obvious I needed some practice. I couldn't understand him but from his gesturing I guessed that he wanted the axe. I handed it over and he proceeded to hack away at the branches I had gathered. He had a great technique and in no time had chopped up more than I had managed in two hours. Stevie was pissing himself with laughter that an old man twice my age and half my size had shown me how to chop wood.

I thanked the man and tried to give him five Deutschmarks for his troubles. He shook his head and said no. But it was the least I could do: I would have been there for another two hours hacking away for less and I was getting very bored with it. I spoke to the man in German and told him thank you. He immediately understood and said thanks, but the money was too much. I looked at his clothes. The suit was threadbare and the elbows and knees had been patched with a different woolly grey material. It occurred to me that he probably only earned about ten Deutschmarks a week and this was a huge sum to accept for a few minutes' work. Five Deutschmarks was nothing to me, just two beers in the EFI, but I didn't have anything smaller. I didn't want to insult his pride by appearing condescending so I went into the 9×9 and brought out a few sachets of compo coffee and a tin of boiled sweets and gave them to him. He was very grateful and thanked me for the gift. I was taken aback by his humble nature and wished him good luck.

The next morning he came back but this time stopped and said hello. We gave him a cup of hot chocolate and got talking to him. With mine and Stevie's limited German we discovered that he walked for 10k each day to get to work. On a map he showed us where he lived and where he worked. He was an ethnic Hungarian, probably a leftover from the vast Austro-Hungarian Empire that had ruled the area before the Great War, and didn't want to meet up with any of the armed Serb gangs that controlled the main roads and villages in case they took him away. So he walked the long way to work through the forests and hills every day, no matter what the weather, and then back. On his way home he stopped and chatted again. He asked us about the wood cutting but all I could show him was a pitiful stack of twigs at the back of the 9×9. He said he would help us and went over to the treeline. He took off his raggedy jacket and pulled a small hatchet from his belt. Stevie and me stood there in awe as this tiny old man chopped enough wood to see us through the night and all of the next day in just half an hour. This time we made him take the five Deutschmarks and gave him some more compo coffee powder. He was overjoyed with our generosity and kept shaking our hands and saying thank you. He walked off waving and smiling, and left me with a warm feeling inside.

That feeling soon left me though when the man with the AK turned up again, this time with a friend. The other Serb had an old up-and-over shotgun cradled in his right arm. It wasn't broken open so I had to assume it was loaded. The magazine on the AK told me likewise. Both of them were pretty grubby with greasy hair and about a week's growth on their faces. They stopped and looked over at the Rebro. They looked like they were up to no good, especially because of the fact that they were a little unsteady on their feet, just like drunks between pubs. After a brief discussion they came over to the Rebro and started asking questions in Serbo-Croat. I didn't understand a word as they spoke too quickly and slightly slurred. I continued with my attempts at diplomacy and said, '*Dobro vecher*,' but I couldn't remember any of the other sayings on our official handout. I wanted to appear as if we didn't give a toss who they

192

were. I told them in English that we were British soldiers and they both laughed. Shotgun man gave me a nasty look and spat some phlegm on the ground between our feet. What was it with Slavs and gobbing up phlegm all the time? I could smell his breath and felt like throwing up. It was a mixture of raw alcohol, cheap cigarettes and spicy sausage.

I noticed that they both had crude woven unit badges on their sleeves with what looked like a double-headed eagle. It looked like the badges that so called BSA Special Forces wore. The only thing special about them was that these units did most of the cleansing after the front-line soldiers did all the hard work.

They didn't look too pleased and started gabbling away in a slurred Serbo-babble. I smiled and calmly told Stevie to grab his gat if things started to look serious, but otherwise to try and not to do anything to provoke them. Stevie nodded and after a fashion went into the 9×9. I heard him put our rifles close by on the camp-bed and he came out.

I tried to speak German to them but they didn't understand. They pointed at things and asked questions but all we could do was shrug and say we didn't understand. AK man took a dirty glass bottle from the pocket of his combat jacket and offered it to shotgun man. He undid the lid and took a swig, coughed, then passed it back. AK man had a swig and was about to screw the lid back on when he decided that despite us being non-Serbs he should stick to tradition and pass it round. He gestured to Stevie and said, '*Slivovitz.*' Stevie took a big slug and wiped his mouth. He said it was nice but it came out like a hoarse whisper.

Stevie then offered it to me, and not wanting to offend anyone I took a swig. I wasn't expecting something as potent as this. My eyes misted over and my throat burned as it flowed down to make my guts feel like they had just been microwaved. I coughed and tried to say something but all that came out was a silent whisper that was supposed to say, 'fuck!'

Everyone started laughing and passed the bottle around again. I declined and made my excuses. Stevie followed me after another swig and we watched as the Serbs walked back down the track. I gulped down some water to dilute the raw alcohol in my stomach and help wash the taste of paint stripper from my mouth. Stevie, on the other hand, seemed to savour the taste and was licking his lips trying to get at any residue that was left over from the mouth of the bottle!

I didn't trust the two Serbs and hoped that we wouldn't be seeing them or their mates in the future. They had an overconfidence that was common with thugs who were used to getting their own way for too long. I had seen that look too often from some of the villains in certain East London pubs that I had the misfortune to stumble upon. The last thing we needed was bored BSA full of Dutch courage wandering about near the Rebro looking to show how hard they are. Stevie wasn't too happy either and mentioned on more than one occasion that he wished the Light Dragoons would hurry up and find the bloody ZSUs so we could piss off. Safety in numbers was the number-one thought on both our minds.

That night while Stevie slept I stagged on in the commander's hatch. This time I wore as much as I could, including my tank suit. I looked like the Michelin Man and it was lucky I had no plans on going anywhere in a hurry as it was a bit of a tight fit around the hatch opening. It was another freezing-cold Bosnian winter's night, but I was too worried about possible nocturnal visitors to stay inside the wagon. I leaned back on the rim of the hatch and looked into the darkness. Stagging on – I knew it wouldn't be too long til I did this again. My night vision came to me after about ten minutes and I began to focus on my surroundings. I could make out individual trees and the undulations in the track. It was deadly quiet and all I could hear was the soft rustling of fir branches that moved in the wind.

It was the part of stagging on that I really enjoyed. Quiet, absolutely still, camouflaged and smelling like a caveman, I would go undetected by humans and wildlife alike. As a city boy while growing up, the only wildlife I got to see were pigeons, sparrows, domestic pets and the slappers that fell out of the pubs and clubs at closing time. In the field, nature was close up and full of variety. I had seen sheep and cattle graze right in front of me while I was in hides or OPs when normally they would run a mile. I had watched mink and stoats search for food a few feet in front of me, and I had stayed stock-still as insects galore had crawled all over me. This time I got to see something I had only ever seen on wildlife programmes or in horror films.

The sound was very faint at first but it definitely wasn't human. It was the sound of scampering feet on the stony path and it was getting louder as it came closer. A few minutes later a pair of grey wolves appeared at the clearing, sniffing their way along the path with their heads bobbing side to side, searching for any faint traces of tonight's prey. They didn't look up or notice me and the Rebro. It was a good sign that I could hear and see them and that they didn't detect me. The Rebro was in the shadow of the hill and was covered in darkness, which wasn't just good luck but tactically sound positioning considering where we were.

I was enjoying observing such a dangerous wild animal at close quarters when a burst of celebratory made them start and scamper off back down the track. I checked my watch: it was coming up to half three in the morning, a bit late for the pubs to be shutting. Unless it was a lock-in, if they had lock-ins in Boz. It didn't matter; it was loud enough for me to guess that it was close by. I ducked down and checked the radios, which were fine. I called in the news and was greeted by a sleepy 'Roger oot.' It carried on intermittently, rather like suppressive fire, for the best part of half an hour. The net remained quiet, and after a few single shots that signalled an end to tonight's fun or a stoppage, so did the rest of the night.

About an hour before daybreak a mist rolled down the hill and swallowed the Rebro. Visibility was between five to ten metres and I couldn't see the track. My legs and back were a bit stiff from standing in the same spot for the last five hours, but more worrying was the need to take a slash. Undoing a dozen layers of clothing with numb hands was a nightmare: after unzipping the tank suit, my combat jacket and my trousers, I pulled up my Norwegian and T-shirt, then pulled down my long johns, and finally scrabbled inside my boxers where my dick was doing a very good impression of a Walnut Whip. It was a blessed relief when he was finally free to do his business.

Stevie was still asleep, so I gave him a hint that he was on next by switching on the engine. We had a brew and a boil-in-the-bag while we waited for the mist to clear. Stevie shivered uncontrollably but refused to put anything else on as he'd only have to take it off again soon, typical squaddie logic. After a few fags, he went into the wagon and stood in the commander's hatch while listening to the net on his headset, still shivering. I refuelled the wagon with the last of the petrol and stored the empty cans in the roof cage. After a wash and shave, I lay down and got some sleep. At midday I was woken by Stevie – we had visitors again.

I grabbed my rifle and poked my head out of the back of the 9×9. I was expecting the two drunken Serbs again but was surprised to see the old man and his family. I slung my rifle over my back and went over to meet them. The old man had brought his daughter, son-in-law and his young grandson. They had walked for about 7k to get here and he wanted them to meet the two soldiers who were nice to him. I was touched by his humility and felt very humble standing next to him. It was cold outside so I invited them into the 9×9 to warm up and made them some coffee.

Stevie was amazed to see them all here and gave them a great welcome. They were very interested in what we were doing and why we were there. We didn't give away anything but told them we were helping some other IFOR soldiers who had trouble talking on the radio and wouldn't be there for much longer. He seemed upset at that news but said he was glad he had made the journey now rather than later. He translated my patchy German to his family and they nodded along with every word. Stevie got some chocolate bars from his webbing and gave them to the grandson who beamed ear to ear when he tasted it. The old man said it was the first time he had tasted chocolate, which made the moment really special. We spent an hour chatting about the local area and heard about how glad they were that we had come to stop the fighting. The old man had lost some good friends and was worried that his son-in-law might be taken away to fight as he could not support the family on his own. I looked at all of them. Their clothes were very clean, but were old and worn and had long since been out of fashion back home, and I bet they had dressed up to visit us. The old man's skin was extremely wrinkled and dark, and his son-in-law's complexion wasn't far off that. Even the daughter's face was creased in places, but there was a hint that at one time she might have been a looker. Apart from the fresh but thin features of the grandson, they all looked much older than they were. It must have been a very hard life for the country people of Bosnia and the war could only have accelerated the ageing process.

I heard on the loudspeaker that the Light Dragoons had finished their mission and were on their way back to us. Stevie acknowledged and we started saying our goodbyes. I gave the family the last of our compo coffee and the grandson a full tin of chocolate bars. His face lit up like it was Christmas. The old man said he would be the envy of his friends now. As they got up they all shook our hands while the old man told us he was grateful for our kindness and hospitality.

I watched them leave with a good feeling inside me. It was nice to do something for others, especially those who we had come to help, even if it was such a small thing as a few friendly words and some spare compo. It was a happy ending to a tense few days.

We packed away everything apart from the masts and waited for the Light Dragoons. Stevie sat by the jimpy smoking while I emptied the stove. As I was taking down the 9×9, AK man and shotgun man appeared. They looked agitated and a little annoyed that we were packing up. They started up a noisy dispute over something and from their gesturing it looked we were the main subject. It looked like they were disappointed we were leaving, like they had something planned for us. This time we didn't wave and contrary to our earlier attempts at being non-confrontational and peaceful I openly carried my rifle. With Stevie puffing away and stroking the butt of the jimpy, they got the message that we weren't in the mood to play around. Shotgun man pulled out his bottle of slivovitz and waved it at Stevie but he ignored the offer. The last thing we wanted was to get too close to a pair of drunken and bored former psychopaths. They didn't get the hint straight away but the arrival of a few Scimitars of the Light Dragoons soon had them disappearing down the track.

The Light Dragoons seemed to be in a bit of a hurry and wanted us to follow on ASAP. I called Zero and asked permission to shut down which was quickly given. I don't know if the LDs managed to track down the ZSUs, but I was glad we were leaving this place. I dropped the masts and had a quick area sweep, then climbed up the body of our Sultan and sorted myself out in the commander's seat.

It was like *Wacky Races* on the way back to Banja Luka and I found out why when we reported back in. There was to be a CSE show in the cookhouse and it was on in an hour. I had just enough time to hand my gat into the armoury and buy two cans of beer before we took our seats.

It was an excellent show, with a comedian and a band. I had never heard of the comic but he had us rolling around with laughter. The band was made up of session musicians and was brilliant. They were backed up by a very sexy dance troupe of four young girls, whose gyrations definitely raised the temperature in the cookhouse that night. The Support Company Serjeant Major tried to stop people from dancing but gave up after Mac McGee got up and refused to sit back down. The lead singer loved it and encouraged everyone to stand up. The Support Company Serjeant Major knew when he was beaten, and we carried on dancing. Actually dancing might not be the correct term if you've ever seen squaddies in a disco, but we moved about a bit anyway!

The band's finale was a cover of the Animals' 'We gotta get out of this place.' It was the right song at the right time and really summed up how we felt about our conditions in Bosnia. They had us all singing along by the end, and for about another two minutes they carried it on a cappella, with the whole place singing, 'We gotta get out of this place, if it's the last thing we ever do!'

The show was all over in two hours, and everyone headed off while the roadies started to pack up. I went backstage and had my photo taken with the dancers, who were hanging around in their skimpy tops and combat 95 trousers waiting to be taken to the serjeants' mess. I must have looked and smelled like shit after four days in the field, but the girls were nice about having their photo taken and posed with me and Private Judge, who, despite stagging on in Main for the last week, looked as if he had been out on the op with me!

I tried to have a shower before getting some kip but the water was off again. I was wrecked, so got into my minging doss bag and closed my eyes thinking of those CSE dancers, but the two beers and tension of the op must have got to me because I fell into a deep and exhausted sleep.

The next day I handed my doss bag in for cleaning and was amazed to hear that a mobile shower unit had set up on a concrete hard standing area at the back of the factory. I thought that they were a joke unit, just like the Women's Auxiliary Balloon Corps from *Blackadder Goes Forth*, but it was here and real. I joined the queues of Cavalry, Gurkhas and Light Infanteers and enjoyed the most amazing shower I ever had in my life. The showers were in large canvas interconnecting tents and had wooden duckboards for a floor. There were dozens of shower heads, and the water was hot and plentiful. The Gurkhas looked funny, showering while still wearing their underwear, but each to their own. I stood under the shower and washed about three times. I scrubbed at my legs with a nail brush, hoping to get rid of the mass of combat zits, and even shaved under the water. I didn't care how long I took; I wasn't due back on duty for a few hours yet and the Army owed me this moment a hundred times over.

Outside and dressed in fresh combats, I walked back to the Sigs tent feeling like a new man. I packed away my wash kit, hung up my towel to dry and took my dirty washing to the stores. I reported to the RAP to carry out a few days of maintenance on the 432s, which in the main meant cleaning them. During the tea break I heard that the RAMC medic who treated my burned hands had been flown back to Germany. The Med Serjeant had carried out a spot check of the drugs stores and found that dozens of morphine syringettes were missing. Only a few staff in the RAP had access to the drugs cabinet and a quick investigation led them to the medic. He had been involved in exhuming bodies from mass graves and the horrendous and sickening scenes had affected him badly. The only way he could cope with the nightmares it gave him and to be able to carry on with the job was to jack up on morphine, even though he knew it would be only a matter of time before he was caught. It was the end of his career, and the Army quickly moved him out of theatre. The surprising thing was that everyone I spoke to in the RAP understood why he did it, but didn't suspect a thing. He had hidden it well and carried on with the exhumations, even though he knew he was suffering badly because of it. He was devoted to the job, but his refusal to get help was his downfall. He was a big loss to the RAP, and it was a shame to see such a talented and dedicated soldier go. I hoped he would recover quickly.

The atmosphere in the RAP was subdued to say the least, so I was pleased to get back on duty in the Ops Room a few days later. It was still Rupert Central during the day, but despite the importance of the job it was doing it was a relaxing place to work. Dress was casual and we were allowed to wear our LI tour sweatshirts. To be different I wore my RGJ sweatshirt as a reminder that it was a team effort.

By all accounts the search for the ZSUs was a success. I didn't hear if they were caught, but from then on they were no longer a threat to our helicopter flights in the area. As a reward I was given the drag stag in the Ops Room for a few days. The platoon might have thought it was the worst duty, as it was eight hours long and nothing really happened at night, but it gave me time to relax after a trying operation and prepare for the next one. I must have looked too cheerful when going on stag because a few others copped on how eager I was to stag on and managed to get themselves put down on the next lists. One in particular was Mac McGee, who found it gave him time to catch up on all the jazz mags hidden in Main's battle box!

The end of February saw some real progress in our AOR. Hungarian Army Engineers erected a pontoon bridge at Bos Gradiska, linking the Bosnian Republic of Srpska with Croatia in the north. The UN Envoy Karl Bildt visited Banja Luka, and the old airfield outside the town was reopened. A RAF Herc landed safely, raising hopes that the remaining R&R parties could bypass the long road journey back to Split by taking a Herc back to Germany directly.

I was on the second-from-last leave party, but the Crabs were slow to utilise the local airfield. Instead they sent a Chinook to come and pick us up. So after we collected our civvy holdalls and changed into something more comfortable, we all assembled outside the Metal Factory and waited in the snow. We were all looking forward to two weeks at home, either back in the UK or Germany. Two weeks away from the cold, wet and dirt. Two weeks where we could relax and recharge our batteries. After standing in the snow for an hour, with most of us just wearing tracksuits and trainers, we were told that the RAF considered the weather too bad to fly. I looked up at the sky. It was cloudy but in places it was clear. Was it that bad in Split?

A convoy of four-tonners arrived and we were told to board. They were our transport to Mrkonjić Grad, where we would carry on with the remainder of the journey in a coach. The Croat coach drivers refused to cross the Confrontation Line so we sat huddled together in the back of the Bedford and suffered for two hours in the freezing cold.

The manky coaches were a blessing after nearly catching pneumonia in the back of the four-tonners, and even the gypsy music playing on the radio was a luxury. As we headed away from Mrkonjić Grad someone spotted a lone Chinook flying overhead. It looked like the Crabs had been telling porkies. It really pissed us off, especially when we had to wait overnight in Split to get the next flight. So our first night of leave was spent in the same awful transit accommodation as we had stayed in when we first arrived. Thanks a bunch, Crab Air!

The next morning we boarded a RAF Tristar transport aircraft and took our seats facing the back of the plane, a safety feature that never caught on in the real world of passenger airlines. Once airborne, the crew handed out horror boxes and soft drinks. It was weird to be given mine by a WO2. In fact most of the crew were senior NCOs, a job that could easily be done by junior ranks. They had it too cushy in the RAF.

After we dropped off the pads in Germany, the rest of us flew on to RAF Brize Norton. From there I took the train to London and arrived at my sister's at 11 p.m. So far two days of my leave had been lost in transit. I soon forgot about the trouble getting home and began to relish small comforts like hot water, clean bed sheets and being able to stay warm inside a building.

I knew it was pointless trying to see my kids, and my ex didn't disappoint me. She refused point blank and left me thinking that the only way now was to go through the Courts. It was the only sour part of a pretty good leave; I even got to see West Ham beat Middlesbrough 2–0 at Upton Park. The news rarely mentioned Bosnia now that we had won the peace. It was good in a way; it meant we had achieved something, but the lack of news made me think about my mates who were still there and made me feel guilty about enjoying myself while they were still in danger and suffering from the still raging Bosnian winter. It was a strange feeling, wanting to return to such a savage place, but I wanted to finish the tour and leave Bosnia when my adopted battalion were relieved. So it wasn't with dread that I packed and left London, but with a determination to go back and see the job through.

I returned to Brize the day before we were due to fly out, another stupid Crab Air rule, even though the flight was at midday and Brize was easy to get to by mainline train. We were put up in the RAF's very own version of the Holiday Inn, and I waited in the TV lounge watching West Ham lose away to Newcastle 3–0 live on *Monday Night Football*. Of all the teams! I hoped Mac was on a Rebro when I got back.

Again we flew to Germany to pick up the pads. This time we had the

200

renowned TV chef Keith Floyd as a passenger. He was to make a TV show for the BBC about cooking with the Army in Bosnia. I doubted if he would get as far as Banja Luka or the company outposts, so it would be a REMF show, but at least it was a bit of prime-time publicity for the Army in Bosnia.

I arrived back in Banja Luka to find out what had happened during my absence. The main news was a private had been killed when he accidentally shot himself in the head. It was a shock to everyone, especially his platoon who witnessed the unfortunate event. A Lynx had crashed with no serious casualties, while the first delivery of a new Corimec village arrived in the Metal Factory. BSA mine-clearing T55s were allowed into the Anvil to help clear minefields, but it seemed that their training wasn't up to much because casualties were commonplace. Snap VCPs were set up to catch PIFWC, more commonly referred to as war criminals, while members of the International Police Task Force were being met with suspicion by the locals. Tac had moved into Mrkonjić Grad in preparation to let the Serbs back into the Anvil, while the companies and squadrons were catching the BSA trying to sneak heavy weapons in. The Signal Platoon had sent a Rebro back into the Anvil to upgrade comms, while C Company and 77 Squadron RE set up blocking positions to ensure the move went smoothly and the BSA didn't get too close to HVO or BiH positions.

North of Banja Luka, planned civil disturbance by the Serbs resulted in some IPTF members being detained against their will, but negotiations with IFOR soon had the startled coppers free. The IPTF were drawn from dozens of police forces around the world and were in Bosnia to monitor and advise the local police forces. It was also a huge source of intelligence and as they got closer to the locals than we ever could.

In the Ops Room things were hotting up as NATO prepared for the former warring factions to enter all the areas vacated by their former enemies under the terms of the Peace Accord. In the Anvil the battle groups were on standby and monitored the reoccupation. After a tense two days the units were stood down and the operation was declared a success.

We also had many visitors in the Metal Factory: very senior officers, politicians, religious leaders and, on some days, what seemed like the world's press. On one particular VIP visit, a US ambassador and a ridiculously large entourage arrived in a couple of US Navy Sea Stallion helicopters escorted by a whole troop of SEALs. At lunch, the SEALs came into the cookhouse and queued up along the servery. It was our first look at the US military's finest. They were all tall, over six foot, had high and tight haircuts, and were dressed in tight grey jump suits. They wore black assault vests and webbing belts, with pistol holsters and water bottles strapped to their thighs. Some of them had pump-action shotguns or sniper rifles slung over their backs, as well as their issue Colt Commando assault rifles. I didn't know if they were ready to assault an embassy or audition for the Village People! It was totally over the top. Even John Major, the British Prime Minister, on his recent visit to Sarajevo only got a couple of plain-clothes SAS troopers for protection!

The whole room went quiet as we looked at the SEALs waiting at the servery to get served. I don't know how they took it, but the grubby British squaddies sitting down and filling their faces suddenly burst out laughing at the macho pantomime in front of them. Red-faced, the SEALs got their food and, to save any more embarrassment, were seated in the SNCOs' section.

At the end of March we started to relax the Force profile. It didn't mean a reduction in our armoured escorts or manpower, but rather we were allowed to wear berets in soft-skinned vehicles and on patrol, as well as carry out some hearts-and-minds exercises. We were even officially encouraged to carry on waving at the local kids again. It was one of Higher Command's ways of saying that the threat had been reduced. It was nice of them to say that, but it wasn't that safe for us out there yet. We still had another deadline from the Peace Accord to oversee, the withdrawal of all forces and heavy weapons into barracks, on D+120 (18 April 1996). Then there was the problem with DPs trying to cross the IEBL, the removal of dead bodies, the discovery of new mass graves, civil disturbances, the discovery of still more air defence assets and the ever-present problem of being sniped at.

In the battalion we seemed to be getting back to some of the bullshit normally associated with barrack life. We were paraded one morning in the Factory and the OC of HQ Company came over and launched into a mother of a bollocking. Was the security of the base compromised? Were squaddies buying black-market AKs? Was somebody selling fuel on the black market? Were there complaints from Brigade about how dirty we looked? No, it was far worse than that. We were using glossy magazines for toilet paper!

The toilets had become blocked and the culprit was pages of jazz mags that squaddies were using because there was no toilet roll. The OC HQ Company carried on like a Victorian Methodist minister, just as if we were whoring and drinking on duty. His voice quivered and stuttered as the pitch got louder and louder. How dare we clog up the toilets with such filth? (No pun intended!) Why we couldn't use the toilet tissue provided was beyond him! But he never bothered finding out why we had to revert to newspapers and glossy mags.

The HQ Company storemen did restock the toilets each day, but two rolls per trap wasn't going to last long with over two hundred squaddies using the two toilet ISOs. It was bad drills by the storemen and could lead to hygiene problems. It wasn't as if toilet rolls were in short supply, they had boxes of the stuff, but the Army is notoriously mean when it comes to issuing kit or supplies. Those running the stores are always joking that stores are for storing, issues are for issuing. It looked like their peacetime attitudes had followed them from Germany.

There was no point trying explaining the facts, so we just stood there listening to this senior officer talk down to us like we were naughty children. It was times like this I felt sorry for the Light Infantry soldiers who had to put up with this carry on week in and week out in Germany.

Chapter 18

The Last Rebro

My last Rebro duty was at H21D at the Serb Lisina Radar Complex, between Banja Luka and Prijedor. I had spoken to our Int Cell and found out that it was hit by 13 Tomahawk cruise missiles fired from a US Navy warship in the Adriatic on 11 September 1995. Eleven hit the target, two had been shot down. The Rebro had been relocated closer to the bombed-out building after a stand-off with some BSA soldiers who wanted to occupy the Rebro site, but that had ended just like most BSA harassment since we changed to IFOR, with the visit of a few Warriors.

On the way up to H21D we passed the Rebro and CP sites from the Light Dragoons, Queen's Royal Hussars, Artillery and Canadians. At the top, the mountain track levelled out where the Radar Complex was located. We pulled up in front of H21D and unloaded all the fuel and food we would need for the next few days. We said our farewells and sorted our kit out. This time I had Private Mac McGee as my operator. He had made sure his stint on the Rebro was going to be productive and had brought about twenty dog-eared jazz mags which he placed lovingly next to the logbook on the map table.

After we had settled in, I made my way through a small gate and into the Radar Complex. Even though it had taken eleven hits from cruise missiles, a large section was still standing. There was no way inside and from the scale of the collapse I doubt if anyone got out alive either. The winter had probably prevented the bodies from decaying but that might change when the weather turned. At least we would be spared that. Parked next to it was a Ptarmigan node site from the Royal Signals. I went over and introduced myself to the Det Commander, a young sergeant, who in turn introduced me to his crew of two corporals and a signaller. They operated from the back of two four-tonners but had set up inside the remains of the complex. Here, they had set up their camp-beds in some spare rooms and had set up an old TV that they linked to a video recorder in one of their wagons. Their organisation and kit might not have been as good as the Canadians, but it still made ours look like something out of *The Flintstones.*

I had operated with the Royal Signals before on exercises with the Brigade HQs of 19 Mech and 24 Airmobile, and had got on well with them. They were very professional about their job and were easy going.

The Ptarmigan Detachment was the same, and we were soon invited to move into the building with them. It was much warmer than the back of the Rebro and the Royal Signals lads had a major advantage over us – they were living on fresh rations!

As part of a deal with the Local Serb authorities, NATO had agreed to rent the radar site to prevent any misgivings about IFOR being an army of occupation. Along with the deal came two middle-aged Serbs who were sent there as maintenance men, but they did sod all apart from lurk around and spout on about Serb Nationalism and the curse of the Turks (Muslims). They were often spotted peeking into the backs of our wagons, and constantly followed us around, making sure we didn't venture into the remains of the complex. They never did a stroke all day and their furtive behaviour gave us the impression they were secret police or at least Serb Nationalist Party members sent to keep an eye on us.

A new arrival at the complex confirmed our suspicions. A Royal Artillery radar unit set up not too far from H21D. It was set up in a box body on the back of a four-tonner and had a big circular dish on top. Immediately they put up a razor-wire perimeter and trip flares. I know the Serbs tried their best to get close, but even we weren't allowed to look inside. In fact, the gunners running it wouldn't even tell us what it was used for. I knew from my early days as a gunner that it wasn't ground radar like M-Star or a mortar-locating radar like Cymbeline, and I couldn't think of anything else that the gunners needed radar for. Maybe it was looking for more BSA air defence radars? One thing I did know was that we started to padlock the gate between us and the complex to keep the Serbs as far back as possible.

As the end of our tour was coming to an end, we started to relax more. Apart from a few visits and resupply runs, we had a relaxing time. We did experience one more blizzard where we were snowed inside the Rebro for two days, but from then on the weather improved, so that by the start of week two most of the snow had disappeared and the sun started to show its face.

It was strange to be able to wear our issue combats without having to

206

add our own extra layers, which made moving around and sleeping much more comfortable. We went straight from winter to summer. I don't think they had a spring or autumn in Bosnia; at least they didn't when we were there. There might still have been a lot of cloud cover, but we soon began to feel the warmth of the sun's rays again after a very hard winter. Going home was now the only thought in our minds.

The Royal Signals lads were sad to see us leave and decided to throw us a smoker. They ordered fresh steaks and sausages and even managed to get a few crates of pivo from the village at the bottom of the mountain. The food would be brought up on the next supply run, but before that we were given a potentially suicidal task to carry out.

On the next peak, about five hundred metres away, was another part of the Lisina Radar Complex. Like the part we were at, it had been hit by cruise missiles and was thought to be unoccupied. That was until one of the Royal Signals lads spotted an early-morning troop handover. It was a few days past the D+120 (18 April 1996) deadline for the withdrawal of all former warring factions' forces and heavy weapons into barracks. It had to be called in, but to our surprise Brigade ordered the Ptarmigan Det to go over and tell the Serbs to leave.

The Det Commander was expecting to be told that a platoon of Warrior or maybe a troop of Scimitars would be sent, and definitely wasn't expecting to be ordered to do it himself! He came over and asked if me and Mac would join them to make up the numbers.

'Fook off, man!' was Macs reply. 'I'm not going to do something stupid this close to going home!'

I understood his feelings. We had a week to go and then we were out of there. He didn't want to compromise that by walking up to a doubtless well defended Serb EW site. The complex had been classified top secret before and during the war and was out of bounds to the locals, and we knew that the Serbs used to guard their secrets jealously. It was probably why one of the Serb maintenance men had insisted that he tag along as an interpreter. I looked at the four signallers putting on their body armour and banging magazines onto their rifles.

They didn't look too confident so I told them to wait while I got ready. Mac told me I was mad to go, it wasn't our problem and we should stay at the Rebro, but I couldn't let them go alone. They were technicians and not combat soldiers. They wouldn't be used to this kind of work and needed someone who understood infantry tactics in case it all went pear-shaped.

For some reason Higher had got a bee in its bonnet about Serbs flouting the conditions of the Peace Accord and insisted that the Serbs be told immediately that IFOR wouldn't tolerate them staying. I don't think that the Rupert at the other end of the line considered the possible dangers he was sending us against. It went against SOPs and common military sense. Higher should have sent a Warrior platoon against a fortified position and not a squad of techies. We should have carried out a proper recce and the QRF was over an hour away – twice that if it was still made up of 432s! The order to remove them was given with the casualness of telling the signallers to change frequencies rather than go and evict armed men from a top secret site!

I switched off from all thoughts of negligent Brigade Watchkeepers and concentrated on the job in hand. As I had the only SUSAT on my rifle I carried out a visual recce. I talked out loud as I scanned the route so that the signallers could all have an appreciation of what I saw. There was a dirt track that went from our site up to the other one and we knew that the grassed fields either side were mined. The track went down into a valley and was quite steep. It was joined by a road near the top so we knew that once we started down the track we would have nowhere to go if we got bumped, apart from back. To the left of the path at the bottom of the valley was some wreckage that looked like one of the crashed cruise missiles. If we got bumped on the way up we would have no option but to fight our way towards the site. Either way we were totally exposed. And on our own.

We removed our helmets and hung them on our webbing. We needed to send out the right signals and look non-threatening so we wore our berets instead. As it was a Royal Signals show they would lead, with me in the rear, but if the shit hit the fan they would look in to me for orders. The younger signallers looked a bit nervy and were holding their weapons a bit too tightly. I didn't blame them for being nervous; it was a stupid thing for Brigade to order them to go up alone and confront the Serbs, especially as the last time NATO sent them a message it was by special delivery courtesy of the US 6th Fleet!

We cocked our weapons and started down the track at a quick pace, so I told them to slow down and spread out. We didn't want to look like we were attacking the complex and we would need to save our energy for the steep climb up the other side. While the signallers concentrated their stares on the main gates, I kept an eye on everything else. The ground to the sides of the path was covered in wild grass, but now and then I could make out PNM anti-personnel mines, their light-green paint jobs not quite blending in with the darker greens of the grass. At the bottom of the valley we passed the wreckage of one of the cruise missiles that never found its target. It was riddled with shell holes and had obviously been shot down by a radar-controlled triple A gun, probably the same ZSUs that we had been looking for a month ago. None of us were sure what the Yanks put into those things and we didn't want to get too close to find out, so we veered away from it and moved quickly on.

On the way up things started to get real scary. We knew we had passed the point of no return and could only go up, no matter what happened. We kept silent and strained our ears to listen to any strange or alien sounds. Ahead of us the complex looked intimidating, like a medieval keep. It had dozens of windows where someone could be following us with the sight of their weapon. The entrance was a set of big rusting double mesh gates with some signs in Cyrillic that were not likely to be the visiting hours! Either side of the gate was a long chain-link fence with bushes growing up against it, ideal for hiding OPs or machine gun nests. Inside the compound we could make out sandbagged bunkers and weapons pits. The main building looked in pretty good nick considering the cruise attack and still had a mast full of antennas sitting on top.

Closer to the gate the path crested and partially hid us. It was so silent and unnerving, like the quiet before the storm. We were now fifteen metres from the gates, where the path joined the stony track. At least we now had another option if we were bumped. The ground had levelled out and we were skylined against the valley. This was when we were at our most vulnerable. I could see the gate was chained and padlocked, but there was a small door set into the right-hand one of them. Seeing the padlock the signallers hesitated, but I pointed to the smaller door and we carried on. It was brass-neck time!

We were in luck. The door wasn't locked. The Serbs evidently didn't expect anyone to simply walk up to them. My heart rate was going through the roof and sweat was running down the small of my back like a waterfall. I nodded at the Sergeant and he looked at his lads. It was now or never. We rushed into the compound and fanned out in all-round defence. The compound was empty but the footprints and sounds told us we weren't alone. From a bunker to our right we could hear an electronic voice, like a radio. It had to be occupied. Leaving two signallers outside to cover us we rushed inside and completely surprised some BSA soldiers who were sitting around smoking and drinking some awful smelling coffee. The shock on their faces was a picture and for a full minute they just sat there looking at us with their mouths open.

The inside of the bunker was laid out like an observation post. There was a slit in the side of the bunker facing the valley. An RPK74 light machine gun was lying next to it on a ledge, its huge cumbersome curved 75 round magazine caught up in some camouflage netting that had blown in from the outside. Beside it were two pairs of binoculars. Radios were set up on a table opposite, and there were a few AK74s stacked against some wooden ammo boxes, with dozens of spare orangey plastic magazines stacked beside them. In one corner was an old black-and-white portable TV showing a Serb news programme, its picture full of lines and interference.

The Royal Signals Sergeant called in our interpreter and told him to explain why we were here. The conversation between the Serb and the BSA soldiers was longer and more excitable than we expected. It seemed to me that the Serb civvy was giving the soldier an almighty bollocking. We listened, not understanding a word that was being said, covering the Serbs in case they went for their weapons. The interpreter said the BSA soldiers insisted we leave as we were trespassing and illegally here, but it sounded like it just came from him. The Sergeant told them we could arrest them and take them away forcibly, but we weren't going to do that and he should radio his superiors for confirmation of the agreement and to arrange to vacate the site. The Serb soldier, now realising that he wasn't going to be taken prisoner, visibly relaxed and picked up a handset and started talking. I went outside to see how the other two were getting on.

It was still quiet and no one else had appeared. I took a short walk over to a bombed-out anti-aircraft pit. The remains were so mangled I couldn't begin to make out what type it was. The sandbagged protection and bits of kit were scattered over a wide area. I walked over to a door on the side of the main building. I tried to open it but it wouldn't budge. I couldn't see a lock and had the feeling that it was bolted from the inside. I went back over to the OP and joined up with the signallers. The BSA soldier was still on the radio while the interpreter told the Sergeant the gist of what was being said. When the soldier finished the interpreter told us that all was in order and the base would be evacuated the next day. The Sergeant agreed and went on to tell the Serbs that if they didn't leave by tomorrow we would send some Warriors and get them. The translation of the last part soon had them all nodding to each other in agreement.

We left the Serbs to sort out their eviction and followed the path back up to our location, Once we reached the safety of the Ptarmigan site we unloaded our rifles and made safe. The Sergeant got into the Ptarmigan wagon and phoned Brigade. I said my goodbyes and went down to relieve Mac on the Rebro. I changed my sweat-soaked T-shirt and drank greedily from a carton of water. I was back safely and it was only now that I began to think about how fortunate we were. The Royal Signals Sergeant came down and chatted about the successful conclusion of the task. He thanked me for going along with them and said that Higher wasn't too happy that the Serbs were still there but accepted the outcome as long as we monitored it.

I looked at him and told him we were lucky, very bloody lucky. It could have turned into a major clusterfuck. In reality we had forced an enemy unit to surrender and stand down. We had surprise on our side and we caught them napping. If we had done that a few months ago, before the Peace Accord, we would all be up for a gong! He looked at me and let the enormity of what we just accomplished sink in.

I suppose for the Royal Signallers it was an opportunity to do something a bit more exciting than their normal routine of running a tactical mobile phone mast. It was no wonder he jumped at the chance without thinking it over, but now it was over and he had time to reflect on his hastiness he looked more than a bit relieved that it had gone OK. I told him not to worry; we had got the result we went up there for. He agreed, but the smile on his face wasn't matched by the self-conscious look in his eyes.

The next day we kept an eye on the Serbs across the valley and watched as four open-backed trucks entered the gates. An hour later they left, I looked through my SUSAT and could see a few dozen men in the backs. It sent a shiver down my spine to think that the base was full of BSA troops. They were probably in the main building, probably signallers and technicians, but they were still armed. I spoke to one of the Royal Signals corporals who was stagging on and told him what I had just seen. He phoned Brigade with the news and was told that another callsign would investigate. Not even a word of thanks. Later that day we watched as a pair of Scimitars drove up to the gates and confirmed the base was empty. At least that bit of excitement was over.

That evening we held our smoker beside the bombed-out remains of the Radar Complex. We told Zero that we wouldn't be available for a few hours to answer any calls as we had to carry out maintenance, and locked up the 432. Up at the Ptarmigan the smell of barbecued sausages and steak was mouthwatering. The sun was beginning to set and it was warm enough not to bother with jumpers or combat jackets. The signallers had made the barbecue with bricks from the rubble of the Radar Complex and cooked over the embers of a wood fire. The food was wonderful and they had kept the beers cold in a bucket full of icy water. If it wasn't for the surroundings and the fact that we had our weapons close by, it could have been a barbecue back home. We had a great few hours shooting the shit and telling funny stories about our time in green. It was a great way to relax after the previous day's events but I knew it wouldn't be until we had landed back in Paderborn that we could unwind totally.

The next day we had a visit from Fred. He brought with him a corporal from the Worcestershire and Sherwood Foresters who was going to take over the Rebro from us and we were to look after him for a day while he acclimatised. Fred seemed to be smiling more than normal and I realised why after he had left. The Woofer didn't have a clue about signals or the 432! Why he was sent up to take over a Rebro I didn't have a clue. All he did was talk about how many girlfriends he had left behind in Tidworth, something his ugly boat told me was pure fantasy. He continually boasted about how successful his career was and went on about how many times he had been jailed, not realising the contradiction. After a few hours I had had enough of his dodgy war stories and told him to stow his kit with the Royal Signals lads in the building, as we needed to carry out a CES check. We didn't, but I wanted to keep him out of the way until I was relieved. The last thing I needed was to baby-sit a boring Brummie suffering from verbal diarrhoea.

The next day we signed over the 432 and signals installation to the Woofer. He didn't have a clue what he was signing for and the ever sly Fred secretly removed a few items that were missing on some of our other wagons. It wasn't a nice or professional thing to do, but it was his battalion's fault for sending the muppet up here in the first place. They would learn the hard way.

We left Mac with him for one more day so he wasn't totally on his own, and so that while we still controlled the net comms wouldn't go down on us. When Mac returned to the Metal Factory he couldn't help mentioning how useless the Woofer was, and it wasn't long before the Ops Room lost comms with the Rebro. I hoped for the sakes of the Woofers that they would replace him soon as more of them were turning up in theatre.

For the last few days before we flew out, we carried out handovers with the Signal Platoon of the Woofers and packed away our own signals kit. We milled around waiting for tea breaks and scoff, and generally made the place look untidy. Contractors started work on a new Corimec village on the side of the factory, a sure sign that the MND was moving up here. There was no point moaning about it now, we were leaving, but it reeked of them and us. After doing all the hard work, Division could have waited a week until we were gone, but I suppose if they had a care about us in the first place we would have had decent accommodation all along.

More new faces arrived, replacing the old familiar ones. Men of the Queen's Lancashire Regiment had taken over from the Royal Fusiliers. The big yellow backing behind their cap badges stood out like traffic signs and their new and unfaded soldier 95 uniforms heralded their status as newcomers. Platoons of Woofers arrived along with their Warriors, allowing the tired and dirty Light Infanteers to stand down. Troops of Queen's Royal Hussars set up camp and parked their Challenger tanks in an ever-growing vehicle park, while Royal Signals troops erected huge satellite dishes, masts and antenna farms. Squat Gurkhas stood guard on the gates, and Royal Engineers began building a helicopter landing site and FARP in the field to the right of the factory. It looked as if Butlins was coming to Banja Luka.

We were all looking forward to leaving and letting the newcomers take over. The RAF had finally agreed to use Banja Luka airfield to fly us out of theatre, providing the perimeter was surrounded by armoured protection. Everything was looking rosy. We would be back in Paderborn in a few hours rather than the few days we expected. It was just the news we wanted to hear.

As we were when we first arrived in Bosnia, the Signal Platoon of the Woofers was their first fully operational sub unit. That meant our lads could leave as soon as the flights were sorted. The RSO managed to get most of us on the first flight back, and on the night before we were due out none of us could get to sleep and for the last time we stretched the 'two can' rule a little!

Banja Luka airfield might have been a dingy-looking place, but to us it was better than going first-class through Heathrow. The terminal was nothing more than a dirty-white single-storey shed with a rusting red tin roof. The runway looked small but we knew the Herc was built for short take-off and landings. We were ferried out on four-tonners escorted by Scimitars from the Light Dragoons, who went off and secured the perimeter as soon as we arrived.

Clerks from the AGC stood in as airline check-in clerks, and we handed back our IFOR ID cards as they ticked off our names on the list. Then we waited for twenty minutes until the Herc landed and taxied to a stop outside the terminal. Ninety fresh-faced Woofers got off and were duly greeted with cheers and jeers. We were all overexcited because we were leaving, and even the usual kit checks, head counts and unnecessary delays by the miserable Crab Police, who wanted to show us who was in charge while 'airside', didn't detract from our buoyant mood.

Once we got the all-clear, we boarded and found a seat. A loadie checked that we had our seat belts on and explained that because of the possible threat of Serb air defence missiles we would be making a tactical jet-assisted take-off. We would be in a steep climb for about ten minutes but when the aircraft levelled out we would be out of range.

The dangers that the loadie mentioned didn't seem to bother anyone too much. We were all too hyped up because we were leaving. The lads were mucking around and jumping out of their seats to give dead legs and arms to each other. It wasn't until the rear ramp closed and we taxied to the end of the runway that the fooling around stopped. The engines revved up and the plane vibrated madly while the brakes held us stationary. Once the engine noise became a scream the Herc jumped forward and began to hurtle down the runway. It only seemed that we had started the run when we felt the pull of gravity when the Herc's wheels left the ground. We kept in a steep climb just like the loadie said and eventually levelled out. Some of the lads cheered and we all began to relax. I realised that I had achieved what I set out to do a year ago when I volunteered to join 2LI. I had helped in some small way to bring peace to Bosnia. I could carry out my job just as well in war zone, and even though I was scared at times I wasn't afraid. I never took a step back, in fact on more than one occasion I seemed to be going in the opposite direction.

The short spell of tension during take-off was quickly forgotten as the realisation that we had survived Bosnia swam over us in a huge wave of relief. It seemed to trigger something in our subconscious as one by one our brains shut down and we succumbed to some form of mental exhaustion and fell into a deep sleep.

Chapter 19

The Bitter-sweet Farewell

Arriving back in Paderborn was a bit of an anti-climax. We queued up in the gym and handed back our ID discs. At the Support Company stores we got the keys for our rooms and unpacked everything. There wasn't much to do in the first few days apart from hang around the platoon office and go drinking at night. Paddy Murphy's was quiet, probably because they now had a ban on all members of the Light Infantry. The D&Ds had been using it for the last six months and the bar manager thought that trouble might break out if we mixed and didn't want to see it trashed. As a Royal Green Jacket I didn't think it applied to me, and nor did Jamie Ross, an RGBW. I don't think the manager had anything to worry about. It was still the best pub in town and soon was full of trouble-free LI squaddies trying to get over the horrors of Bosnia the only way they knew.

As soon as the battalion had all returned, it started to get back to barrack life. The RPs started pulling people up for minor dress offences and the jail started to fill as NCOs got back at the privates that had pissed them off in Bosnia. The mood in the battalion was pretty subdued and would need something to take the lads' minds off the past six months. It was hard to switch from the excitement and danger of active service to the slow and boring pace of barrack life.

The Signal Platoon ISOs with all the signals kit in turned up two weeks after we got back and we spent a few days unloading, cleaning and testing the kit. It was hard work but the team effort from Boz still hadn't left us and even the corporals lent a hand. The smells from the kit reminded everyone of the place, and now and then a broken or damaged piece of equipment would bring back memories of how it happened and where someone was at the time. Those two days were the last time the platoon worked together as a whole. Soon the orbat would change as people's careers and postings took them in different directions.

I knew that in less than two months I would be transferred back to my parent battalion. For me and scores like me, this was just a posting and I would be leaving the platoon that I had shared the last ten months with. We had trained together, gone off to a war in a distant land and had come home safely. I had made friends with many of them and would miss them when I left. The RSWO and RSO asked me if I would consider staying and transferring permanently. It was very tempting. All I had to do was say yes and they would arrange everything. For the rest of the week I gave it some serious thought. I had made some good friends, loved the life in Germany, and the battalion wasn't too bad either. Most of the other attachments were asked to stay as well, and just like me most seemed to be thinking about it seriously. If I decided to stay, the formalities would be sorted after the medals parade, in one month's time.

I was looking forward to the medals parade. I had always been a bit of a drill pig and loved the ceremonial side of soldiering. Some of my best memories were of being the Guard of Honour for the Lord Mayor of London at the annual November Show, when we marched in full Number Ones and behind the Band of the Light Division in front of a crowd of tens of thousands of Londoners and tourists. The following day we were part of the Honour Guard at the Cenotaph on Remembrance Sunday. It was a proud and emotional moment, especially when the veterans marched past, and something that I'll never forget.

To celebrate our safe homecoming and the culmination of a job very well done the Signal Platoon held a smoker in the NAAFI. It was on a Friday and everyone attended. The RSO made a speech and told us that he had been to see the CO who had singled out the Signal Platoon above all the others for praise. We had performed far in excess of our usual role and enbabled the CO to maintain control the battalion in all of its tasks. We never let the battalion down no matter the enormity of the task, and in some of the worst conditions imaginable. It was a deciding factor in the battalion's ability to carry out a dangerous and demanding mission and secure peace. We had also achieved an enviable reputation in theatre for being able to communicate anywhere, and it became known that if you couldn't get through, copy the Light Infantry. The RSO had been invited to give a lecture in the Staff College at the School of Infantry about our record-breaking Rebro chain, but he was gracious enough to let us know he would be doing it on our behalf. We all cheered, and after he had sat down we began to seriously unwind!

It was a great night and we all felt good about ourselves. At closing time about a dozen of us carried on with the celebrations in town, ending

216

up in the Black and White Nightclub, where I met up with Jamie Ross, Chris Emmins and most of the Paras. It was so good to relax in their company, and we laughed as the Bosnia veterans of 2LI tried their hardest to chat up the local girls, then, having failed, resorted to a few hours of squaddie dancing, in the hope that would impress them!

The following Monday morning I was called in to the RSWO who told me to report to Battalion HQ. He didn't know what it was about, so I went along wondering what was up and found that about fifty other squaddies were waiting outside. When I got closer I could see that they were all attachments, and just like me, they hadn't a clue why we were here.

Soon we were all herded into the corridor outside the AGC offices and listened as a staff sergeant explained that we would be leaving Germany in a few days and returned to our units. There was a stunned silence and disbelief amongst us. The clerk went on to say that flights had been arranged, that we were to hand in our surplus kit and to close our German bank accounts. We couldn't believe what we had just heard. The battalion was getting shot of us! That sparked a flood of questions, like why? We still had two months of our attachments to serve. What about the medals parade? What about those who wanted to stay on? The clerk gave us the usual bullshit of 'It's nothing to do with me' and 'I'm just passing the message on' crap. He was a senior clerk and knew exactly what was going on. He went on to say that if we wanted to stay for the medals parade we could arrange it with our companies but we would have to pay our own way back to the UK as the Army would only pay for the flights we were given. If we wanted to stay with 2LI then that would have to be put in a transfer request with our parent units after we got back to the UK. In the meantime we had to deal with our company clerks to sort out the admin side of things. It was total bollocks, but we were too stunned to argue.

We left the building and slowly walked away. How could the battalion treat us like that? We had volunteered to help them out when they desperately needed us and now, after we returned, they didn't want to know us any more. Every one of us standing there guessed the answer though. We were being treated like outcasts. We were an embarrassment to them now, like a relative that lives on the wrong side of town. Because we came from the Territorial Army.

I felt like I had been kicked in the stomach and felt sick. I couldn't get my head around the sudden change of events and started to get very angry. I needed to calm down so I stopped off in the NAAFI for a brew before I went back to the platoon. I knew we would get a hard time when we joined, but that had soon changed when the regulars got to know us. We had proved our worth and had become indistinguishable from them, did the same job, suffered the same hardships and all with enthusiasm. Even the warring factions in Bosnia didn't mind who they were shooting at. And now, just before the battalion celebrated its outstanding success with a medal parade, we were being told thanks for turning up but we don't really want you to be seen with us. It was a shitty way to be treated and I didn't like it one bit.

I thought about the origins of 20 Armoured Brigade, formed in East Anglia in 1940 by Territorial battalions when the Army was in a desperate struggle against Nazism. It was ironic that we had been asked to help them out in another European War, but that was lost on the regulars who had needed our help yet again.

The RSWO was still at his desk when I told him that Battalion HQ had arranged for me to leave in a few days. He was shocked with the news and asked me why it was so soon, but I had no answer to that. He mentioned the medal parade but all I could say was we had our marching orders and the flights were confirmed. I could have told him that I could stay, at my own expense, but the battalion had made it quite clear how they felt about us.

Over the next few days we handed in our kit. They even took the one-off issue stuff we were supposed to keep. It didn't matter though. The mood of the TA lads was let's just get out of here. We closed down our bank accounts and packed away our personal belongings. The final humiliation was our own version of the medals parade, when we signed for our medals from the stores. We were given two small flat cardboard boxes, one with a UN medal, the other with the newly-minted NATO medal. It should have been a proud moment, but being told to 'sign here' instead of a handshake and 'well done' didn't have the same ring to it.

For those of us in Support Company we had our final parade in front of the CSM. Like most CSMs he was a hard man and difficult to please. He said we might have been STABs but did a bloody good job and he was sorry to see us go. He told us if it wasn't for the TA attachments the battalion wouldn't have had the numbers to go to Bosnia, and we should remember that. He wished us good luck and dismissed us.

Later on I said my farewells to the Signal Platoon. The RSWO didn't say much and probably thought I was snubbing the platoon by leaving them as soon as we got back from Bosnia. I hoped one day he would find out the truth. In the accommodation saying goodbye to my room-mates was harder to do. We promised to keep in touch but we knew that those small words, even though well intended, would be impossible to keep.

My last sight of 2LI was the same as when I arrived just under a year ago, the sign at the front gate that said 2nd Battalion the Light Infantry. Only this time the doors were closing after me.

Chapter 20

Endex

There were no fanfares or cheering crowds waiting for us when we got back to the UK. No heroes' welcome. Not even a pat on the back. At least the lads from 10 Para had a mini bus to pick them up. I was left on my own. On the train home I was just another traveller. No one passed me a second look. I didn't exist, just took up a seat. The newspaper headlines were of Mad Cow Disease and the latest goings-on of the pop group Oasis. The world and the press had moved on. I sat back and watched as my fellow passengers got on with their lives, safe from harm or terror. It was a world apart from Bosnia where I had witnessed history at first hand and seen the harsh reality behind the headlines. I was home, but it didn't feel like home. I didn't know if my experiences would change me, but I did feel good about myself, probably for the first time in my life.

I had been back in the UK for a few weeks, still officially a regular soldier, when I noticed that I hadn't been paid properly. My pay was short, so I went to see the Chief Clerk from my parent battalion, the 4th Battalion the Royal Green Jackets, in his office in Battalion HQ in Davies Street, opposite Bond Street Tube Station. Once the home of the Queen Victoria's Rifles, it was now home to HQ Company 4RGJ and the London HQ of the Royal Green Jackets. He took down my details and promised to contact the Army pay office in Glasgow to sort out the problem. I was happy that it would be sorted out and left in a good mood. I revisited Battalion HQ again one day after my regular service officially ended and signed on as a TA soldier again, so that I wouldn't have broken service. I took over my previous job of the Company Signals Detachment Commander of A Company, based in the Cedars TAC, in West Ham Park, and visited my QPSI, Tony Finnegan, to get kitted out again. There were some major changes since I had been away. Some of the lads had been promoted or left, and we had a new OC, CSM and SPSI. Lt Fox had stayed on with 2LI, so a new fresh-faced platoon commander was posted to take his place, a Mr Greengrass.

I was happy to be back but my pay problems were to get worse. My final month's pay never materialised in my bank account. It meant I was short about a thousand pounds and I immediately went to see the Chief Clerk again. Normally if there was a discrepancy in pay it was resolved by the next pay day. However, this problem involved corresponding between Germany, Glasgow and London. It was a messy process and from the sound of things it would take months to sort out.

In the meantime I settled back into my company and prepared for annual camp. I had only been back for a month when we went off to Sennybridge in the Brecon Beacons for two weeks of exercises and live firing. It was a hard camp and a shock to the system. I had become soft as an armoured infanteer and was back to manpacking everything again, like a real soldier.

When we returned from Wales I went to see the Chief Clerk again. I was told that according to the 2LI clerks I had withdrawn the money in theatre, and they had only balanced the books after we had left. I told him I was sure I would have remembered getting that amount, even in the small sums that we were allowed to withdraw. I told the Chief Clerk there was a mistake and to ask for dates when I signed for the money. I knew something was up and made a point to ask Chris Emmins, Colin Nufer, Bob House and Perry Tuson if they received their last month's wages. The next drill night I drove over to Support Company at Mile End but only saw Bob House. He hadn't been paid and told me that Nufe hadn't either. Something didn't add up, and it wasn't just the 2LI clerks' accounting.

When I got back from camp I also re-enrolled back at my local college in Newham. Like a lot of students I took a year off in the middle of my construction engineering course, but unlike the usual work experience or trip around the world that students do in their year out I did it differently. The way I had been treated by 2LI when we returned had put me off joining them. Now all I wanted to do was get back to college and finish my studies. Money was tight but by doing as many TA exercises and courses as possible I managed to make ends meet. Getting back into civvy life after peacekeeping and enforcing in Bosnia was difficult to start with, but being a part-time soldier helped with the transition.

I did manage to meet up with some of the other TA lads who served with me in Bosnia. At the Courage Trophy military skills competition at the Longmoor training area in Hampshire, I met some of the Paras. Martin Hooper recognised me straight away and congratulated me on my award.

He was always a bit of a joker and I thought he was taking the piss, but for once he was being serious. I asked him to explain what he was on about and he went on to tell me that Private Fluker had been awarded a GOC's commendation for his actions at the kitchen fire in Banja Luka. Fluker was in Northern Ireland with 3 Para when he received it, and the lads had automatically assumed that as it was me that had saved the kitchen and its occupants from being blown up I would get something. I knew medals and awards sometimes took a while so maybe something was in the pipeline. It was good news for Martin Fluker. I looked down at my hands. The scarring had almost healed. I wondered if I would get an award. Mind you, the way the TA were treated, probably not.

Talk of awards and the surprise of meeting up with them almost made me forget about my pay, but just before I said my goodbyes I asked Martin Hooper if he got his last wages from 2LI. The answer was, as I expected, no.

It was the same answer from Jamie Ross. I met up with him when I was on an RSDC course at the School of Infantry in Warminster. Jamie lived in Pusey, a village not too far from there. Like me he had rejoined his battalion as soon as his regular service had ended and, like everyone else I had spoken to, had not been fully paid yet. It was now a year since we had left and none of us had got anywhere with our enquiries, and it didn't look like we were going to either.

I also met up with my old RSWO, John Thirlwell, who was now a senior instructor at the Signals Wing. He looked happy and asked me to visit him when I had a break, but TA courses are condensed from six weeks to two, which meant I had very little spare time. I did manage to get to his office on a few occasions, but he was always out on the training area with his class. It was a shame because I would have liked to find out how the rest of the LI lads were doing. I did get to see a few of their faces on the course photos that lined the walls outside the classrooms. I was pleased to see them doing well, and for a few moments I felt kind of homesick and wished I was back in 2LI with them.

I passed the course with flying colours and came top of the class, but unfortunately I didn't get awarded the best student prize as it went to a lad with the same cap badge as the course RSO. It was a joke but things like that happen all the time in the Army, and there was no point getting upset over it. Cap badge favouritism was the only downside of the regimental system and was as old as the Army. I did get made up to full Corporal not long after though, finally getting the rank for the job I had been doing for three years.

223

When I got back to London I was asked to see the Chief Clerk. He had a list of dates when I withdrew cash in Bosnia and showed it to me. I had to laugh. Most of the dates were when I was on Rebros, and only had visits from my platoon mates on resupply runs or Serbs! I told the Chief Clerk the list was false and he should send it back to Glasgow with my explanation, and besides, where could I spend money? Did anyone ever see a shop on the top of a mountain or in the middle of a minefield!

The more I thought about it the more I realised that someone might have arranged for the TA attachments to leave Germany long before we were supposed to so that we could be swindled out of our pay. I know it sounds outrageous, but I doubt if it happened to the other members of 2LI. For a start the pads' wives would have caused a riot in Battalion HQ! If we had stayed in Germany it might have been different. I never did get my money, and nor did anyone else I spoke with. I was very bitter about it and for a long time it sullied my memories of 2LI. But time is a great healer, and as I write this account ten years after my time with them I only have fond memories. It was a unique time and we achieved something that has had a lasting effect on the country and people we left behind. I am proud to have served with the Light Infantry, and of being part of the British Army's outstanding success after years of hardship and sacrifice under the flag of the UN.

I even got to have my medals presented on a proper parade. The London Borough of Newham decided to honour the TA volunteers in the borough who served in Bosnia at a medal parade. It was to take place at my first unit, 289 Commando Battery, Royal Artillery, based in Vicarage Lane, East Ham. My old Battery Sergeant, Barry Exley, was surprised to see me back there. He was the Battery Captain now and welcomed me back with a sly grin and a very hardy handshake. My sister Mandy was also there among the crowds of family and well-wishers. It was a shame my parents weren't alive to see it as well.

I waited outside the drill hall with a dozen commando gunners who had served with the ARRC. We were all wearing Number Two dress uniforms, but whereas they had khaki badges, brass buttons and berets, I stood out with the gold-braid corporal's chevrons, peaked cap, and black belt and buttons of a Rifle Regiment. 289 Battery had arranged for their medals to be presented by their Honorary Colonel, in the presence of the Mayor of Newham, who presented everyone with a certificate of gratitude from the people of the borough. It seemed fitting that I was there on this occasion, where I had first worn green. The gunners were presented their medals first, but out of respect to the Mayor of Newham it was decided to let him present me with my medals.

The Mayor was a former sapper in the Royal Engineers and was honoured to carry out the duty. It was unique that someone who served in the ranks was in a position to present medals to another ranker, a job normally associated with senior officers and royalty, and he was overcome by the situation. His eyes welled up and his hands shook as he pinned them on, but I could see it was a proud moment for him and that made it all the more special. It was a memorable moment, and something I will always treasure.

I found out that I had passed my college exams while I was on duty in the ammo bunker in ATR Pirbright. 4RGJ was sponsoring the annual Bisley shooting competition and we were responsible for its admin for the six weeks it was on. I now had a choice to make and it was going to affect the rest of my life.

I had previously written to dozens of companies and filled out scores of application forms, but had only a handful of replies and a few interviews. One of them came with a very good job offer, but it would mean moving overseas and leaving the TA. It was the hardest decision I had to make since joining the TA and it took a lot of agonising deliberation before I made up my mind.

In the TA I was successful. I was in line to take over as Sergeant in the Sigs Platoon and I was due to get the TA Efficiency Medal for long service. My TA career was looking good and I had everything going for me. On the other hand I had studied hard for four years and had passed my college course. I desperately wanted a proper career and to get that would mean giving up the one thing that I loved to do above anything else.

Handing my kit back for the final time was one of the hardest things I have ever done. It left me feeling naked and emotionally stunned. I had a few drinks in the bar and went home. Walking out of the big steel gates for the last time made me feel like an orphan being sent out into the big bad world. I hoped I wouldn't regret my choice.

It's now 2006, and everyone has moved on. Many of the old 2LI Signals Platoon have transferred or left the Army. A few stayed. Martin Carney became RSWO, as did KD Walters. The RSO, Mark Winston-Davies, was promoted to Major and is now a Company Commander. Phil Fox was also promoted to Major and picked up an MBE on the way. He commanded a company in Iraq and is now at the Ministry of Defence. The Adjutant, Johnny Bowron, also became a Company Commander and won the DSO in Iraq. He is now a Lieutenant Colonel and commands 1LI in Paderborn.

2LI's CO in Bosnia, Ben Barry, was awarded the OBE and is now a Brigadier. He returned to Bosnia as Commander, Multinational Brigade North West in 2003 and is now at the MoD. Stevie Locke and Chris Emmins were part of the invasion of Iraq on Op Telic, still serving TA members and still helping out the regulars. Box left 10 Para after it was merged to form 4 Para. Martin Fluker was invalided out of the Army after getting injured in Northern Ireland. Colin Nufer re-joined 2RGJ and as a Sergeant was awarded the Queen's Commendation for Bravery in Northern Ireland. My old battalion, 4 RGJ, was reduced to two companies under the Strategic Defence Review and merged with the London Regiment, an ill thought hybrid of light and heavy infantry. A Company at West Ham survived and became G Company again, just as they were when I first joined them. Now those Green Jackets are back in a Rifle regiment, the Royal Rifle Volunteers, and a lot happier for it. In February 2007 they become the 7th battalion the Rifles, part of the new Light Division large regiment. 2LI are now based in Edinburgh, and are looking forward to 2007, when they become the 4th battalion of the Rifles.

My Aunt Nell once remarked that I was 'army barmy'. I was ten years old at the time. I think she was right. I loved every minute of my time in green, especially being a *Rifleman* and all it represents. Of all my experiences in life, the army, regular and TA, has been the most profound and influential. I was tested to the limit and beyond, and came out the other end smiling. I still miss being in green, sometimes more than others, but I don't regret my decision to leave. I had to do it sometime and I believe that was the right time. I am very happy. Life goes on and with it come new challenges. I am doing very well in my career. I joined a project management company as a Clerk of Works and oversaw the construction of a new office block for AIG, the large American insurance company. I worked on other major projects, including one for the European Commission, and I won national awards from the Institute of Clerks of Works for my work in 2003 and 2005. In March 2005 I married an amazing woman, Ela, who gave birth to a little angel, Jessica, in May 2006. Napoleon wrote *'once you have made up your mind, stick to it; there is no longer any if or but.'* Good advice. I'll second that.

Glossary

ØB	Zero Bravo – Callsign of a Unit OC's vehicle
ØC	Zero Charlie – Callsign of a Unit 2I/C's vehicle
2I/C	Second in command
9 × 9	Nine foot by nine foot canvas tent usually used as a CP
12 × 12	Twelve foot × twelve foot general purpose canvas tent
90	Land-Rover 90 – short wheel base
110	Land-Rover 110 – long wheel base, pronounced 'one-ten'
320	UK PRC 320 HF man-portable radio set
321	UK VRC 321 HF vehicle-mounted radio set
353	UK VRC 353 VHF vehicle-mounted radio set
404	UK PTC 404 field telephone
AAA	Automatic Anti Aircraft – or triple A
AAC	Army Air Corps
ABCD	Airways, Breathing, Circulation, Deformities – the four basic principles of first aid in use at the time of Bosnia operational training
ACIO	Army Careers Information Office
Actions on	Drills used when you come under fire
AFV	Armoured Fighting Vehicle
AGC	Adjutant General's Corps
AK47	*Avtomat Kalashnikova* 1947 – Russian designed 7.62mm assault rifle
AKS74	*Avtomat Kalashnikova Skladyvayuschimsya* 1974 – newer version of the AK47 but chambered for 5.45mm
AMX 10 RC	French wheeled armoured amphibious reconnaissance vehicle
AOR	Area of Responsibility
APC	Armoured Personnel Carrier
APWT	Annual Personal Weapons Test
ARAB	Arrogant Regular Army Bastard
Area Sweep	The British Army method of leaving areas clear of rubbish and kit

ARRC	Allied Rapid Reaction Corps
AS90	Self-propelled gun in service with the Royal Artillery
ATO	Ammunition Technical Officer
ATR	Army Training Regiment – based on the old training depots
AVLB	Armoured Vehicle Launcher Bridge – used by the Royal Engineers to bridge streams and small rivers.
ARRV	Armoured Recovery & Repair Vehicle – used by REME in tank recovery and repair
AVRE	Armoured Vehicle Royal Engineers – an armoured assault vehicle, usually seen with bundles of plastic tubes on top
BAOR	British Army of the Rhine
Bash the bag	Wet the bed
Batco	Battlefield Code – a unit-level encrypted message system
battle box	The CP stationary set – usually kept in an old artillery ammo box
BATUS	British Army Training Unit Suffield – a large military training area close to Calgary in Canada
BCH	Boots Combat High/Boots Cardboard High – standard-issue high-leg boots
BFBS	British Forces Broadcasting Service – garrison TV and radio
BFT	Battle Fitness Test – 3 miles in 25 minutes (approx – depending on age)
BGHQ	Battle Group Headquarters
BiH	*Bosnia i Herzegovina* – the country, but also used to denote the Bosnian Muslim forces
Bison	Canadian 8 × 8 APC – part of the Mowag family of vehicles
Blue on Blue	An exchange of fire between friendly forces
bluey	Forces mail – so called because of the blue paper they are printed on
BMP	*Boyevaya Mashina Pehoti* – Soviet Mechanized Infantry Vehicle
Bn	Battalion
BOV-M	Wheeled 4 × 4 APC used by the Serb-run Yugoslav People's Militia, a paramilitary internal security force of the Former Yugoslavia
Boxhead	Nickname for Germans
BRITFOR	British Forces in Bosnia
BSA	Bosnian Serb Army
BTR	*Bronyetransporter* – Soviet class of wheeled armoured vehicles
BV	Boiling vessel – a boxlike water boiler found in armoured vehicles
BV 206	Wide-tracked lightly armoured troop carrier primarily used by the Royal Marines in Arctic warfare

C130	Hercules turbo prop transport aircraft operated by most of NATO
Casevac	Casualty Evacuation
CDT	Compulsory Drug Test
CEFO	Complete Equipment Fighting Order – full combats, webbing, personal weapon and helmet
CEI	Communications Electronic Instruction – the list of frequencies and callsigns issued daily to units
CES	Complete Equipment Schedule
CET	Combat Engineer Tractor – Royal Engineers specialist vehicle that clears obstacles, digs pits and prepares barriers
Challenger 1	British Army main battle tank
cheese possessed	Tinned compo processed cheese – it was a play on words but once tasted you knew why!
CMT	Combat Medical Technician
CO	Commanding Officer – usually a Lieutenant Colonel
coax	coaxial – mounted machine guns or cable for transferring the signal from a mast to the radio set
colourboy	Nickname for the Company Quartermaster Sergeant
Compo	Composite rations
Contact	An exchange of fire with an opposition
Cpl	Corporal – also known as a full screw
CP	Command Post
CPU	Commander's Personal Unit – connects crew member's headset to the vehicle's radios
CQB	Close Quarter Battle
CQMS	Company Quartermaster Sergeant
Crab Air	Royal Air Force
Crabs	RAF personnel – nickname given due to the resemblance of the colour of their uniforms to crab ointment
CSE	Combined Services Entertainment – organisation dedicated to entertaining HM Armed Forces around the world
CSM	Company Sergeant Major
CSS	Combat Service Support
CVRT	Combat Vehicle Reconnaissance Tracked
Cymbeline	Mortar-locating radar used by the Royal Artillery
D10	Cable used in line communications
D&Ds	Devon and Dorset Regiment
Det	Detachment
Dixies	Pots and pans
DM	Deutchmark – former German currency
doss bag	Sleeping bag
DP	Displaced Person
DPM	Disruptive Pattern Material – British camouflage

DROPS	Demountable Rack Offload & Pickup System – removable pallets for stores using specially adapted trucks
DS	Directing Staff – Army course instructors
Ech	Rear Echelon – the logistic support of a battalion
EFI	Expeditionary Forces Institute – pronounced 'effy' and the active service version of the NAAFI
Endex	End of Exercise – the most eagerly awaited command given over the net when on exercise
EOD	Explosive Ordnance Disposal
EW	Electronic Warfare
FAMAS	*Fusile d'Automatique Manufacture d'Armes de Saint-Étienne* – French 5.56mm assault rifle
FARP	Forward Air Refuelling Point
Felix	Nickname for an ATO – derived from his old callsign
FIBUA	Fighting In Built Up Areas
FFR	Land Rover fitted for radio
four-tonner	Bedford 4×4 truck
FTX	Field Training Exercise
full screw	Corporal
FV 432	Obsolete Armoured Personnel Carrier first seen in service in 1962 – still in service and in process of being re-issued
FV 434	REME Recovery version of the 432
gat	Nickname for your personal weapon
Gazelle	Light Battlefield Helicopter – primarily used in reconnaissance
GDs	General Duties – the Army's version of being a dog's-body
GOC	General Officer Commanding
Gyros	German for 'kebab' (pronounced geeross)
GPMG	General Purpose Machine Gun – 7.62mm belt fed; *see* jimpy
HD	Heavy Duty
Herc	Nickname for the C 130 transport aircraft
Hesco	Large version of the humble sandbag
Hexy	Hexamine blocks – solid-fuel tablets used for cooking in the field
HF	High Frequency
HGV	Heavy Goods Vehicle
HMG	Heavy Machine Gun
Horror box/bag	Packed lunch – so called because you didn't know what horrors you would find inside until you opened it
Humvee	HMMWV – High Mobility Multi-Purpose Wheeled Vehicle
HVO	*Hrvatsko Vijeæe Obrane* – Croat Defence Council

ICTY	The International Criminal Tribunal for the Former Yugoslavia
IEBL	Inter-Entity Boundary Line – the old Confrontation Line
IFOR	Implementation Force
IFV	Infantry Fighting Vehicle
IPTF	International Police Task Force
IRA	Irish Republican Army – the paramilitary wing of Sinn Fein
ISO	International Standardisation Organisation – also the name given to the universal steel container used for transporting goods
IWS	Individual Weapon Sight – a night-sight for the SA 80
JCO	Joint Commission Observers – Special Forces
jimpy	Affectionate name given to the GPMG
JNA	Yugoslav People's Army – the regular army of Yugoslavia
JNCO	Junior Non Commissioned Officers – lance and full corporals
Jamrep	Jamming Report of enemy radio interference
KFS	Knife, Fork and Spoon
L37	Turret-mounted GPMG
LAD	Light Aid Detachment
lance jack	Lance Corporal
Last Four	Last Four digits of your Army Number
LI	Light Infantry
light role battalion	Non-Armoured or Mechanised – usually lorried or air-portable troops
LO	Liaison Officer
loggie	RLC personnel
Logsitrep	Logistics Situation Report – daily stocktake of ammo and stores
LSW	Light Support Weapons – a SA80 with a bipod and extended barrel
Lynx	Medium battlefield helicopter
M4	Colt Commando – shortened version of the M16
M16	US 5.56mm assault rifle
Main	The main body of a Battalion HQ
manpacking	The art of carrying all your equipment on your back
MFO Box	Military Freight Only – small cargo boxes for personal kit
MILAN	Missile Infantry Light Anti Tank – Wire Guided Anti Tank Missile System; also used as the name of the Anti Tank Platoon
MIRA	Medium Wave Infrared Array – thermal sights used on the MILAN missile system
MNB	Multi National Brigade
MND(C)	Multi National Division (Central) – part of NATO's ARRC

MND(SW)	Multi National Division (South West) – NATO AOR in Bosnia controlled British Forces
MO	Medical Officer
MoD 90	Army Identification Cards
Monkey	Nickname for a Royal Military Policeman
monkey	Heavy steel tube with arms used for erecting steel pickets
MSTAR	Moving and Stationary Target Acquisition and Recognition – a lightweight ground surveillance radar
MT	Motor Transport
MTO	Motor Transport Officer – usually a captain commissioned from the ranks
NBC	Nuclear, Biological and Chemical warfare
NCO	Non Commissioned Officers – Lance Corporal, Corporal, Sergeant and Colour/Staff Sergeant
ND	Negligent Discharge – an unauthorised shot from a weapon
NGO	Non Government Organisation – charities and aid organisations
NI	Northern Ireland
Nig	New in Germany/Green – a nickname for soldiers straight out of Depot
Norgie	Norwegian olive-green roll-neck sweat top
Norwegian container	Thermal food containers used for feeding troops in the field
OC	Officer Commanding; Company Commander, usually a Major
OOM	Order of March
OP	Observation Post
Opcom	Operational Command
Op Eval	Operational Evaluation – a series of tests used to check a unit's readiness for operations
ORs	Other Ranks – generally used to denote privates and NCOs and WOs
Orbat	Order of Battle – the list of names and appointments within a unit
P-Company	Parachute Company – pre-parachute selection course
Para	Parachute Regiment
PIFWC	Person(s) Indicted for War Crimes
pivo	Bosnian beer
PMR	Yugoslav copy of the Soviet POMZ stake-mounted trip-activated anti-personnel mine
PNM-1	Soviet anti-personnel mine
PoW	Prisoner of War
Powdered cow	dehydrated milk substitute
PRI	President of the Regimental Institute – a unit-run shop selling

	regimental items and kit; normally based in barracks and training depots
PRO	Public Relations Officer
Ptarmigan	Tactical Trunk Communications System providing fully secure digital communications
PVR	Premature Voluntary Redundancy
pyro	Pyrotechnics and explosives
PTI	Physical Training Instructor
QLR	Queen's Lancashire Regiment
QPSI	Quartermaster Permanent Staff Instructor – C/Sgt attached to TA units to manage stores and equipment
QRF	Quick Reaction Force
R&R	Rest and Recuperation – Leave in UK forces
racing spoon	Used to eat rations in the field – probably got its name due to the speed with which squaddies wolf down their food while out on exercise
RADC	Royal Army Dental Corps
RAF	Royal Air Force
RAMC	Royal Army Medical Corps
RAP	Regimental Aid Post
Razzman	Nickname of the RSM
RE	Royal Engineers
Rebro	Radio Rebroadcast; also the name given to the facility that provides it
reccy mech	Recovery mechanic
REME	Royal Electrical and Mechanical Engineers
Resup	Re-supply
RGBW	Royal Gloucestershire Berkshire and Wiltshire Regiment
RGJ	Royal Green Jackets
RHF	Royal Highland Fusiliers
RLC	Royal Logistics Corps – nicknamed the Really Large Corps due to the initials and size
RoE	Rules of Engagement
RP	Regimental Provost staff – the battalion's own police
RPK74	*Ruchnoi Pulemet Kalashnikov* 1974 – light machine gun, a version of the AK74
RRF	Royal Regiment of Fusiliers
RSDC	Regimental Signals Detachment Commander
RSM	Regimental Sergeant Major
RSO	Regimental Signals Officer
RSWO	Regimental Signals Warrant Officer
RTU'd	Returned to Unit
Rupert	Nickname for an officer

RWF	Royal Welsh Fusiliers
SA80	Standard-issue 5.56-calibre British assault rifle
SAM	Surface to Air Missile
SAS	Special Air Service
Saxon	Wheeled British Armoured Personnel Carrier
SCBC	Section Commander's Battle Course
Scimitar	Reconnaissance variant of the CVRT family of vehicles
SCRA	Single Channel Radio Access – mobile sub-system of the Ptarmigan network
screech	Powdered orange and lemon drinks that were coarse and bitter
SEAL	Sea Air Land – US Navy Special Forces
Serjeant	The original spelling of sergeant that is still used by the Light Infantry
Silverman's	A well-known Army surplus store in Mile End, East London
SISU	Danish 6×6 APC
Sitrep	Situation Report
Slop Jockey	Nickname for cooks of the AGC
Smoker	A barbecue and piss-up in the field – normally carried out after a major exercise; so called because of the smoke from the fires
SNCO	Senior Non Commissioned Officer – Sergeant, Colour Sergeant and Warrant Officers
SOPs	Standard operating procedures
SPSI	Senior Permanent Staff Instructor – Regular SNCO attached to TA units for training
Spartan	Specialist variant of the CVRT
STAB	Stupid TA Bastard
Stag	Any type of sentry or watch duty
Stuyer Aug	Austrian 5.56mm Assault Rifle
S-Type	Type of attachment to the Regular Army
Sultan	Command variant of the CVRT
SUSAT	Sight Unit Small Arms Trilux – the optical sight on the SA80
T 55	Soviet main battle tank – produced from 1946 to 1981
TA	Territorial Army
TAB	Tactical Advance to Battle – a forced march usually wearing heavy kit
Tac	Tactical Headquarters – the forward element of Bn HQ
TAC	Territorial Army Centre
Tac Signs	Tactical signposts
TAM	Tactical Aide Memoire – an issue booklet with useful command subjects
TMA-3	Soviet anti-tank mine
TMM-1	Soviet anti-tank mine
TOA	Transfer of Authority

TOETS	Test of Elementary Training Standards
TOW	Tube-launched Optically-tracked Wire-guided missile
UBRE	Unit Bulk Refuelling Equipment
UN	United Nations
UNHCR	United Nations High Commission for Refugees
UNICEF	United Nations International Children's Emergency Fund
U/S	Un-serviceable
VAB	*Véhicule de l'Avant Blindé* – French wheeled APC
VBL	*Véhicule Blindé Léger* – French armoured 4 × 4
VCP	Vehicle checkpoint
VPK	Vehicle Protection Kit – applied GRP armour fitted to Land Rovers first used for civil disturbances in Northern Ireland
VRS	Army of the Republic of Serpska
Warrior	British Infantry fighting vehicle – designated FV 510 but never used
watchkeeper	Duty officer in an HQ or CP
WO1	Warrant Officer First Class
WO2	Warrant Officer Second Class
Woofers	Nickname for the Worcestershire and Sherwood Foresters Regiment
Zero	The control station of a radio net
ZOS	Zone of Separation
ZSU-23-4	*Zenitnaya Samokhodnaya Ustanovka* – Anti-aircraft self-propelled gun with 4 × 23mm radar-controlled guns